The Rise and Fall of Critical Legal Studies

EDINBURGH CRITICAL STUDIES IN LAW, LITERATURE AND THE HUMANITIES
Series Editor: William MacNeil, University of Queensland
Senior Deputy Editor: Shaun McVeigh, University of Melbourne
Deputy Editor: Daniel Hourigan, University of Southern Queensland

With a global reach, this innovative series critically reimagines the interdisciplinary relationship between legal and literary (or other aesthetic) texts through the most advanced conceptual frameworks and interpretive methods of contemporary theory available in the humanities and jurisprudence

Editorial Board
Dr Maria Aristodemou (Birkbeck, University of London)
Associate Professor Fatou Kine Camara (Université Cheikh Anka Diop de Dakar)
Professor Daniela Carpi (University of Verona)
Dr Susan Chaplin (Leeds Beckett University)
Professor Andrew Clarke (Victoria University)
Dr Stella Clarke (University of Melbourne)
Professor Penny Fielding (University of Edinburgh)
Mme Justice Hon Jeanne Gaakeer (Erasmus University Rotterdam)
Professor Peter Goodrich (Yeshiva University)
Professor Elizabeth Hanson (Queen's University at Kingston)
Associate Professor Susan Sage Heinzelman (University of Texas at Austin)
Professor Bonnie Honig (Brown University)
Professor Rebecca Johnson (University of Victoria)
Dr Orit Kamir (Hebrew Union College)
Associate Professor Lissa Lincoln (American University Paris)
Professor Desmond Manderson (Australian National University)
Professor Panu Minkkinen (University of Helsinki)
Dr Anat Rosenberg (IDC Herzliya)
Professor Renata Salecl (Ljubljana/Birkbeck London)
Professor Austin Sarat (Amherst College)
Dr Jan Melissa Schram (University of Cambridge)
Professor Karin Van Marle (University of Pretoria)
Dr Marco Wan (University of Hong Kong)
Professor Ian Ward (University of Newcastle)
Professor Alison Young (University of Melbourne)

Titles available in the series:

Judging from Experience: Law, Praxis, Humanities
Jeanne Gaakeer

Schreber's Law: Jurisprudence and Judgment in Transition
Peter Goodrich

Living in Technical Legality: Science Fiction and Law as Technology
Kieran Tranter

Imagined States: Law and Literature in Nigeria 1900-1966
Katherine Isobel Baxter

Outlaws and Spies: Legal Exclusion in Law and Literature
Conor McCarthy

Criminality and the Common Law Imagination in the Eighteenth and Nineteenth Centuries
Erin L. Sheley

Sensing Justice through Contemporary Spanish Cinema: Aesthetics, Politics, Law
Mónica López Lerma

The Play of Law in Modern British Theatre
Ian Ward

Earthbound: The Aesthetics of Sovereignty in the Anthropocene
Daniel Matthews

A Theological Jurisprudence of Speculative Cinema: Superheroes, Science Fictions and Fantasies of Modern Law
Timothy D. Peters

Character: Writing and Reputation in Victorian Law and Literature
Cathrine O. Frank

The Lawful Forest: A Critical History of Property, Protest and Spatial Justice
Cristy Clark and John Page

The Corporation in the Nineteenth-Century American Imagination
Stefanie Mueller

The Faustian Pact in International Law
Edwin Bikundo

The Rise and Fall of Critical Legal Studies: Law, Politics, Culture
James Gilchrist Stewart

Visit the **Edinburgh Critical Studies in Law, Literature and the Humanities** website at http://edinburghuniversitypress.com/series-edinburgh-critical-studies-in-law-literature-and-the-humanities

The Rise and Fall of Critical Legal Studies

Law, Politics, Culture

James Gilchrist Stewart

EDINBURGH
University Press

For Christopher and Christina.

Edinburgh University Press is one of the leading university presses in the UK. We publish academic books and journals in our selected subject areas across the humanities and social sciences, combining cutting-edge scholarship with high editorial and production values to produce academic works of lasting importance. For more information visit our website: edinburghuniversitypress.com

© James Gilchrist Stewart, 2024, 2025

Edinburgh University Press Ltd
13 Infirmary Street
Edinburgh EH1 1LT

First published in hardback by Edinburgh University Press 2024

Typeset in 11/13pt Adobe Garamond Pro
by Manila Typesetting Company

A CIP record for this book is available from the British Library

ISBN 978 1 3995 1531 3 (hardback)
ISBN 978 1 3995 1532 0 (paperback)
ISBN 978 1 3995 1533 7 (webready PDF)
ISBN 978 1 3995 1534 4 (epub)

The right of James Gilchrist Stewart to be identified as the author of this work has been asserted in accordance with the Copyright, Designs and Patents Act 1988, and the Copyright and Related Rights Regulations 2003 (SI No. 2498).

Contents

List of Figures	vi
Preface: How Do You Solve a Problem Like Critical Legal Studies?	vii
1 Reimagining Critical Legal Studies	1
2 Untangling Critical Legal Studies	22
3 Death on the Books	48
4 Searching for Death	54
5 Theoretical Ghosts and Spectres	73
6 The Haunting of Critical Legal Studies	92
7 Navigating US-CLS	126
8 American Gods	148
Bibliography	166
Index	179

Figures

2.1 *Family Tree: Broad versus Narrow* 25
2.2 *Family Tree: Broad, Complete* 26
2.3 *Family Tree: Narrow US-CLS, 1977* 27
2.4 *Family Tree: Narrow UK-CLS, 1984* 28
2.5 *Family Tree: Narrow US-CLS, 1977–1995* 30
2.6 *Family Tree: Narrow PCLS* 31
2.7 *Family Tree: Complete* 47
6.1 *The US-CLS Timeline* 96

Preface: How Do You Solve a Problem Like Critical Legal Studies?

"[I]ntellectual histories may aim to be 'affectionate' but they also aim, with the movement outsider's characteristic ressentiment, to sting the insiders."[1] Duncan Kennedy's assessment of those writing on the Critical Legal Studies movement (CLS) during the mid-1980s probably still rings true today. I don't believe I've been affectionate in this history of Critical Legal Studies, and if I suffer from ressentiment, that is very much for someone else to diagnose. However, to move beyond the lines of reification and envy, this book deliberately takes a disinterested approach to CLS, using the distance of time and location to assess what CLS was and continues to be.

There are flaws in Critical Legal Studies, and these are discussed in detail, to learn from and move past. There is also real value in the ability to speak truth to power, and this intellectual history may be understood as taking a CLS approach to CLS. At its core, this is a work to demystify the US Critical Legal Studies movement, and to clarify and discuss questions that often fall outside the dominant history of the movement.

This history starts with the first Conference on Critical Legal Studies in the late 1970s. Those in attendance drew on the counterculture and progressive views of the time, as well as continental philosophy and the recent history of American legal realism, in their critiques of law. The newly emerged "Crits" used tools from other disciplines and developed their own versions to uncover law's hidden power structures. At the heart of the movement, the Crits demystified law. In the 1980s, CLS spread to other jurisdictions and boomed in the US. However, by the end of the decade, CLS was in decline. The histories diverge slightly here, with CLS either in permanent decline, or dead. There are implications for each description, but the dominant history

---

[1] Duncan Kennedy, "Psycho-Social CLS: A Comment on the Cardozo Symposium" (1985) 6(4) *Cardozo Law Review* 1,013, 1,016.

is largely unchanged: remnants remain,[2] but the power CLS had, has ended. Outside the US, other jurisdictions developed their own versions of CLS; these flourished and changed, and have not suffered the same fate.

In any history reduced to an extended paragraph, there is no real space for nuance or subtlety, but especially so in a history of CLS. Kennedy and Karl Klare give some insight into why:

> Critical Legal Studies embraces disciplines other than law, and . . . many Critical Legal Studies articles cut across traditional legal categories . . . [w]e have made no attempt to define what CLS is. The CLS movement has been generally concerned with the relationship of legal scholarship and practice to the struggle to create a more humane, egalitarian, and democratic society. CLS scholarship has been influenced by a variety of currents in contemporary radical social theory, but does not reflect any agreed upon set of political tenets or methodological approaches. Quite the contrary, there is sharp division within the CLS movement on such matters. CLS has sought to encourage the widest possible range of approaches and debate within a broad framework of a commitment to democratic and egalitarian values and a belief that scholars, students, and lawyers alike have some contribution to make in the creation of a more just society.[3]

As Kennedy and Klare highlight, the breadth of approaches and understandings that fall under "Critical Legal Studies" is seemingly limitless. And yet, in spite of this, there are identifiable trends, and dominant works, theorists, relationships, and conflicts. The discussion and reconciliation of these areas creates a new version of CLS history, one that is complementary to but challenges existing assumptions and narratives.

In keeping with Kennedy and Klare's articulation of the movement, this book uses a range of theoretical lenses to unpack and engage with CLS. Chapter One recategorises CLS as a legal subculture, before Chapter Two presents a family tree to understand the main limbs of Critical Legal Studies. The family tree highlights the death of CLS, and argues that this has resulted in two types of US Critical Legal Studies, one before and one after the event: CLS and Posthumous Critical Legal Studies (PCLS). Chapter Three investigates the death of CLS, and where this event is remembered. Chapter Four builds on this analysis and questions how CLS is remembered in reference

---

[2] Samuel Moyn, "Legal Theory among the Ruins" in Justin Desautels-Stein and Christopher Tomlins (eds), *Searching for Contemporary Legal Thought* (Cambridge University Press, 2017) 101.

[3] Duncan Kennedy and Karl E. Klare, "A Bibliography Of Critical Legal Studies" (1984) 94(461) *Yale Law Journal* 461, 461–2.

material, identifying a feedback loop in CLS's dominant history. Chapter Five focuses on the specific nature of the death of CLS, and what this means for posthumous critical works. Chapter Six discusses the significant differences evident in similarly themed CLS and PCLS works. Chapter Seven takes critiques of CLS seriously, identifying CLS's failures and successes. Chapter Eight is a direct CLS critique of CLS, building on the previous chapters to better contextualise those behind the movement.

In a concentric manner, this history is focused on the US Critical Legal Studies movement. Other types of CLS are touched upon, but only to contextualise the US variant. Within US-CLS, Duncan Kennedy is the primary focus. Other Crits and their work are addressed throughout, but Kennedy is the link between them all. In the penultimate chapter, Patricia Williams is the primary interlocutor.

Acronyms and initialisms are also used, as well as abbreviated titles for repeated works. These should be clear in context, but the main ones used are:

CLS: Critical Legal Studies
Brit Crit: Adherent of UK-CLS
CCLS: Conference on Critical Legal Studies
Crit: Adherent of US-CLS
Fem-crit: Feminist critical theorist
PCLS: Posthumous Critical Legal Studies
UK-CLS: British Critical Legal Studies
US-CLS: United States Critical Legal Studies movement

Ideas, theories, and elements of this book have been presented and published elsewhere. Chapter One expands on "Panic at the Law School! A Critical Case for Legal Subcultures", published in *Law and Critique*, volume 33.[4] This paper was also presented at UC Berkeley and Cardozo Law Schools in February 2020; I am grateful for the feedback and discussions this piece garnered. Chapter Two draws on "Demystifying CLS: A Critical Legal Studies Family Tree", published in the *Adelaide Law Review*.[5] Chapter Five builds on the concept published as "CLS is Haunted!" in *Law and Literature*.[6] Elements in Chapter Six were presented at the Post-Critical Perspectives on Critical Legal Studies conference at Cardozo Law School in 2022. My sincere thanks

---

[4] James Gilchrist Stewart, "Panic at the Law School! A Critical Case for Legal Subcultures" (2002) 33(2) *Law and Critique* 195.

[5] James Gilchrist Stewart, "Demystifying CLS: A Critical Legal Studies Family Tree" (2020) 41(1) *Adelaide Law Review* 121.

[6] James Gilchrist Stewart, "CLS Is Haunted! A Perspective on Contemporary Critical Legal Studies" (2020) 36(1) *Law and Literature* 135.

to all reviewers, editors, discussants, and organisers who assisted with the publication of these pieces.

A number of people are owed individual thanks for their assistance with this project in a variety of capacities and ways: Peter Goodrich, Bill MacNeil, Corinne Blalock, James Martel, Paul Babie, Peter Burdon, Megan Beatrice, Kyriaco Nikias, Daimeon Shanks, Matt Steilen, Peter Rush, Alison Young, Tim Peters, Ben Howe, Peter Gabel, Bob Gordon, and Duncan Kennedy. Sincere thanks to the team at EUP, Laura, Sarah, Helena, Judith, Fiona, and Sam. My deepest thanks to my brothers, Angus and Rupert, and my father, Christopher. And last but never least, Lizzy.

1

Reimagining Critical Legal Studies

[A]n intellectual critique is not a disembodied text but is rather always spoken or written by a living being who exerts his own presence through it and toward his listener or reader, and that it is on this meta-plane of reciprocity, of being-together and seeing the object of critique together in a new light, that a better world starts to be born each time that it happens.

Peter Gabel, "The force that through the green fuse drives the flower" (2015)

The US Critical Legal Studies movement (CLS) is often remembered through its development of theory and practice: actions of trashing, arguing law as politics, and addressing the indeterminacy of law. These actions are synonymous and often interchangeable with "demystification", "delegitimation", "debunking",[1] and "deconstruction".[2] Using these and other methods of legal critique and pedagogy, CLS sought to demystify dominant legal structures and institutions. However, this focus on theory and practice leaves a noticeable gap in the position of Critical Legal Studies—or, to put it another way, in determining the space that CLS operated within. As nature abhors a vacuum, this gap is often filled with two broad descriptions: first, CLS as a self-proclaimed network and political location that provided like-minded legal scholars with a place to converge;[3] and second, CLS as a counterculture or countercultural

---

[1] Alan D. Freeman, "Truth and Mystification in Legal Scholarship" (1981) 90(5) *Yale Law Journal* 1,229; Mark Tushnet, "Critical Legal Studies: An Introduction to its Origins and Underpinnings" (1986) 36 *Journal of Legal Education* 505, 506.

[2] Clare Dalton, "An Essay in the Deconstruction of Contract Doctrine" (1985) 94(5) *Yale Law Journal* 997, 1,007; Jerry L. Anderson, "Law School Enters The Matrix: Teaching Critical Legal Studies" (2004) 54(2) *Journal of Legal Education* 201, 209.

[3] Tor Krever, Carl Lisberger, and Max Utzschneider, "Law on the Left: A Conversation with Duncan Kennedy" (2015) 10(1) *Unbound* 1, 23; Mark Tushnet, "Critical Legal Studies: A Political History" (1991) 100 *Yale Law Journal* 1,515, 1,517.

movement.[4] The first description addresses the relationship between Crits and their fellow travellers, mirroring the disjointed but connected nature of CLS work and the scholars who dabble in it. The second describes the relationship between CLS, society, and the institutions it operated within. However, the second descriptor gives an inaccurate understanding of Critical Legal Studies. Despite clear connections to the broader 1960s countercultural movement, CLS was not a counterculture, it was a legal subculture.

The relationship between the 1960s countercultural epoch and CLS is woven into the movement's general history, buried amongst other uncontroversial and seemingly undisputed elements. Conversely, there is only a brief published mention of CLS as a subculture, in which Cornel West uses and repeats the phrase, "academic left subcultures like critical legal studies".[5] Whilst initially it may appear to be a relatively minor linguistic difference, the reimagination of CLS as a legal subculture provides several points of clarification. First, for the general demystification of CLS, the very position and relationship of a legal subculture clarifies where and how CLS operated: in operation below the dominant culture, but engaged with it. This contrasts with the position of a counterculture, which operates outside an existing legal framework *countering* it.

The second point of clarity comes with a more meaningful understanding of the relationship between the 1960s–70s counterculture and CLS, specifically unpacking the terminology and imagery associated with Critical Legal Studies. The final point of clarification comes through the associated lens of a "moral panic", a sociological method which codifies a series of reactions common to all subcultures. The identification and discussion of a CLS moral panic presents a rationale for the dominant reactions to the movement both within and outside the academe.

The categorisation of Critical Legal Studies as a subculture is uncommon. When West called CLS a subculture, the framing or importance of the term was not discussed. Instead it appears to have been an accurate but unimportant categorisation of CLS; in context, West presents CLS as emblematic of left-wing disruptive approaches in academia. West's choice to use the term "subculture" is more logical in this context, when other leftist movements could not all be categorised as "countercultural". Understandably, West's brief mention of "subculture" pales in comparison to the common conflation between the 1960s counterculture and CLS. In a less literal application than "CLS is a counterculture", this

---

[4] Juhana Mikael Salojärvi, "A Counter-Culture of Law: Jurisprudential Change and the Intellectual Origins of the Critical Legal Studies Movement" (2019) 59(4) *American Journal of Legal History* 409.

[5] Cornel West, "Reassessing the Critical Legal Studies Movement" (1988) 34 *Loyola Law Review* 265, 267.

categorisation can be read as a placeholder to make sense of CLS's origins. Given the way in which CLS came about, as well as its shared values and adherents,[6] there is a clear logic to the application and use of the term "counterculture".

The Crits were also reluctant to position themselves under any specific title or school of thought, so as to avoid conflation with unnecessary and doctrinal structures; in that sense, the idea of a counterculture fits with their broad ideology. Addressing the development and connection between the early Crits, Duncan Kennedy states that, "Many had been activists or counterculturalists of one kind or another and/or had been exposed to critical theory in the humanities or social sciences in one of its myriad American forms of the 1970s."[7]

Clearly, the counterculture created space for CLS. As Robert Gordon articulates:

> Critical Legal Studies is basically a movement of legal intellectuals, originating in intellectual quarrels with their own legal education. Most activist students of the 1960s who were involved in radical or left-liberal politics found the studiedly anti-political teaching of that time simply irrelevant to their concerns; they scrounged such slim practical pickings from law school as they could, got the degree, and moved on. But the 1960s law students who went on to form the core of cls mostly became teachers themselves, and so were motivated to engage with the content and style of orthodox doctrinal teaching and scholarship.[8]

Kennedy adds to Gordon's explanation with a reflection on two branches of CLS:

> I guess critical legal studies has two aspects. It's a scholarly literature and it has also been a network of people who were thinking of themselves as activists in law school politics. Initially, the scholarly literature was produced by the same people who were doing the law school activism. Critical legal studies is not a theory. It's basically this literature produced by this network of people.[9]

---

[6] Salojärvi (n 4); Kimberlé Williams Crenshaw, "Twenty Years of Critical Race Theory: Looking Back to Move Forward" (2011) 43 *Connecticut Law Review* 1,253; Laura Kalman, *Yale Law School and the Sixties: Revolt and Reverberations* (University of North Carolina Press, 2005) 7.

[7] Duncan Kennedy, *Legal Education and the Reproduction of Hierarchy: A Polemic Against the System* (New York University Press, 2004) 205.

[8] Robert W. Gordon, "Critical Legal Studies as a Teaching Method, against the Background of the Intellectual Politics of Modern Legal Education in the United States" (1989) 59 *Legal Education Review* 59, 75.

[9] Gerard J. Clark, "A Conversation with Duncan Kennedy" (1994) 24(2) *Suffolk University Law School Journal* 56, 56.

From both Gordon and Kennedy's accounts, the developing picture of Critical Legal Studies is a network of left-wing activists, focused on legal education and law more generally. Beyond this, their categorisation appears unimportant. These initial observations manifest in Kennedy's self-published *Legal Education and the Reproduction of Hierarchy: A Polemic Against the System*. As the title implies, the book is a challenge to the systemic way in which American law schools taught and interacted with law and the legal profession. In the preface to the first edition, Kennedy presents an overview of the text, which affirms the position he and Gordon identified above:

> This is an essay about the role of legal education in American social life. It is a description of the ways in which legal education contributes to the reproduction of illegitimate hierarchy in the bar and in society. And it suggests ways in which left students and teachers who are determined not to let law school demobilize them can make the experience part of a left activist practice of social transformation.[10]

While there is some unity within Kennedy's *Legal Education and the Reproduction of Hierarchy* and Gordon's "Critical Legal Studies as a Teaching Method", CLS was not confined to one target or one method. Instead, the self-described network was rhizomatic in its development, refusing to be static or easily defined. The Crits prided themselves on this, as fellow Crit Mark Kelman discusses when identifying the unique approach of CLS: "What differentiated Critical Legal Studies, especially in comparison with left academic movements of the past is its focus on ambiguity, its resolute refusal to see a synthesis in every set of contradictions"[11]—a point which Gordon confirms:

> For perhaps the most central CLS tenet is that the legal system is not a single, integral system at all. Rather it is a teeming jungle of multiple, overlapping, contradictory systems, each pregnant at every historical moment with multiple alternative interpretations, possibilities and trajectories of future development. Each alternative is perfectly consistent with the system's operating premises and processing logic but only a few in any given moment are selected for adoption.[12]

Viewing law as a multifaceted and contradictory series of systems, rather than one unified or synthesised model, offers some explanation for the wide breadth of critiques that fell under the CLS banner. In 1984, an example

---

[10] Kennedy, *Legal Education and the Reproduction of Hierarchy* (n 7) 15.
[11] Mark G. Kelman, "Trashing" (1984) 36(1/2) *Stanford Law Review* 293, 296.
[12] Gordon (n 8) 77.

of the breadth of CLS was presented in the ambitious "A Bibliography of Critical Legal Studies", compiled by Kennedy and Karl Klare.[13] However, the sheer number of different and disparate works in this article mirrored Gordon's view of the legal system, with CLS a teeming jungle of systems and approaches.

In 2005, China Miéville outlined this issue and the unwanted ramifications that came from the CLS approach, stating: "There are lacunae and problems with . . . the CLS approach in general. One problem lies in the very eclecticism which some see as CLS's strength. This can lead to a blunting of analysis, as a plethora of conflicting influences are lumped together."[14] Miéville takes his analysis further, outlining that the lack of a unified base or a doctrinal method hinders CLS: "The sometimes indiscriminate attitude to theory comes at a price. The profusion of influences has left CLS scholars with powerful critical tools, but a poverty of systematic *theory*".[15]

Miéville's critique of Critical Legal Studies is understandable and offers a way to address this issue through the implementation of a systemic or doctrinal grounding for CLS. However, any attempt to ground CLS in this way pulls it closer to the apparatuses it identified and railed against in other methods and institutions.[16] Even where CLS reflected the varied and multiple systems in law itself, it never succumbed to a definitive structure. Kennedy reflects on this aspect of the organisation, seen in CLS's approaches to critique and scholarship more broadly:

> Don't forget the brilliance of CLS scholarship and the creativity of the organizing strategy, which eschewed both formal organizational structure and the development of any kind of CLS program or manifesto but nonetheless managed to avoid being co-opted by the smug liberal elitists or destroyed by the authoritarians and random crazies who are drawn like flies to honey by apparently unboundaried left ventures.[17]

Kennedy's reflection on this success fails to consider or reconcile how the measures put in place to protect CLS actively excluded, and continue to exclude, contemporary applications by those sympathetic to its cause.

---

[13] Duncan Kennedy and Karl E. Klare, "A Bibliography of Critical Legal Studies" (1984) 94(461) *Yale Law Journal* 46.
[14] China Miéville, *Between Equal Rights: A Marxist Theory of International Law* (Brill, 2005) 55.
[15] Ibid 56 (emphasis in original).
[16] Kennedy, *Legal Education and the Reproduction of Hierarchy* (n 7).
[17] Ibid 206.

One argument for why this wasn't rectified throughout the lifetime of CLS can be seen in founding Crit Roberto Unger's understanding that CLS was only meant to be something temporary: "Critical legal studies was never intended to generate a permanent genre of legal writing, or to take its place among a standing cast of schools of legal theory. It was a disruptive engagement in a particular circumstance".[18] While one might respect this founding Crit's view on the *intention* of Critical Legal Studies, his position is not reflective of its impact or influence. From Unger's perspective, the categorisation of CLS as an "extension of sixties activism"[19] would be justified. However, it ignores the continuing and posthumous versions of CLS, as well as the wants of those, like Miéville, who cannot access something concrete from the Crits.

What can be taken from these reflections on the origins of CLS is that there was not any unified self-identification of category, and that while the categorisation as a counterculture is understandable, it is at best limited and at worst aids the mystification of CLS. Instead, the recategorisation of CLS as a legal subculture allows for, and explains, the movement's history. There is a necessary balance, then, between the imposition of a structure that betrays the Crits' understanding of CLS, and a recategorisation that ignores the influence of 1960s counterculture on CLS. An effective middle ground is the presentation of CLS as a legal subculture birthed by a broader counterculture.

* * *

Before continuing, a clear distinction needs to be drawn that, while similar, a counterculture and a subculture are not synonymous. This distinction can be clarified through the prefix to culture in each word: either "counter" or "sub". As the names denote, a counterculture exists in opposition to a dominant culture—it *counters* it—while a subculture occurs under or below the dominant culture. When these terms are applied to CLS, its location within university law schools is problematic for a counterculture which "poses itself in total opposition to the dominant culture. It takes the values of the dominant culture and redefines them negatively".[20]

For CLS to be a true counterculture, it would need to be positioned in opposition to law schools, not within them. "Subcultures represent 'noise'

---

[18] Roberto Mangabeira Unger, *The Critical Legal Studies Movement: Another Time, a Greater Task* (Verso, 2015) 4.
[19] Kalman (n 6) 7.
[20] Ralph W. Larkin, "Counterculture: 1960s and Beyond" (2015) 5 *International Encyclopedia of the Social & Behavioral Sciences* 2nd Edition 73, 73.

(as opposed to sound) [and] interference in the orderly sequence";[21] they are disruptive and challenging, but fundamentally *under* and within the dominant culture. This argument on the location and relation of CLS to the dominant culture of law and the law school underscores the argument that CLS was not a counterculture. Again, it is important to note that this distinction does not deny the effect of the 1960s counterculture on CLS. Instead, it should be understood as forming an important part of CLS's status as a legal subculture, sharing common goals and understandings:

> As a movement, the counterculture was admittedly disjointed, with its followers embracing everything from yoga to shamanism to McLuhanism. Yet if there was one common thread, it was a rejection of the existing society, which many labelled "The Establishment", their main critique being that everyday life in the Western world had come to resemble the workings of a massive industrial corporation.[22]

The similarities of the 1960s counterculture to Critical Legal Studies are immediately clear, but they exist microcosmically, with a focus on law and the law school rather than on the existing society more broadly. Through the influence of the counterculture, other elements of CLS make contextual sense. For example, the first published edition of Kennedy's *The Rise and Fall of Classical Legal Thought* states, "For this edition I've added this preface, a bibliography and a rudimentary index".[23] What at first appears to be an innocuous statement highlights that the original self-published history of American legal thought refused to conform to even the most common and useful structures.

Similarly, Unger's *The Critical Legal Studies Movement* presents as a standard book, and draws on a body of existing theory, but has no citations: this can be read as defying a similar convention. The obvious downside to these actions is the way they add to the mystification of CLS, especially when one is approaching the work years after it was presented in context. However, whilst these examples demonstrate some structural relationships between CLS and the counterculture, the counterculture's influence is perhaps most evident in the specific language used by the Crits.

A common thread in assessments of CLS, was the Crits' use of language: "This body of writing has been correctly described as 'dense and difficult and

---

[21] Dick Hebdige, *Subculture: The Meaning of Style* (Routledge, 1989) 90.
[22] Meghan Warner Mettler, "'If I Could Drive You Out of Your Mind' Anti-Rationalism and the Celebration of Madness in 1960s Counterculture" (2015) 9(2) *Journal of Literary & Cultural Disability Studies* 171, 173.
[23] Duncan Kennedy, *The Rise and Fall of Classical Legal Thought* (BeardBooks, 2006) vii.

often inaccessible' and as having produced some of the most provocative and perplexing legal scholarship of the past several years."[24] The inaccessibility of CLS's language was not only due to the style of the work, but also to the specific terminology used.[25] The use of this specific language demonstrates the interconnectivity between the influence of the counterculture and the position of CLS as a legal subculture.

The CLS buzzword "trashing" offers insight into the influence of the counterculture, whilst also reiterating the deliberate difficulty in defining elements of CLS. Starting with the eponymous "Trashing", Mark Kelman's article offers a somewhat opaque definition of the term:

> Here's one account of the technique that we in Critical Legal Studies often use in analysing texts, a technique I call "Trashing": Take specific arguments very *seriously* in their own terms; discover they are actually foolish ([tragi]-*comic*); and then look for some (external observer's) *order* (*not* the germ of truth) in the internally contradictory, incoherent chaos we've exposed.[26]

Kelman expands on the term, drawing on Michel Foucault's discussions of power, stating:

> Many of us (arguably influenced by Foucault) have been interested in understanding power in its most local manifestations . . . for me, trashing is above all a technique of seeing (and undermining) illegitimate power in the most comprehensible and immediate institutions I see—the law schools where I've studied and worked.[27]

In the second quotation, Kelman's expansion on trashing highlights the use of "foolishness" in the original definition, and the need to both see and undermine illegitimate power. Despite their non-doctrinal aim, Kelman's approach does follow an earlier explanation of trashing by Alan Freeman:

> That trashing may reveal truth seems significant if one's mission as a scholar is to tell the truth. If telling the truth requires one to engage in delegitimation, then that is what one ought to be doing. Trashing is also liberating . . . The goal of trashing, however, is not liberation into nihilist resignation . . . The point of delegitimation is to expose possibilities more truly expressing reality, possibilities of fashioning a future that might at least partially realize

---

[24] J. Stuart Russell, "The Critical Legal Studies Challenge to Contemporary Mainstream Legal Philosophy" (1986) 18(1) *Ottawa Law Review* 1, 3.

[25] See, for example, Peter Gabel and Duncan Kennedy, "Roll Over Beethoven" (1984) 36(1/2) *Stanford Law Review* 1.

[26] Kelman (n 11) 293 (emphasis in original).

[27] Ibid 321.

a substantive notion of justice instead of the abstract, rightsy, traditional, bourgeois notions of justice that generate so much of the contradictory scholarship.[28]

Freeman's account of trashing, which also addresses issues of power, elucidates the themes taken up by Kelman. At the heart of Freeman's trashing is a type of liberation that cannot be achieved by side-stepping dominant approaches to legal issues. At the same time, Freeman highlights that works addressing rights or other notions of justice within this existing framework only bolster the dominant culture, rather than challenging it. Although the reading of both papers together provides a basic understanding of trashing, the more logically titled "Trashing" relies on existing knowledge or supplementary texts (both Foucault and Freeman in this case) to fully appreciate or apply trashing to a subject. Even Freeman's much more clear account, which also relies on Karl Marx and Foucault, is a short, ten-page article that challenges fellow Crits rather than offering a "how to" trash.[29] However, the difficulty in clarifying what trashing is, or how to trash, is not only related to the lack of descriptions given, but to the term trashing itself.

The verb "trashing" arose in the in the early 1970s in relation to specific vandalism by university students in the United States . The era, locations, and reasons for the vandalism position the students accused and associated with acts of trashing within the same broad counterculture that birthed the Crits.[30] For CLS more specifically, the idea of trashing incorporated the term's roots in vandalism and desecration, but also drew from its application in counter-culture literature, specifically the titular character from the comic *Trashman*.

The character of Trashman, created and drawn by Spain Rodriguez, was originally featured alongside other countercultural cartoonists such as Robert Crumb in the *East Village Other*, or *EVO*. With the *EVO* considered "a New York Newspaper so countercultural that it made *The Village Voice* look like a church circular",[31] the cartoon—which features sex, drugs, and violence—reflects a number of other countercultural themes and styles of the time.[32] Alleged to have been reflective of the author's own social and political beliefs, *Trashman* is set in an American dystopia "with a totalitarian form of

---

[28] Freeman (n 1) 1,230–1.
[29] Ibid 1,237.
[30] Helen Lefkowitz Horowitz, "The 1960s and the Transformation of Campus Cultures" (1986) 26(1) *History of Education Quarterly* 1, 10–13.
[31] Margalit Fox, "Walter Bowart, Alternative Journalist, Dies at 68", *The New York Times* (online, 14 January 2008) <https://www.nytimes.com/2008/01/14/arts/14bowart.html>.
[32] See generally counterculture comics such as "The Fabulous Furry Freak Brothers" and "Fat Freddy's Cat".

government, mass poverty, repressive social control systems, a large military-like police force, a lack of individual freedoms, and continual warfare or violence".³³ Trashman is an agent of the Sixth International, a nod to the Third International and a denotation of Trashman's Communist allegiance. Although Trashman does not actively trash those he fights against, the people inspired by his disdain for oppressive or fascistic structures—who opt to challenge similar structures of their choosing—may be understood as "trashing".

It should be noted that while comics also played a large part in the way CLS was presented, in both their *Critical Legal Studies Newsletters* and the work of their students,³⁴ there is little assessment given to the importance of this graphic culture.³⁵ Building on the visual as well as the linguistic connection, the link to Trashman is strengthened with a description of Kennedy from the 1996 *Harvard Law Bulletin* discussed by Peter Goodrich in his review of Kennedy's *Critique of Adjudication (fin de siècle)*. In his assessment of Kennedy's image, Goodrich states that the Carter professor of general jurisprudence "is dressed for urban combat, he is everyday cool, sympatico but with attitude, and in the accompanying text he talks of adopting 'a kind of intellectual guerilla warfare' against the institution",³⁶ a description which would be equally fitting for a similarly presented Trashman. However, while Goodrich's assessment circles around similar visual connections, the link to the obscure counterculture comic book hero is not addressed. Nor should it be: it is unlikely, despite the seemingly obvious influence of *Trashman* on CLS, that the Crits would have noted it, or thought it worthy of noting. Much like Kennedy's lack of bibliography or index, or Unger's lack of citations, the Crits not only avoided existing conventions but importantly, like most subcultures, they were organic and responsive, rather than strategic. This is something that Kennedy was seemingly aware of:

> I've been asked a million times why CLS "failed", but it seems a more interesting question how such an overtly leftist, anti-mainstream academic movement, with no outside funding of any kind, could take off, expand

---

33 Steven M. Fox, "The Collected Trashman" (2013) *Underground Comix Joint* <https://comixjoint.com/collectedtrashman.html>.

34 Duncan Kennedy, "Remembering Keith Aoki's 'Casual Legal Studies: Art During Law School'" (2012) 45(5) *University of California Davis Law Review* 1,817.

35 For current rather than historical works on comics and law, see: Thomas Giddens, *Graphic Justice: Intersections of Comics and Law* (GlassHouse Routledge, 2015); Thomas Giddens, *On Comics and Legal Aesthetics: Multimodality and the Haunted Mask of Knowing* (GlassHouse Routledge, 2018).

36 Peter Goodrich, "Duncan Kennedy As I Imagine Him: The Man, the Work, His Scholarship, and the Polity" (2001) 22 *Cardozo Law Review* 971, 974.

so quickly, and last for about fifteen years as a highly visible factor in legal academia (of all places).[37]

Kennedy's position is similar to the point made earlier by Unger that CLS was "never intended to generate a permanent genre of legal writing".[38] Instead it was reactionary, a method that intended to engage with an immediate issue, not an ongoing solution to a problem. The lack of explanations, the reactionary nature, the specific language, and (for Kennedy specifically) a certain dress sense demonstrate the features of a subculture.[39]

The term "trashing" as a legitimate way to critique law is a recognition of the influence the counterculture had on the legal subculture: "Notions concerning the sanctity of language are intimately bound up with ideas of social order."[40] For the Crits, the use of the term "trashing" began to undermine the existing order, removing the politeness that a term like "critique" implies. In turn, for the universities and non-Crits, the use of "trashing" challenged the sanctity of the law school and the profession of law: "[V]iolations of the authorized codes through which the social world is organized and experienced have considerable power to provoke and disturb."[41] These reactions worked simultaneously, so that while the Crits were delegitimating an existing legal argument, they were also provoking and disturbing the existing social order. The effectiveness of this approach is much harder to maintain from a countercultural position, one which is outside the dominant culture rather than operating within it and subverting it from below.

* * *

Arguing that CLS was influenced, birthed, and/or shaped by the 1960s counterculture, but was not itself a counterculture, does not automatically lead to the conclusion that it was a subculture. In some ways the emerging field of minor jurisprudence provides a logical position for CLS. Objectively a legal subculture and a minor jurisprudence are not the same thing, and either could characterise CLS better than a counterculture. However, despite their similar names, minor jurisprudence is less applicable for what CLS was and continues to be, and instead provides a characterisation for what CLS could or should have been.

---

[37] Kennedy, *Legal Education and the Reproduction of Hierarchy* (n 7) 204.
[38] Unger (n 18) 4.
[39] Hebdige (n 21) 90–99.
[40] Ibid 91.
[41] Ibid.

The legally specific term "minor jurisprudence" was developed in the 1990s to recognise historic and contemporary "rebels, critics, marginals, aliens, women and outsiders who over time repeatedly challenge the dominance of any singular system of legal norms".[42] This description, by Goodrich, comes directly from a critique of the US-based Critical Legal Studies, identifying where and how it "failed in its radicalism".[43]

Whilst Goodrich presents a clear outline of who he sees fitting within his description, the concept of a minor jurisprudence can be traced from three sources leading to its application to CLS. Originating from Gilles Deleuze and Félix Guattari's classification of "minor literature",[44] the term was adapted and reimagined in its application to law. This adaptation was made separately by both Goodrich and Panu Minkkinen, as "two distinct incarnations".[45] However, all three sources aid in understanding CLS as a form of minor jurisprudence.

Deleuze and Guattari defined a minor literature with reference to Franz Kafka, as "not the literature of a minor language but the literature a minority makes in a major language".[46] The authors categorise minor literature with three characteristics: the deterritorialisation of the language, the connection of the individual and the political, and the collective arrangement of utterances.[47] Chronologically, Minkkinen's adaptation came next, and while he and Goodrich tackle the same original text, Minkkinen focuses more on Kafka's role as a minor jurisprudent. Minkkinen sees the transition between literature and law as evident in Kafka's texts, stating that Kafka was able to "unravel the essence of law and see the legal phenomenon as it truly is".[48] He argues, "Outside the realms of all major literary traditions, Kafka cannot be read merely as an author trying to describe a particular life and its circumstances but, rather, as the initiator of a political program."[49]

---

[42] Peter Goodrich, *Law in the Courts of Love: Literature and Other Minor Jurisprudences* (Routledge, 1996) 2.
[43] Ibid 186.
[44] Gilles Deleuze and Félix Guattari, "What is a Minor Literature?", tr. Robert Brinkley (1983) 11(3) *Mississippi Review* 13, 16. See also Gilles Deleuze and Félix Guattari, *Kafka: Towards a Minor Literature*, tr. Dana Polan (University of Minnesota Press, 1986) [trans of: *Kafka: pour une literature mineure* (1975)].
[45] Christopher Tomlins, "Law As ... IV: Minor Jurisprudence in Historical Key. An Introduction" (2017) 17 *Law Text Culture* 1, 2.
[46] Deleuze and Guattari, "'What is a Minor Literature?'" (n 44) 16.
[47] Ibid 18.
[48] Panu Minkkinen, "The Radiance of Justice: On the Minor Jurisprudence of Franz Kafka" (1994) 3 *Social & Legal Studies* 349, 358.
[49] Ibid 357.

While Minkkinen's, and Deleuze and Guattari's readings of Kafka could be applied to CLS, it is Goodrich's focus on law more generally which creates the applicable framework:

> A minor jurisprudence is one which neither aspires nor pretends to be the only law or universal jurisprudence. Its referent is a law whose jurisdiction is neither jealous of other jurisdictions nor fearful of alternative disciplines. It represents the strangeness of language and so the possibilities of interpretation as also of plural forms of knowledge. A minor jurisprudence . . . is a challenge to the science of law and a threat to its monopoly of legal knowledge. *It challenges the law of masters, the genre and categories of the established institution of doctrine and its artificial and paper rules.*[50]

For CLS, the application of the last line is the most pertinent, while those before it fit in some but not all applications. Thus, the applicability to CLS is good, but not perfect: Goodrich's own development of this framework comes from a critique of CLS, presenting what it could have done better and how to achieve the full aim of minor jurisprudence. From this perspective, there is still merit in thinking about CLS through the lens of minor jurisprudence; however, so far, the term is underutilised, and as such lacks the cachet and development that "subculture" has benefitted from.[51]

In 2016, the idea of minor jurisprudence was revisited through a symposium, with the papers collated by Christopher Tomlins and published in *Law Text Culture* as "Law As . . . Minor Jurisprudence in Historical Key". While some of these papers present new ways to think of, and on, minor jurisprudence, they do not offer the structure needed to classify CLS. What this symposium and its papers do highlight, however, is a structural clarity similar to a legal subculture and opposed to a counterculture, where critique comes from within rather than outside the dominant framework. This geography may render "minor jurisprudence" a preferred term for legal-specific subcultures in the future, but given its history and current status, classifying CLS as a legal subculture is the preferable way to represent it.

* * *

---

[50] Goodrich, *Law in the Courts of Love* (n 42) 2 (emphasis added); see also Deleuze and Guattari "'What is a Minor Literature?'" (n 44) 17 for their use of "master".

[51] Contra, Elena Loizidou, "Sex @ the End of the Twentieth Century: Some Re-Marks on a Minor Jurisprudence" (1999) 10(1) *Law and Critique* 71; Olivia Barr, *A Jurisprudence of Movement: Common Law, Walking, Unsettling Place* (GlassHouse Routledge, 2016).

A benefit to reimaging Critical Legal Studies as a legal subculture is the inherent clarity this shift brings. Aside from demonstrating the influence of the 1960s counterculture on CLS's language and image, a subculture comes with a history of associated terms and reactions. Notably, the idea of a moral panic is intrinsically linked to subcultures. This sociological construct relates to the perception of subcultures and their adherents, positioning the latter as deviants.[52] In categorising CLS as a legal subculture, its adherents, the Crits, assume the role of legal deviants. Whilst law school professors are not likely to be the first group associated with the term "legal deviant", the proposal of the Crits' deviancy is not new, even if the lens through which it is presented is. The deviant nature of CLS has been noted, perhaps most literally but also imaginatively by Patricia Williams. In a critique of CLS, Williams describes the Crits leaving an allegorical walled city of law, the "Celestial City", demonstrating a literal deviation of the Crits from law's form and structure.[53] Whilst this deviation may seem insignificant when contrasted with other societal deviancy, it still leads to a moral panic.

The concept of a moral panic was developing several years before the first Conference on Critical Legal Studies. A sociological construct to make sense of disproportionate reactions to deviants, the term has been used widely since its inception.[54] However, in its original context, there are interesting crossovers of counterculture influence between CLS and the subcultural groups who were both the subjects and instigators of the term "moral panic". For example, Jock Young, credited with creating the phrase, applied it initially in *The Drugtakers: The Social Meaning of Drug Use*, an assessment of the 1960s hippies and counterculture in Notting Hill, UK.[55] Similarly, Stanley Cohen refined the idea of the moral panic in *Folk Devils and Moral Panics: The Creation of the Mods and Rockers*, addressing the media and political portrayals of these two youth subcultures in Brighton, UK.[56]

In a similar approach to CLS, Young and Cohen focused on phenomena that related to the cultural change they were witnessing. Though not directly connected, there were shared cultural values in the work of the Crits and

---

[52] Jock Young, "Moral Panic: Its Origins in Resistance, Ressentiment and the Translation of Fantasy into Reality" (2009) 49(1) *British Journal of Criminology* 4.
[53] Patricia J. Williams, "Alchemical Notes: Reconstructing Ideals From Deconstructed Rights" (1987) 22 *Harvard Civil Rights–Civil Liberties Law Review* 401, 401–2.
[54] Eugene McLaughlin, "See Also Young, 1971: Marshall McLuhan, Moral Panics and Moral Indignation" (2014) 18(4) *Theoretical Criminology* 422.
[55] Jock Young, *The Drugtakers: The Social Meaning of Drug Use* (MacGibbon and Kee, 1971).
[56] Stanley Cohen, *Folk Devils and Moral Panics: The Creation of the Mods and Rockers* (Paladin, 1973).

specifically those of Young. Reflecting on the importance of when this took place, Young states:

> It is important to stress how a younger generation of sociologists identified with the process of cultural change that pivoted around 1968. We were all moved by the times: the possibility of social change, the worlds of diversity that the new bohemia promised, the youthful colonization of leisure and the rejection of austerity and discipline in a world seemingly in fast-forward, all of which made the choice of being on the side of progress well nigh inevitable.[57]

Similarly, Kennedy reflects on the effect this time had on him; leading him from being a left-liberal undergraduate to becoming a radical law student:

> In the first year of law school, this was 1967–68, I had the classic generational experience of radicalisation. I started law school as a disillusioned Cold War leftliberal, anti-Communist, and then there was this realisation: the Soviet Union was a paper tiger; with the Prague Spring in 1968, it was obvious that the Soviet Union under Brezhnev had had it; I was happy not sad or alarmed by the successes of the North Vietnamese Tet offensive. The whole anti-Communist construct was now nothing but an aspect of conservatism in America, and the liberal commitment to anti-Communism was a major source of America's inability to deal with the real problems, the war and the ghetto. In the course of a year I switched back to a position much more like that of my teenage self and have been there more or less ever since.[58]

While revisionist cultural artefacts such as films, books, and television depict this trope as dominant within the 1960s, those in this progressive space were far from the majority: "Usually portrayed as having rejected traditional values, or at least as having redefined them, only a small minority of young boomers were actually involved in radical politics or the hippie movement."[59] Despite this, "a small percentage of a huge number is still a lot; and this fraction of the baby boomer generation clearly very much made its mark on how the 1960s are perceived."[60] This perception was then magnified as it resonated

---

[57] Young, "Moral Panic" (n 52) 8.
[58] Krever, Lisberger, and Utzschneider (n 3) 6.
[59] Phil Rose, "'Love Is All You Need': Why There Will Never Be Another Beatles", in Brian Cogan and Thom Gencarelli (eds), *Baby Boomers and Popular Culture: An Inquiry Into America's Most Powerful Generation* (Praeger, 2015) 225, 234.
[60] Ibid.

beyond national boundaries: "The counterculture . . . bonded internationally through shared values and sensibilities".[61]

In its original usage, moral panic was seen as occurring in the interaction between certain subcultures and society more broadly, for example, hippies and drugs, or the violence between mods and rockers and their contrast to "decent" society. This juxtaposition lies at the heart of a moral panic, influenced by previous work on moral indignation which threatened identity and conformity:[62]

> One may also join with others in righteous puritanical wrath to mete out punishment to the deviants, not so much to stamp out their deviant behavior, as to reaffirm the central importance of conformity as the basis for judging men and to reassure himself and others of his attachment to goodness.[63]

The development of the concept of the moral panic drew on the work of Marshall McLuhan, who highlighted the effect of the media, and how indignation could transform into panic.[64] In recent years, this framework has been more formally structured through the work of Stanley Cohen, who, it has been argued, "launched the term moral panic as a means of characterizing the reactions of the media, the public, and agents of social control to the youthful disturbances".[65] In this more formal approach, there are seven actors or events in a moral panic: the press, the public, law enforcement, politicians and legislators, action groups, folk devils, and an analogy to disaster.[66] With minor adaptations to its law-school context, this list can be applied to CLS, reinforcing its position as a legal subculture and highlighting that the reactions it received were to be expected.

Traditionally, moral panics were societally based and focused on national reactions. In contrast, the CLS moral panic was institutionally based, with a smaller, interested audience. For CLS, its location was law schools; however, for those outside the movement, CLS was primarily aligned with its "home", Harvard Law School.[67] While the identification of law enforcement or politicians and legislators for purposes of a moral panic is difficult in the context of CLS, that does not mean that their equivalents were not present. For CLS,

---

[61] Ibid.
[62] Young, "Moral Panic" (n 52) 10.
[63] Ibid.
[64] McLaughlin (n 54) 424.
[65] Erich Goode and Nachman Ben-Yehuda, *Moral Panics: The Social Construction Of Deviance* (Wiley-Blackwell, 2nd ed, 2009) 22.
[66] Ibid 23–7.
[67] Kalman (n 6) 7.

the "agents of social control" can be seen to mirror the deans, boards, and alumni of the university.[68] With this contextual clarification, it can be posited that the reaction to CLS followed the formula of a moral panic.

The first actor in a moral panic is the press. The press covered CLS, with a number of articles appearing in the *New York Times*, the *New Yorker*, and the *New Republic*. However, it is not enough that a subject is covered: it must be given far more attention than is deserved and the seriousness be overstated. From inside CLS, Kennedy highlights this event: "[T]he national media decided that Harvard Law School was a 'story', the story of sixties radicals reemerging with tenure to disrupt everything good and true."[69] Objectively, it is a strange occurrence for a group of legal academics and their pedagogical methods to be reported on, let alone repeatedly in a paper of record like the *New York Times*. However, the seriousness of the claims against CLS can be seen in this excerpt from the *New Republic* in 1986: "it [Critical Legal Studies] operates with no expectation of developing a theory of politics or the state. No target is out of bounds, since whatever exists helps maintain the ideological hegemony of the powers that be, and is thus deserving of disrespect."[70] Within the same article, the terms "nihilist" and "elite" are levelled at the Crits, as well as records of staff wanting to leave Harvard Law School due to the presence of CLS and its adherents.[71] The threats, if one were to take the words at face value, were the anti-ideological promulgation of disrespect in all facets of "normal" or "decent" society—with the added threat that if it can happen at Harvard, it can happen anywhere.

The related aspect of the public—those who read the press and react to it—also needs to be considered in terms of its application to CLS. Although the publications that wrote on CLS were national papers and magazines, the panic was likely to affect only those within the broader legal community. In the original positioning of "the public" in moral panics, the panicked response of the public was due to the relatability to the act of deviancy, for example, the drugs in question rather than the specific users, and the acts of "disdain, rebellion and indecency" from youths, rather than the groups specifically in Brighton:[72] "[t]he events themselves were not as important as what they seemed to represent".[73] For the public concerned with CLS—that

---

[68] Goode and Ben-Yehuda (n 65) 22.
[69] Kennedy, *Legal Education and the Reproduction of Hierarchy* (n 7) 216.
[70] Louis Menand, "What is 'Critical Legal Studies': Radicalism for Yuppies" (17 March 1986) *The New Republic* 20.
[71] Ibid 21.
[72] Goode and Ben-Yehuda (n 65) 25.
[73] Ibid.

is, the broader US legal community—the reactions were numerous. However, Paul Carrington, dean of law at Duke University, summed up the fears of this community, offering this damning statement on CLS and the Crits:

> The nihilist teacher threatens to rob his or her students of the courage to act on such professional judgment as they may have acquired. Teaching cynicism may, and perhaps probably does, result in the learning of the skills of corruption: bribery and intimidation. In an honest effort to proclaim a need for revolution, nihilist teachers are more likely to train crooks than radicals. If this risk is correctly appraised, the nihilist who must profess that legal principle does not matter has an ethical duty to depart the law school, perhaps to seek a place elsewhere in the academy.[74]

The effect of the public reaction was felt most harshly at Harvard Law School, with influential alumni stating that Kennedy and the Crits "represented a kind of professional barbarism" compared to Harvard's civilised place within the legal profession.[75] Similarly, the agents of social control effected a change, actively avoiding hiring Crits:

> Critical Legal Studies' faculty members would find a place here [Harvard Law School] if the only concern of the faculty was scholarship. But, what has happened now is many people will vote "for" or "against" thinking how that person will turn out to vote in the future.[76]

This open secret received wide attention with the denial of tenure to Crits Clare Dalton and David Trubek. Although there was no express statement that their denial was due to an anti-CLS stance, earlier statements by faculty members help to frame it as such. The effect of this practice quelled the growth of CLS at Harvard Law School, despite an expansion in faculty more generally.

Moved by pieces they saw in the press, action groups such as the John M. Olin Foundation were so panicked by CLS that they contacted sympathetic Harvard faculty to see what could be done to stop them.[77] The result of this action group was the creation of the Law and Economics centre at Harvard Law School, which would be the recipient of over $18 million from the

---

[74] Paul D. Carrington, "Of Law and the River" (1984) 34 *Journal of Legal Education* 222, 227.
[75] Steven M. Teles, *The Rise of the Conservative Legal Movement: The Battle for Control of the Law* (Princeton University Press, 2008) 193.
[76] Miguel Rodriguez, "'Politicized' Faculty Affects Tenure, Teaching, Research", *Harvard Law Record* (Cambridge, 9 March 1984).
[77] Teles (n 75) 193–4.

Olin Foundation.⁷⁸ This specific type of actor is described as a "moral entrepreneur", offering solutions to panics they believe are not being dealt with by existing remedies.⁷⁹ The moral entrepreneurs behind the action groups are often moved by the image of the *folk devil*, "the agent responsible for the threatening or damaging behaviour or condition".⁸⁰

In general terms the folk devil relates to stereotypes, that is, the images conjured by "decent society" when a certain type of deviancy or criminal activity is mentioned. Where there is no such clear image, the folk devil will still incite similar panics if it is given a title. For example, terms like "leftist" and "radical" are folk devils to conservatives: "To conservatives, leftists and radicals are great as folk devils; even today, they do terrible things like desecrate the flag, the symbol of our country".⁸¹ Whilst there is no defined image of a "leftist radical", the title applied to a person will incite the relevant panic.

For CLS, the folk devil was the Crit, often exemplified by Kennedy. For example, under the title of "Invasion of the Punk Professors",⁸² the front page of the *New Republic* featured a caricature of Kennedy in sneakers and a turtleneck, in front of a lectern, gesturing vigorously to an audience of bashful and confused law students. While this image is less radical than that of Kennedy as Trashman, the image of the folk devil is still there.

The final element in a moral panic is the analogy to disaster, where preparations are made in a similar way to those before, during, and after a natural disaster. However, unlike natural disasters, people gravitate towards these analogous events. The strength of this analogy can be seen in the rhetoric used by those responsible for the disaster, with Kennedy using similar terminology to describe CLS:

> It is often said that we destroyed Harvard—that Yale's ascendency was caused by what we did beginning in the late 1970s. The common view is that Yale Law School triumphed because it was not disrupted internally by the radicals, who they purged. I think this is largely correct. That is, I think the Yale Law School's current intellectual prestige is directly based on the reaction of the law professoriate to the disruption of Harvard Law School through the 1980s.⁸³

---

⁷⁸ John J. Miller, Karl Zinsmeister, and Ashley May, *Agenda Setting: A Wise Giver's Guide to Influencing Public Policy* (Philanthropy Roundtable, 2015) 40.
⁷⁹ Goode and Ben-Yehuda (n 65) 26.
⁸⁰ Ibid 27.
⁸¹ Ibid.
⁸² "Invasion of the Punk Professors", *The New Republic* (Washington DC, 17 March 1986) 1.
⁸³ Krever, Lisberger, and Utzschneider (n 3) 34.

Kennedy's account plays into the moral panic of CLS, as he accepts and genuinely uses hyperbolic terms when remembering what took place. As a response to a moral panic, the reactions to CLS were contextually reasonable.

While in general CLS does not cause such reactions now, the panic does occasionally return when the influence of CLS is used to explain a legal or political position. For example, although more prominently levelled at his connections to critical race theory (itself seeing a revival in its moral panic) and specifically to Derrick Bell,[84] Barack Obama's time at Harvard from 1988–1991 resulted in criticisms that he was influenced by Critical Legal Studies. From the *Chicago Tribune*:

> It is probably no coincidence that President Barack Obama's executive orders stretched the law and Constitution to new lengths, often beyond the breaking points. He went to Harvard Law School in an era when critical legal studies, which challenge and overturn accepted legal norms and standards and practices, were at their zenith.[85]

Evidently, CLS not only satisfies but exemplifies the necessary elements of a moral panic. The reimagination of CLS as a legal subculture also leads to a better understanding of the current status of CLS, with the final stage of a subculture beings its normalisation: from an "other" to something reduced and accepted. In more famous subcultures, this process of transition relates to commodification, for example, the sale and acceptance of the once-subcultural ripped tee shirts and leather jackets of the punks. There is a process of "freezing" the subculture through commodification: "As soon as the original innovations which signify 'subculture' are translated into commodities and made generally available, they become 'frozen'."[86]

Although not commodified in a strict sense of the word, the more that CLS's approaches and methods were separated from the subculture and accepted, the more CLS itself became frozen. This can be seen through the adaptation of CLS concepts, presented without the pragmatic and activist base of the original legal subculture. This in turn leads to a weaker, accepted version. For example, a throwaway line in *The Atlantic* stated: "No one lives

---

[84] Fred A. Bernstein, "Derrick Bell, Law Professor and Rights Advocate, Dies at 80", *The New York Times* (online, 6 October 2011) <https://www.nytimes.com/2011/10/06/us/derrick-bell-pioneering-harvard-law-professor-dies-at-80.html>.

[85] Stephen B. Presser, "What American Law Professors Forgot and What Trump Knew", *Chicago Tribune* (online, 17 November 2016) <https://www.chicagotribune.com/news/opinion/commentary/ct-law-professors-trump-scalia-supreme-court-conservative-perspec-1118-md-20161117-story.html>.

[86] Hebdige (n 21) 132.

on Mount Olympus. Government lawyers, judges, journalists are all fallible. They are all vulnerable to bias and self-interest."[87] This weakened version of the indeterminacy thesis is not only presented as common and accepted knowledge, but with the added effect of there not being anything that can be done about it.

---

[87] Peter Beinart, "Why Trump Is Accusing Obama of Wiretapping', *The Atlantic* (online, 8 March 2017) <https://www.theatlantic.com/politics/archive/2017/03/why-trump-is-accusing-obama-of-wiretapping/518793>.

2

Untangling Critical Legal Studies

One's ideas must be as broad as Nature if they are to interpret Nature.
Arthur Conan Doyle, *A Study in Scarlet* (1887)

Critical Legal Studies has ground to a halt. The movement is a memory, remembered historically as leftist intelligentsia against legal liberalism.[1] This is not a controversial statement to make, nor is it unique to CLS, with a number of academic theories, movements, and positions melding, moving, and transitioning to new incarnations, or to nothing. What makes CLS unique is that while the movement may have ended, other Critical Legal Studies—those concerning fields of legal inquiry posed to analyse law from a critical position, or through a critical lens—have branched out and developed.[2] Such is the multifaceted nature of the title "Critical Legal Studies" that specific differentiations often rest on necessary further identification of themes, theorists, and locations.

Despite some similarities and a shared "critical" approach, the varied Critical Legal Studies are not the same. To understand the CLS that this book is concerned with, it is necessary to situate it in relation to other Critical Legal Studies. Given the inherent confusion in differentiating Critical Legal Studies in a narrow sense from other Critical Legal Studies more broadly, the situation will be represented visually, borrowing in format from a family tree. This diagram is therefore a simple genealogy of Critical Legal Studies.

---

[1] Peter Goodrich, *Law in the Courts of Love: Literature and Other Minor Jurisprudences* (Routledge, 1996) 185; See, e.g., E. Dana Neacsu, "CLS Stands for Critical Legal Studies, If Anyone Remembers" (2000) 8(2) *Journal of Law and Policy* 415.

[2] See especially Cassandra Sharp and Marett Leiboff (eds), *Cultural Legal Studies: Law's Popular Cultures and the Metamorphosis of Law* (Routledge, 2015); see also Matthew Stone, Illan rua Wall, and Costas Douzinas (eds), *New Critical Thinking: Law and the Political* (Routledge, 2012).

However, given Michel Foucault's specific use of the term "genealogy",[3] and his influence on CLS,[4] it would be remiss not to qualify the difference in application.

Foucault, drawing on Friedrich Nietzsche's *The Genealogy of Morals*,[5] applies the term "genealogy" to reinterrogate histories that are often overlooked,[6] those in the most "unpromising places, in what we tend to feel is without history".[7] Focusing on the different applications Nietzsche has for words related to "the start" (origin, ancestry, and beginning),[8] Foucault argues that it is possible to travel past ideals of "lofty origins" to "lowly beginnings", and in turn reveal new historical perspectives.[9] In contrast, the genealogy undertaken here is a mapping exercise, an extraction of the varied Critical Legal Studies.

This family tree draws from existing work in this area by Margaret Davies, and Costas Douzinas and Adam Gearey. Douzinas and Gearey categorise different Critical Legal Studies through national identities:[10] they identify similarities between national varieties, but address each's individuality based on geographic lines, particularly looking at different Critical Legal Studies in the USA,[11] Great Britain,[12] Australia,[13] and South Africa.[14]

Taking a different approach to the same problem, Davies designates broad and narrow categories to Critical Legal Studies: for example, designating the US Critical Legal Studies movement as narrow, and critical race theory as broad.[15] However, while Douzinas and Gearey's, and Davies's approaches provide some clarity, they have limitations, and can be developed further.

Douzinas and Gearey's categorisation becomes muddied with the (re)location of the Critical Legal scholars they assign to specific locations—a

---

[3] Michel Foucault, *The History of Sexuality: Volume One an Introduction*, tr. Robert Hurley (Pantheon Books, 1978).
[4] See, e.g., Duncan Kennedy, "The Stakes of Law, or Hale and Foucault!" (1991) 15(4) *Legal Studies Forum* 327.
[5] Friedrich Nietzsche, *On the Genealogy of Morals*, tr. Michael A. Scarpitti (Penguin Classics, 2013).
[6] Michel Foucault, "Nietzsche, Genealogy, History", in John Richardson and Brian Leiter (eds), *Nietzsche* (Oxford, 1978) 139–164.
[7] Ibid 139.
[8] Ibid 140–1.
[9] Ibid 142.
[10] Costas Douzinas and Adam Gearey, *Critical Jurisprudence: The Political Philosophy of Justice* (Hart, 2005) 229–258.
[11] Ibid 229.
[12] Ibid 239.
[13] Ibid 247.
[14] Ibid 253.
[15] Margaret Davies, *Asking the Law Question* (Thomson Reuters, 4th ed, 2017) 191.

point which the authors themselves identify.[16] Their acknowledgement of this issue highlights the placeholder nature of their categories, rather than creating a definitive structure. Similarly, Davies's approach imposes a dichotomy wherein a particular Critical Legal Studies is either broad or narrow. Both approaches offer useful ways to think about the categorisation of different Critical Legal Studies. The Critical Legal Studies family tree faces similar issues, imposing strict boundaries on malleable theories and individuals. However, it is used here as a tool to reduce complication and assist in the exploration of Critical Legal Studies' complexities. It is not presented as a definite and permanent structure.

The Critical Legal Studies Family Tree

A discussion of Critical Legal Studies requires the term to be unpacked, to provide an understanding of its origins, impact, and legacy. However, when we ask the seemingly simple question, "What is Critical Legal Studies?" the answer given depends on a number of factors, including the time, location, and associated theorists, with each combination providing a range of different answers, ones that demonstrate the breadth of Critical Legal Studies. Appreciating this breadth contextualises the existing work that has been undertaken to differentiate the various Critical Legal Studies. For example, Davies's framework provides a way to separate the narrow category of Critical Legal Studies as a title from the broad category of Critical Legal Studies as a description. The narrow category focuses on the Critical Legal Studies movement,[17] which Davies restricts to the one that existed within the United States from the 1970s to the early 1990s.[18] In contrast, Davies applies the broad category to areas of legal theory which take a critical approach to law, including critical race theory and feminist legal theory.[19]

The division of Critical Legal Studies into broad and narrow categories should be understood as clarifying the term, rather than separating two distinct areas of study. Davies demonstrates that these two readings of Critical Legal Studies can be identified; however, the influence of the narrowly defined Critical Legal Studies on the broadly defined,[20] and to some extent the

---

[16] Douzinas and Gearey, *Critical Jurisprudence* (n 10) 239, nn 26.
[17] Roberto Mangabeira Unger, *The Critical Legal Studies Movement* (Harvard University Press, 1983).
[18] Davies (n 15) 191.
[19] Ibid.
[20] See Patricia J. Williams, "Alchemical Notes: Reconstructing Ideals From Deconstructed Rights" (1987) 22 *Harvard Civil Rights–Civil Liberties Law Review* 401; David M. Trubek, "Foundational Events, Foundational Myths, and the Creation of Critical Race Theory, or How to Get Along with a Little Help from your Friends" (2011) 43(5) *Connecticut*

inverse,[21] is accepted within the literature. This interwoven relationship between both broad and narrow Critical Legal Studies means that the distinction Davies draws is not always immediately clear. This lack of clarity demonstrates the nuanced relationships between a number of broad and narrow Critical Legal Studies, although it should be noted that this link is not present in all Critical Legal Studies works.[22] The broad/narrow distinction does, however, provide a blunt method of categorisation, based on parameters of time, location, and author.[23]

Similarly, Douzinas and Gearey categorise Critical Legal Studies by a series of geographic locations.[24] This method alleviates the dichotomy of Davies's broad/narrow approach, but still presents some foundational issues. The primary issue is acknowledged by the authors in their discussion of Critical Legal Studies in Great Britain and the "Brit Crits": "There is a problem with the 'Brit' Crit. Many of the scholars associated with this position are not British. Although some may have become British through long association with British bad habits, others are resolutely non-British, or even anti-British."[25] Douzinas and Gearey recognise their framework's limitations and do not impose it as a model of firm categorisation. Instead, it is used to differentiate the historical locations of Critical Legal Studies in the authors' larger project of "[c]ritical legal thought", itself a conscious progression from Critical Legal Studies.[26]

The work that Davies, and Douzinas and Gearey have done grounds the Critical Legal Studies family tree. Using Davies's broad/narrow approach as a starting point, the family tree's first two limbs are presented thus:

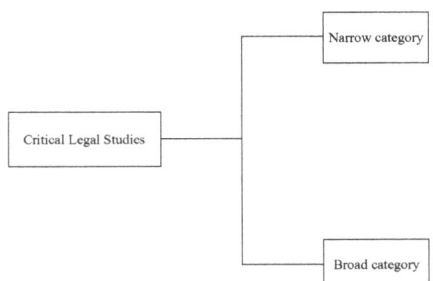

Figure 2.1 Family Tree: Broad versus Narrow

Law Review 1,503; Kimberlé Williams Crenshaw, "Twenty Years of Critical Race Theory: Looking Back to Move Forward" (2011) 43(5) *Connecticut Law Review* 1,253.
[21] See, e.g., Duncan Kennedy, *Sexy Dressing Etc.* (Harvard University Press, 1993).
[22] Crenshaw (n 20); Trubek (n 20).
[23] Davies (n 15) 191.
[24] Douzinas and Gearey, *Critical Jurisprudence* (n 10) 229.
[25] Ibid 239.
[26] Ibid 258.

The focus of the family tree is on the US-based Critical Legal Studies, which is categorised by Davies as narrow; the discussion and refinements of the family tree reflect this. However, this does not mean that there is not further refinement available to the broad category. Instead, it should be understood that substantial discussion of the broad category does not materially affect the US-based Critical Legal Studies. As such, the broad category houses a non-exhaustive list of Critical Legal Studies, including the aforementioned critical race theory and feminist legal theory, but also critical historical scholarship, psychoanalytical theory, postmodernism, law and literature, and queer legal theory, all of which Davies identifies under this heading. In addition to Davies's selection, there are emerging critical fields that should also be included, such as law and popular culture,[27] cultural legal studies,[28] and comics and law.[29]

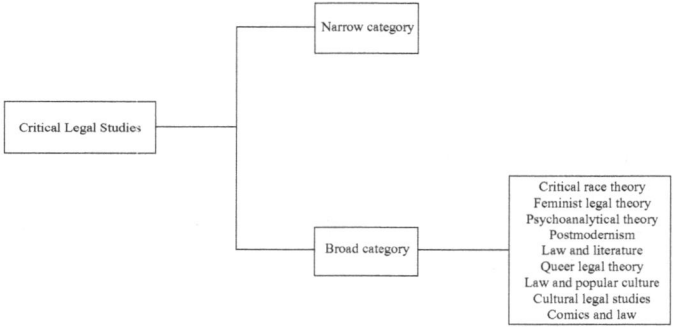

Figure 2.2 Family Tree: Broad, Complete

Having established and identified broad Critical Legal Studies, the next step is to define what distinct areas can be identified under Davies's narrow category. There are specific limitations to Davies's broad/narrow approach and its application to the narrow US-based Critical Legal Studies. Davies draws some distinctions between variants of the narrow Critical Legal Studies; however, these are general and of less importance than the broad/narrow divide itself. For example, Davies provides a location and timeline for the US-based

---

[27] See, e.g., William P. MacNeil, *Lex Populi: The Jurisprudence of Popular Culture* (Stanford University Press, 2007).
[28] Sharp and Leiboff (n 2).
[29] Thomas Giddens (ed), *Graphic Justice: Intersections of Comics and Law* (Routledge, 2015); Thomas Giddens, *On Comics and Legal Aesthetics: Multimodality and the Haunted Mask of Knowing* (Routledge, 2018).

Critical Legal Studies,[30] but her introduction to the very different British Critical Legal Studies is mentioned in a footnote only. However, following Douzinas and Gearey, this difference is clearer. The two dominant narrow Critical Legal Studies are the British and the American approaches.[31] Unlike those in the broad category, narrow Critical Legal Studies are defined primarily by time and geographic location. Despite a crossover of influences, topics, and authors, the Critical Legal Studies of the United States and Great Britain need to be recognised as different. Instead of conflating their similarities and presenting a unified narrow branch, these shared factors create two distinct limbs.

In the foundational years of Critical Legal Studies, this divide may not have been clear.[32] However, its origins are unquestioned, as Douzinas outlined in 2005: "Critical legal thought . . . started in America in the Seventies and was first introduced in Britain in the early Eighties."[33] For the family tree, this positions the US-based Critical Legal Studies as the first limb. The limbs are geographically coded, but with clear acknowledgment of the geographic issues presented by Douzinas and Gearey.[34] As such, the initial limb under the narrow heading is "US-CLS", representing the US-based Critical Legal Studies.

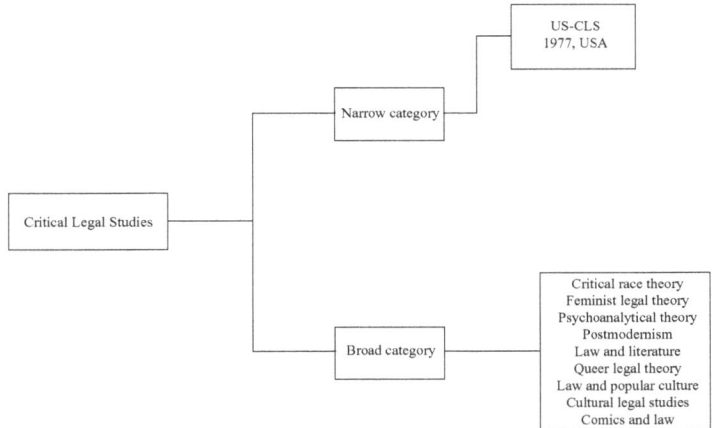

Figure 2.3 Family Tree: Narrow US-CLS, 1977

---

[30] Davies (n 15) 191.
[31] Although other countries have had, and continue to have, critical legal scholarship, it is either less dominant than the US and UK branches, or generally housed within the broad category.
[32] See, e.g., Costas Douzinas, "A Short History of the British Critical Legal Conference or, the Responsibility of the Critic" (2014) 25 *Law and Critique* 187, 189.
[33] Costas Douzinas, "Oubliez Critique" (2005) 16(1) *Law and Critique* 47, 58.
[34] Douzinas and Gearey, *Critical Jurisprudence* (n 10) 229–58.

Initially a distinction between British and US Critical Legal Studies may not have been clear, with "Brit Crit" authors Peter Fitzpatrick and Alan Hunt stating in 1987 that, "Critical legal scholarship has not formed clearly delineated 'national' varieties".[35] However, in 1993, fellow Brit Crit Peter Goodrich presented a paper on the distinctly US-based Critical Legal Studies. Tellingly titled "Sleeping with the Enemy: On the Politics of Critical Legal Studies in America",[36] Goodrich's paper enforces the geographic distinction, questioning the issues faced specifically by US-based Critical Legal Studies compared to legal critique in Great Britain.[37]

By 2005, Douzinas was more confident still, stating that, aside from the name, "not much links the two sides".[38] In terms of categorisation, there is a clear division between the two Critical Legal Studies,[39] and British Critical Legal Studies is presented as "UK-CLS" under the narrow categorisation of the Critical Legal Studies family tree.

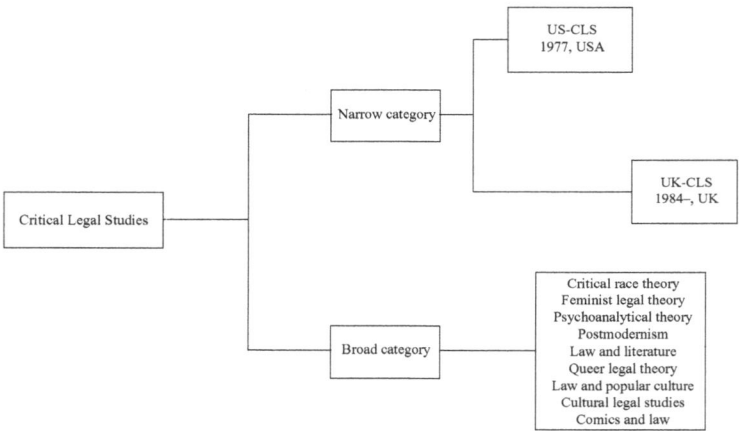

Figure 2.4 Family Tree: Narrow UK-CLS, 1984

[35] Peter Fitzpatrick and Alan Hunt (eds), *Critical Legal Studies* (Basil Blackwell, 1987) 1.
[36] Peter Goodrich, "Sleeping with the Enemy: An Essay on the Politics of Critical Legal Studies in America" (1993) 68(2) *New York University Law Review* 389.
[37] Ibid 186–7, nn 11.
[38] Douzinas, "Oubliez Critique" (n 33) 59.
[39] A number of US-based sources on Critical Legal Studies do not address any variety of Critical Legal Studies outside of the US: e.g., James Boyle (ed), *Critical Legal Studies* (Dartmouth, 1992); Brian H. Bix (ed), *Philosophy of Law: Critical Concepts in Philosophy* (Routledge, 2016) vol 6. This is seen to a lesser extent with later works from the Brit Crits: see, e.g., Costas Douzinas and Colin Perrin (eds), *Critical Legal Theory* (Routledge, 2012), which has no foundational US-CLS papers in the four-volume collection. Instead, Douzinas and Perrin include Pierre Schlag, "US CLS" (1999) 10 *Law and Critique* 199 to address the history of US-CLS.

The creation of the family tree, with the neat categorisation of US-CLS and UK-CLS, comes with its own set of issues; relevant here is the issue of a clear starting point. For example, UK-CLS can potentially be traced back further than 1984, before the introduction of US-CLS, through Zenon Bankowski and Geoff Mungham's 1976 book, *Images of Law*.[40] However, a similar issue arises for US-CLS with Robert Lefcourt's *Law Against the People*, an edited collection on critically demystifying law, published in 1971.[41] Thematically both books could offer theoretical starting points for US-CLS and UK-CLS, although neither should be considered part of the Critical Legal Studies canon. The purpose of this family tree is not to encompass all critical legal works, but only those under the banner of Critical Legal Studies. Therefore, whilst *Images of Law* was influential on UK-CLS specifically,[42] it should be viewed as a separate critical work, rather than a work of Critical Legal Studies.

The starting date given to UK-CLS is drawn from Fitzpatrick and Hunt's *Critical Legal Studies*,[43] which states that, "In Britain the Critical Legal Conference was formed in 1984."[44] With reference to flyers and calls for papers, Fitzpatrick and Hunt's claim can be verified, however the first conference appears to have been somewhat informal and does not conform to what might be understood as a "standard" structured academic conference. In 1985, a one-day conference was discussed at Middlesex Polytechnic in June,[45] and it was held at Birkbeck College that September.[46] In 1986, the Critical Legal Conference (CLC) was considered a "full conference" and was held in September at the University of Kent.[47]

---

[40] Zenon Bankowski and Geoff Mungham, *Images of Law* (Routledge, 1976).
[41] Robert Lefcourt, *Law Against the People* (Random House, 1971).
[42] For UK-CLS, see especially Costas Douzinas and Lynda Nead (eds), *Law and the Image: The Authority of Art and the Aesthetics of Law* (University of Chicago Press, 1999); Peter Goodrich, "Screening Law" (2009) 21(1) *Law and Literature* 1.
[43] Fitzpatrick and Hunt (n 35); Douzinas, "Oubliez Critique" (n 33) 61.
[44] Fitzpatrick and Hunt (n 35).
[45] CLC Organizing Group, "Critical Legal Conference" (Meeting Minutes, 1985) <https://www.kent.ac.uk/law/research/clc-2016/archive.html>.
[46] CLC Middlesex University, "One-Day Conference: What Is Critical Legal Studies" (Call for Papers, 1985) <https://www.kent.ac.uk/law/research/clc-2016/archive.html>.
[47] University of Kent, "Critical Legal Conference, First Annual Conference: Law, Critique and Social Transformation" (Call For Papers, 1986) <https://www.kent.ac.uk/law/research/clc-2016/archive.html>.

In keeping with Davies's initial distinction, the identification and categorisation of UK-CLS is used to outline what US-CLS was not. Whilst certain UK-CLS works will be relevant to the critique and contextualisation of US-CLS, this limb does not warrant further analysis here. Instead, the next limb added to the narrow category is a uniquely American affair: the death of US-CLS.

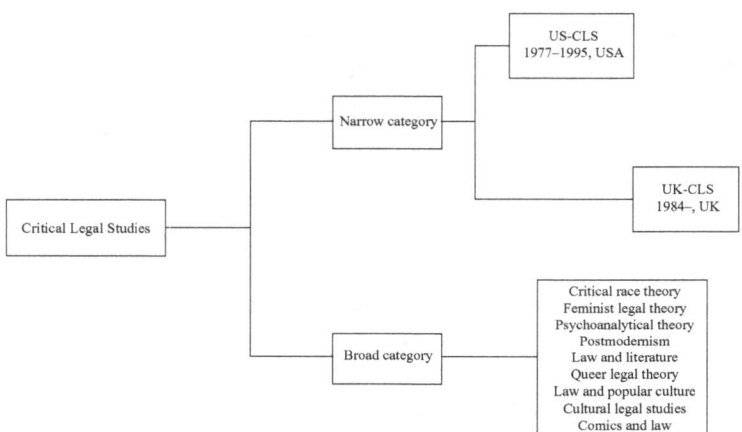

Figure 2.5 Family Tree: Narrow US-CLS, 1977–1995

The death of US-CLS has had two important consequences. First, it further differentiates US-CLS from UK-CLS, which has not suffered a death. Second, the death of US-CLS provides a categorisation for US-based Critical Legal Studies post-1995. For UK-CLS, the Critical Legal Conference is still running, and early UK-CLS works like Hunt and Fitzpatrick's *Critical Legal Studies*,[48] or Douzinas, Goodrich, and Yifat Hachamovitch's *Politics, Postmodernity, and Critical Legal Studies*[49] demonstrate modes of thinking that can still be seen in contemporary UK-CLS works, sometimes from the same authors.[50] US-CLS has not followed this path. Instead, it has transitioned to what has repeatedly

---

[48] Fitzpatrick and Hunt (n 35).
[49] Costas Douzinas, Peter Goodrichm and Yifat Hachamovitch (eds), *Politics, Postmodernity, and Critical Legal Studies: The Legality of the Contingent (and Sport)* (Routledge, 1994).
[50] See, e.g., Ben Golder and Peter Fitzpatrick, *Foucault's Law* (Routledge-Cavendish, 2009).

been called a death. The result of this death is a schism in US-based Critical Legal Studies, resulting in the creation of a new limb: Posthumous Critical Legal Studies, or PCLS.

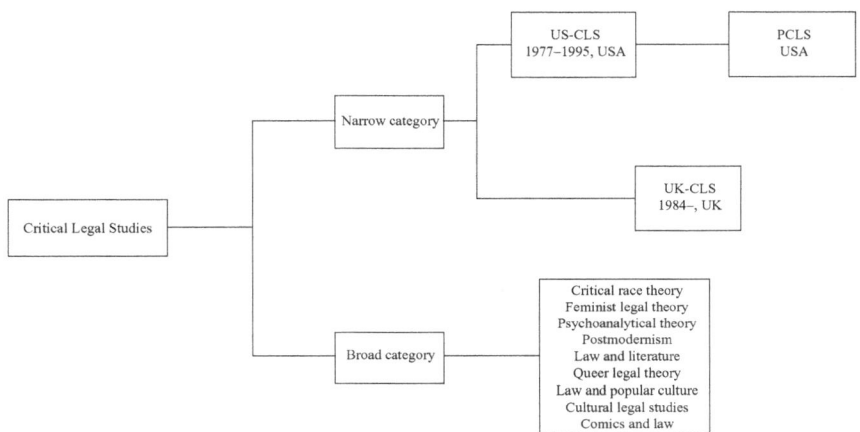

Figure 2.6 Family Tree: Narrow PCLS

Until this point, the divisions presented in the family tree should cause little to no debate.[51] However, the death of US-CLS is not something commonly focused on in other histories of Critical Legal Studies,[52] and the PCLS limb has not been explored elsewhere. This limb should be understood as a contemporary Critical Legal Studies: it follows the categorisation of the narrow US-based Critical Legal Studies, appearing after the death of the original US-CLS. Unlike US-CLS or UK-CLS, PCLS resulted only on the death of US-CLS, rather than through a conference or a grouping of scholars. For clarity, PCLS should also be understood as the US-based Critical Legal Studies that still continues to this day. Investigating how the death of US-CLS occurred, it is possible show the importance of this event and the advent of PCLS.

---

[51] Contra, Davies (n 15) 191–221; See Douzinas and Gearey, *Critical Jurisprudence* (n 10) 229–58.
[52] But see Adam Gearey, "'Change Is Gonna Come': Critical Legal Studies and the Legacies of the New Left" (2013) 24 *Law and Critique* 211, 224.

A Eulogy for US-CLS

The *Harvard Law Record* is a student-run newspaper at Harvard Law School. It publishes student and staff opinions, and enquires into the goings-on at Harvard Law School. In the 1 December, 1995 edition, a student, Hope Yen, penned an article on US-CLS. The article was a response to a perceived lack of engagement by the Crits on development plans for Harvard Law School proposed by the dean, Robert Clark. The article is split over two pages with both headings setting the tone: "As HLS Mulls its Mission, CLS Scholars Remain Quiet"[53] and "Crits at HLS a Dying Breed?"[54] While it is Harvard-centric, Yen's article is an important piece of the US-CLS history. The article's focus on the silence of the Crits allowed Yen to interview Duncan Kennedy and Morton Horwitz, with both Crits referring to US-CLS as dead.[55]

Yen's article offers unique insights into the death of US-CLS: first with quotations from prominent Crits agreeing that a death has occurred, second from the location in which this information was gathered and published, and third with its relation to Clark and his association with law and economics. These three factors are linked throughout the history of US-CLS, with its key actors, their location, and their competing theories of jurisprudence all shaping US-CLS. When Yen captures both Kennedy and Horwitz saying that US-CLS is dead, and Clark stating that he did not kill it,[56] the article can be read as a posthumous discussion of US-CLS itself, rather than of Clark's development plans for Harvard Law School.

The death of US-CLS can be understood and explored through three aspects: the US-CLS founders, their location, and their rivals. It must be noted that—given the organic and loosely affiliated nature of US-CLS, the different universities at which it had clusters, as well as the early relationship between Kennedy and law and economics[57]—these titles are imperfect. However, given what each title denotes, it is possible to understand them as placeholders representative of key issues, rather than as unequivocal terms. The location in question is Harvard Law School; the founders are Kennedy, Horwitz, and Roberto Unger; and the rival is law and economics. Categorised

---

[53] Hope Yen, "As HLS Mulls Its Mission, CLS Scholars Remain Quiet", *Harvard Law Record* (Cambridge, 1 December 1995) 2.

[54] Hope Yen, "Crits at HLS a Dying Breed?", *Harvard Law Record* (Cambridge, 1 December 1995) 4.

[55] Yen, "As HLS Mulls Its Mission" (n 53).

[56] Ibid. (n 53).

[57] See James R. Hackney Jr., *Legal Intellectuals in Conversation: Reflections on the Construction of Contemporary American Legal Theory* (New York University Press, 2012) 22.

in this way, the specific rise and fall of US-CLS at Harvard Law School can be seen as emblematic of US-CLS as a whole.

The US-CLS Founders

Harvard University Law School acted as a microcosm for US-CLS. It was home to some of the most prominent names in US-CLS, which, given its prestige, went a long way towards establishing the movement more broadly. The relationship between Harvard and US-CLS can be traced back to the hiring of three legal theorists in 1971: Kennedy, Horwitz, and Unger.[58] In the framework of the Critical Legal Studies family tree, this act by Harvard Law School predates the beginning of US-CLS. However, the hiring of these theorists serves as a prelude to the movement proper, as Kennedy recounted in a 2012 interview:

> When I got to Harvard Law School, I fell in with Morton Horwitz and Roberto Unger. We were all hired at the same time, and as it very often happens in law faculties, people that are hired in the same year form a kind of cohort. There's a kind of intimacy that comes from arriving at the same time, but it developed quickly way beyond that into a very deep intellectual alliance.[59]

The alliance Kennedy speaks of was manifested through the creation of US-CLS. Kennedy, Horwitz, and Unger all contributed key texts, with their work during the prelude to US-CLS establishing a grounding in areas further developed after the inaugural Conference on Critical Legal Studies (CCLS) in 1977. For example, before 1977, Kennedy published "How the Law School Fails: A Polemic"[60] and "Form and Substance in Private Law Adjudication".[61] Despite the length of these papers—especially "Form and Substance", which runs to ninety-five pages—these works by Kennedy can be considered fairly minor, with his more notable published US-CLS work coming after the first CCLS.[62] Both papers hint, however, at the following US-CLS, with Kennedy's first *Polemic* bearing traceable roots in his more

---

[58] Ibid 28.
[59] Ibid.
[60] Duncan Kennedy, "How the Law School Fails: A Polemic" (1971) 1(1) *Yale Review of Law and Social Action* 77.
[61] Duncan Kennedy, "Form and Substance in Private Law Adjudication" (1989) 89 *Harvard Law Review* 1,685.
[62] See Duncan Kennedy, "The Structure of Blackstone's Commentaries" (1979) 28 *Buffalo Law Review* 209.

famous Polemic,[63] as well as themes of formal and ad-hoc implications of law seen in "Form and Substance".[64] These papers cover issues on the structures of rhetoric and hierarchies within institutions, which feed into the dominant themes throughout Kennedy's later US-CLS work.[65]

The foundational pre-US-CLS work for Kennedy was the 1975 unpublished manuscript *The Rise and Fall of Classical Legal Thought*, which remained in this form until being formally published in 2006.[66] *Rise and Fall* set the tone for a dominant branch of US-CLS with the use of structuralism and critical theory to assess classical legal thought (from 1850–1940).[67] In the 2006 published version of *Rise and Fall*, Kennedy included a preface to the 1975 work, outlining that by discussing structuralism and critical theory with regard to law and legal history, he aimed to provide more techniques for a legal repertoire.[68] Candidly, Kennedy also admits that his hope was for this work to be included in the fields of critical theory and structuralism. Whilst the latter was not clearly achieved, the work's thematic resonance with US-CLS can be seen through the issues Kennedy outlines.

Rise and Fall traces five issues through the period of classical legal thought, which Kennedy identifies as "Legal Consciousness", "The Phenomenological Approach to Legal Reasoning, By Analogy and By Deduction, to Produce a Conception of the 'Mode of Integration of a Subsystem'", "The Notion of Nesting", "The Ontology of Rights and Powers", and "Reason Dies While Giving Birth to Liberalism".[69] For Kennedy, *Rise and Fall*'s structure and subject matter is identifiably a form of Critical Legal Studies, even before the term was coined.

Choosing to publish through Harvard University Press, rather than following Kennedy's self-publication method, Horwitz also released a book on legal history. Published in 1977, *The Transformation of American Law, 1780–1860* won the Bancroft Prize the following year.[70] *The Transformation of American Law* evidenced a different way in which legal history could be undertaken through a broad US-CLS approach. Although they are both historical works, Horwitz's and Kennedy's books differ in both form and

---

[63] Duncan Kennedy, *Legal Education and the Reproduction of Hierarchy: A Polemic Against the System* (New York University Press, 2004).
[64] Kennedy, "Form and Substance" (n 61) 1,685.
[65] Ibid.
[66] Duncan Kennedy, *The Rise and Fall of Classical Legal Thought* (BeardBooks 2006).
[67] Ibid vii.
[68] Ibid xiv.
[69] Ibid xiv–xxii.
[70] Morton J. Horwitz, *The Transformation of American Law 1780–1860* (Harvard University Press, 1977).

methodology. Horwitz also revisits history through a contemporary critical lens, but does not impose a framework in the way Kennedy approaches *Rise and Fall*.[71] Instead, moving away from the dominant jurisprudential focus of constitutional law, Horwitz focuses on the underrepresented analysis of private law. *The Transformation of American Law* identifies a tendency for previous historical work to look at public law as being in the public interest, and for private law to be "private", despite its influence on the distribution of power and wealth in American society. Horwitz challenges this dominant approach, demonstrating a move from the historical ideals of legal realism's critique of public law,[72] to the foundational US-CLS stance which viewed all law as politics.[73]

The approaches taken by Kennedy and Horwitz highlight the very different types of work at the foundations of US-CLS. It is important to note that these differences were also clear at the time, with Kennedy identifying that "[I]n 1975, Morty Horwitz and I were arguing about a series of different methodological issues that had a lot of influence on the first stages of Critical Legal Studies at the intellectual level."[74] These discussions were in regard to the different approaches they took to their historical work, with Kennedy reiterating his structural and critical position, and stating that Horwitz took an approach relative to his Marxist allegiances.[75] Rather than fragmenting or dissolving US-CLS before it began, these differences paved the way for the diverse approaches taken to law under the banner of US-CLS. This diversity is further exemplified by Unger's work, which moved away from the direct legal-historical approach taken by both Kennedy and Horwitz, instead presenting a philosophical approach to law in the pre-US-CLS period.

Beginning with *Knowledge and Politics* in 1975,[76] and continuing with *Law in Modern Society* in 1976,[77] Unger set the tone for the philosophical side of US-CLS. Whilst not strictly a series, Unger notes that *Law in Modern Society* builds upon *Knowledge and Politics*, and both books follow a similar style.[78] In comparison to that of both Kennedy and Horwitz, Unger's works begin more broadly. *Knowledge and Politics* opens with a statement from

---

[71] Kennedy, *Rise and Fall* (n 66) x.
[72] See Oliver Wendell Holmes Jr., *The Common Law* (Dover Publications, 1991).
[73] Hackney (n 57) 27.
[74] Tor Krever, Carl Lisberger, and Max Utzschneider, "Law on the Left: A Conversation with Duncan Kennedy" (2015) 10(1) *Unbound* 1, 24.
[75] Ibid.
[76] Roberto Mangabeira Unger, *Knowledge and Politics* (Free Press, 1975).
[77] Roberto Mangabeira Unger, *Law in Modern Society: Toward a Criticism of Social Theory* (Free Press, 1976).
[78] Ibid v.

the author that the book's purpose is to "help one understand the context of ideas and sentiments within which philosophy and politics must now be practiced".[79] The book is not so much a call to arms as a map one might use to understand the current (in 1975) climate of philosophy and politics. As such, *Knowledge and Politics* covers a wide-range of topics, but with liberalism at the heart of Unger's critique. This theme can be seen directly in the establishing chapters on liberal psychology, liberal political theory, and the unity of liberal thought.

In his follow-up text, *Law in Modern Society*, Unger continues the thread of liberalism, addressing social theory: the underlying aim of the book is a critique of social theory.[80] Again, Unger addresses the topic at hand broadly, demonstrating and positioning law within the realm of modernity, primarily by addressing different cultures,[81] and then assessing how liberalism has effected change internationally.[82] Whilst there is undoubtedly a marked difference between the three authors and their works, with their own voices and styles evident and distinct in this pre-US-CLS time, the central theme of critiquing and questioning liberalism is unifying. In a post-US-CLS world there is an argument that the works themselves were at best tenuously connected in the sense of each being either broadly critical or merely progressive. However, collectively, their unified approach to demystifying liberal notions of law lay the groundwork for US-CLS.

The US-CLS Location

The groundwork for US-CLS by Kennedy, Horwitz, and Unger was undertaken during their time at Harvard Law School, a location that acted as a microcosm for US-CLS: what happened to US-CLS at Harvard Law School impacted US-CLS as a whole. The relationship between Harvard Law School and US-CLS is an intrinsic part of the US-CLS story. Importantly, the relationship between US-CLS and Harvard Law School was new.[83] The instigation of this relationship hinged on a changing sociopolitical climate, and changes in jurisprudence which led to universities hiring legal theorists like Kennedy, Horwitz, and Unger. Inadvertently these factors helped to create and directly affect US-CLS, and specifically its relationship with Harvard Law School. By understanding how this relationship began, it is possible to identify the pressures which led to the death of US-CLS.

---

[79] Unger, *Knowledge and Politics* (n 76) v.
[80] Unger, *Law in Modern Society* (n 77).
[81] See, e.g., ibid 47–133.
[82] See, e.g., ibid 134–91.
[83] Hackney (n 57) 28.

The importance of the 1971 hiring of Kennedy, Horwitz, and Unger cannot be understated, especially when the broad type of critical work undertaken by these impending US-CLS scholars was not historically welcomed at Harvard Law School.[84] Instead, from the early part of the twentieth century, this type of scholarship had been deliberately nurtured at Yale Law School.[85] As Laura Kalman identifies, the hiring of the early Crits by Harvard and not Yale demonstrated a deliberate transition in both institutions:

> Yale, which had embraced forward-looking legal realism in the 1930s, rejected realism's descendant, Critical Legal Studies [US-CLS], at the same time that Harvard Law School, which had once turned its back on realism, made a home for realism's child and for scholarship that represented one logical extension of sixties activism.[86]

Kalman's assessment highlights a series of issues which underpin the relationship between US-CLS and Harvard Law School. It contextualises US-CLS historically as a descendant of legal realism, and then contemporaneously as an extension of 1960s activism; by unpacking this statement, the significance of Harvard Law School as the location for US-CLS becomes clear. The connection Kalman draws between legal realism and US-CLS further illuminates the relationship between US-CLS and Harvard Law School. The implication in Kalman's quotation is that US-CLS would follow a similar path to legal realism and be rejected by Harvard Law School.[87] The hiring of Kennedy, Horwitz, and Unger demonstrated that Harvard Law School was open to "increasing [its] intellectual dynamism";[88] however, its history with legal realism placed the emergence of US-CLS in a precarious position. To appreciate the importance of this position for US-CLS, it is necessary to briefly look at the relationship between legal realism, US-CLS, and Harvard Law School.

Kalman is not alone in her connection of US-CLS and legal realism. Legal realism has been heralded as a predecessor of US-CLS,[89] along with claims that US-CLS is a continuation of legal realism.[90] Legal realism does

---

[84] Laura Kalman, *Yale Law School and the Sixties: Revolt and Reverberations* (University of North Carolina Press, 2005) 7; See Hackney (n 57) 28.
[85] Kalman (n 84) 7.
[86] Ibid.
[87] Ibid.
[88] Steven M. Teles, *The Rise of the Conservative Legal Movement: The Battle for Control of the Law* (Princeton University Press, 2008) 193.
[89] Hackney (n 57) 27; Goodrich (n 1) 209.
[90] Hackney (n 57) 27; Goodrich (n 1) 209; Debra A. Livingston, "'Round and 'Round the Bramble Bush: From Legal Realism to Critical Legal Scholarship" (1982) 95(7) *Harvard Law Review* 1,669, 1,682; Neil Duxbury, "The Reinvention of American Legal Realism' (1992)

differ from some US-CLS approaches,[91] but the focus on exposing judicial subjectivity hidden under the guise of scientific formalism draws a strong correlation. Related to the idea of a specific US-CLS location was legal realism's own relationship with Harvard Law School, notably through former student, Oliver Wendell Holmes, Jr.[92] The legal realists are often exemplified by Holmes and his work in both *The Common Law*[93] and *The Path of the Law*.[94] Within these works, Holmes embodied the critical stance of the legal realists, demonstrating an application of broader philosophical theory and critique of law.[95] This critical stance also included challenging dominant formalist pedagogy, embodied by Harvard Law School's Socratic method. Although legal realism ultimately failed to directly overthrow formalism at Harvard Law School, its influence was felt throughout the twentieth century, culminating in new jurisprudential approaches, including US-CLS.

The legal realists' decision to focus their challenge on Harvard related to the creation of the Socratic casebook method by a former dean of the law school, Christopher Columbus Langdell.[96] Langdell's formalist pedagogical approach, which he instigated at Harvard Law School, transformed and dominated legal education from the early part of the twentieth century.[97] Sometimes referred to as "Langdellianism", the method was embraced heavily by a large number of law schools across the United States.[98] Critically, this method encouraged students to "believe law was separate from morality and preference", in turn draining law of its "ideological political content".[99]

12(2) *Legal Studies* 137, 138; William W. Fisher III, Morton J. Horwitz, and Thomas A. Reed (eds), *American Legal Realism* (Oxford University Press, 1993) xi–xv; Andrew Altman, "Legal Realism, Critical Legal Studies and Dworkin" (1986) 15(3) *Philosophy & Public Affairs* 205; John Hasnas, "Back to the Future: From Critical Legal Studies Forward to Legal Realism, or How Not to Miss the Point of the Indeterminacy Argument" (1995) 45(1) *Duke Law Journal* 84; David Fraser, "What a Long, Strange Trip It's Been: Deconstructing Law from Legal Realism to Critical Legal Studies" (1988–89) 5 *Australian Journal of Law and Society* 35, 38; Davies (n 15) 200.

[91] See Andrew Altman, *Critical Legal Studies: A Liberal Critique* (Princeton University Press, 1990) 77–9.
[92] See Louis Menand, *The Metaphysical Club* (Farrar Straus and Giroux, 2001).
[93] Holmes, *The Common Law* (n 72).
[94] Oliver Wendell Holmes Jr., "The Path of the Law" (1897) 10(8) *Harvard Law Review* 61.
[95] See, e.g., Holmes, *The Common Law* (n 72) 188.
[96] Anthony Chase, "The Birth of the Modern Law School" (1979) 23 *American Journal of Legal History* 329; Kalman (n 84) 17.
[97] Kalman (n 84) 17.
[98] Ibid.
[99] Ibid.

Despite its success,[100] its vacuous nature made it a target for more inclusive modes of legal reasoning. However, this was not exclusive to the legal realists: an early charge against Langdellianism was led (unsuccessfully) by Roscoe Pound, who called for the implementation of a sociological jurisprudence.[101] Although he was also unsuccessful, the movement spurred by Holmes was described as "the most concerted attempt to challenge Harvard's control over legal education".[102] As a result of this effort by the legal realists, their approach was seen as a valid alternative, and was desirable to other schools, most notably when it was taken up at Yale.[103]

Historically, with Harvard's rejection and Yale's acceptance of legal realism, it was not expected that Harvard Law School would hire young critical scholars like Kennedy, Horwitz, and Unger. Their unexpected appointment, paired with the lack of critical roots within the law school, provided an uncertain foundation for US-CLS at Harvard. More importantly to the current analysis, the level of uncertainty allows a challenge to be levelled at the terminology used by Kalman in the second part of her quotation. Kalman begins by stating that Harvard Law School made "a home for realism's child", and qualifies this child as a "logical extension of sixties activism".[104] However, the concept of a home for US-CLS, as an extension of 1960s activism, from an institution such as Harvard Law School is problematic. The term "home" implies certain values that were not evident in the existence of US-CLS, which is why the term "location" has been used here instead. The distinction between location and home moves beyond mere semantics, and removes the implied emotions associated with the designation of a home, which can include ownership, belonging, and safety. The idea of a location is instead one where US-CLS could be practiced, but where it would also be in competition with other models of jurisprudence, specifically law and economics.

The Rivals: US-CLS, Liberalism, and Law and Economics

Following a similar path to the legal realists and their fight against formalism, US-CLS and the Crits also challenged the dominant structure of law. However, transitions in American society during the twentieth century shifted the dominant form of law from formalism to liberalism.[105] Given the breadth of the term, the "liberalism" in question can be understood as "the

---

[100] Neil Duxbury, *Patterns of American Jurisprudence* (Clarendon Press, 1995) 9–18.
[101] Ibid 54; Kalman (n 84) 18.
[102] Kalman (n 84) 18.
[103] Ibid 19.
[104] Ibid 7.
[105] Duxbury (n 100) 32–64.

set of political ideas that had descended from the New Deal and that had shaped the steady postwar expansion of federal social and economic responsibilities".[106] The shaping of these responsibilities was such that liberalism infiltrated all walks of American life, including law and the academe. As historian Alan Brinkley continues, "[f]aith in both the value and durability of liberalism shaped not only the politics, but also much of the scholarship of the postwar era."[107] The Crits' focus, especially that of Kennedy, was inside the law school,[108] and as he later affirmed, "The mainstream of the law school world was not conservatism; the mainstream was liberalism."[109] Collectively, the critique and criticism of liberalism was the primary target of the Crits.

US-CLS was not alone in its critique of liberalism. Notably, and notably much earlier than US-CLS,[110] law and economics had developed similar anti-liberal sentiments. Law and economics formed within the Chicago School of Economics, primarily to offer alternatives to Keynesianism, the economic driving force behind liberalism,[111] and to apply these alternatives to law.[112] At the University of Chicago, law and economics was spearheaded by Edward Levi and Aaron Director,[113] spawning a journal of the same name in 1958. In the third volume of the journal, Ronald Coase published "The Problem of Social Cost".[114] Presenting a mixture of real case law and theoretical economics, Coase's piece attacked existing economic arguments, specifically the imposition of taxes, fines, and restrictions on businesses that harm others. In turn challenging the dominant concept of the Pigouvian tax,[115] and looking at market-based alternatives that would be less economically damaging to businesses which caused harm.

---

[106] Alan Brinkley, *Liberalism and its Discontents* (Harvard University Press, 1998) ix.
[107] Ibid.
[108] Kennedy, "How the Law School Fails" (n 60); Kennedy, *Legal Education and the Reproduction of Hierarchy* (n 63).
[109] Hackney (n 57) 24.
[110] Ibid 22.
[111] Michael Stewart, *Keynes and After* (Pelican, 2nd ed, 1968) 240.
[112] Rob Van Horn and Philip Mirowski, "The Rise of the Chicago School of Economics and the Birth of Neoliberalism", in Philip Mirowski and Dieter Plehwe (eds), *The Road from Mont Pèlerin: The Making of the Neoliberal Thought Collective* (Harvard University Press, 2009) 140.
[113] Ronald Coase, "Law and Economics at Chicago" (1993) 36(1) *Journal of Law and Economics* 239, 247, 251.
[114] Ronald Coase, "The Problem of Social Cost" (1960) 3 *Journal of Law and Economics* 1.
[115] Ibid 28. The Pigouvian tax is named after its founder, Arthur Pigou, who argued for higher taxes on private companies to balance their self-interest with a broader social interest. A Pigouvian tax is a higher tax on businesses that have higher social costs: see generally Arthur C. Pigou, *The Economics of Welfare* (Macmillan, 4th ed, 1932).

"The Problem of Social Cost" transformed the discipline that would come to be known as "law and economics", notably when Coase took over as editor of the journal and openly pushed the approach he had taken in his paper.[116] Coase's influence and change in direction brought in interest from young scholars, including Richard Posner, who, as a prolific author, would further refine law and economics.[117] On its own, the journal, and even the academics at Chicago, were not enough to bring about an end to liberalism; however, the direction implemented by Coase helped to build a foundation against it. Within jurisprudence and the academe, these efforts, paired with the unlikely allies of the civil rights movement and the revolutionary 1960s,[118] helped to destabilise liberalism until "[b]y the end of the 1960s [the] secure liberal universe was beginning to crumble".[119]

Despite their shared target of liberalism, US-CLS and law and economics occupied different political positions from which they led their attacks. Whilst the categorisation of US-CLS as politically left and law and economics as politically right is an oversimplification, it is one which aids the narrative. Ideologically, these classifications broadly describe the politics aligned with both movements. However, there is an implicit binary opposition in them that was not always evident, as US-CLS and law and economics did interact.[120] Nevertheless, as US-CLS developed, it remained opposed to liberalism and kept its distance from law and economics.[121] As liberalism continued to wane, the distance between US-CLS and law and economics clarified their relationship into one of competition. As Neil Duxbury identifies, "[f]ew American academic lawyers seem to dissent from the proposition that ... law and economics and critical legal studies [US-CLS] have been the 'best-organized most ambitious voices in the law schools'."[122]

Given the status and locations of US-CLS and law and economics, their rivalry occasionally left law schools. Notably, this was seen when Mark Kelman's *A Guide to Critical Legal Studies* singled out Posner's approach to law

---

[116] Coase, "Law and Economics at Chicago" (n 113) 253.
[117] Ibid 251; See Richard A. Posner, *Economic Analysis of Law* (Little Brown, 1973); Richard A. Posner, *The Economics of Justice* (Harvard University Press, 1981).
[118] Brinkley (n 106) x.
[119] Ibid.
[120] Krever, Lisberger, and Utzschneider (n 74) 11; See also Richard Rorty, "The Banality of Pragmatism and the Poetry of Justice", *Southern California Law Review* 63 (1990) 1,811, 1,812; Richard A. Posner, *The Problematics of Moral and Legal Theory* (Belknap Press, 1999) 266. Posner unpacks the difference between postmodernism and pragmatism in law, and asks himself: Am I "a right-wing 'Crit'?"
[121] Mark Kelman, *A Guide to Critical Legal Studies* (Harvard University Press, 1987) 114–85.
[122] Duxbury (n 100) 304; contra, Schlag, "US CLS" (n 39) 206.

and economics in a chapter titled "Legal Economists and Normative Social Theory".[123] In the form of a book review for the *Wall Street Journal*, Posner, at this stage an appeals court judge, penned a response to Kelman's claims.[124] Although he compliments Kelman as a critic of mainstream law,[125] Posner calls Kelman out as "too quick to find contradiction, too dismissive of efforts to reconcile apparent conflicts, [and] too contemptuous of practical reason".[126] This bickering in the public eye can be seen as somewhat sporting and even healthy between two competing legal movements. However, the elephant in the room, the dying form of post-war American liberalism,[127] highlights the very real competition of a winner-takes-all situation.

The Slow Death of US-CLS

As the flaws in liberalism began to show more broadly, interest in both US-CLS and law and economics as potential replacements for legal liberalism grew. However, as this interest grew, so did the critiques and criticisms of both legal movements.[128] Aside from the aforementioned factors, the lack of a coherent US-CLS alternative to liberal law failed to instil confidence in those who might have been more politically supportive of other US-CLS aims.[129] In contrast, the election of Ronald Reagan in 1980 and the push towards supply-side economic policy thematically resonated with law and economics. Culturally there was a push towards neoliberalism, which affected politics and institutions alike.[130]

Whilst the wider political climate was moving towards a conservativism that aligned with law and economics, the "extension of sixties activism",[131] US-CLS, was faltering at Harvard Law School. As the notoriety of US-CLS had grown, so had tensions within the law faculty at Harvard. Broadly, this

---

[123] Kelman (n 121) 114.
[124] Richard A. Posner, "Bookshelf: A Manifesto for Legal Renegades", *The Wall Street Journal* (New York, 27 January 1987).
[125] Ibid.
[126] Ibid.
[127] Brinkley (n 106) x.
[128] See, e.g., Richard Bauman, *Ideology and Community in the First Wave of Critical Legal Studies* (University of Toronto Press, 2000); Ronald Dworkin, "Is Wealth a Value?" (1980) 9(2) *Journal of Legal Studies* 191.
[129] Bauman (n 128); Richard Michael Fischl, "The Question That Killed Critical Legal Studies" (1992) 17(4) *Law and Social Inquiry* 779.
[130] Van Horn and Mirowski (n 112); Corinne Blalock, "Neoliberalism and the Crisis of Legal Theory" (2014) 77 *Law and Contemporary Problems* 71; David Harvey, *A Brief History of Neoliberalism* (Oxford University Press, 2005) 13; Wendy Brown, *Undoing the Demos: Neoliberalism's Stealth Revolution* (ZoneBooks, 2015) 10, 122–31.
[131] Kalman (n 84).

tension was between three identifiable groups: the Crits, traditional liberals, and those affiliated with law and economics.[132] Such was the environment that at least one professor left Harvard, after twenty years' service, for Chicago Law School.[133] However, these tensions truly came to a peak in 1987, when Harvard Law School denied tenure to two US-CLS scholars. When David Trubek, a visiting professor, and Clare Dalton, an assistant professor, applied for tenure at Harvard Law school and were denied, the Crits and their sympathisers took this as a direct attack.[134] There was no clear evidence that it was an attack, and no expectation that every application for tenure would receive it, as Trubek had found previously when he was denied tenure at Yale Law School.[135] However, the timing of the denial moved beyond the issue at hand and became representative of US-CLS at Harvard Law School. Whilst tensions had been running high between the different legal factions,[136] the tenure denial was something instigated by the institution, rather than from an individual. In itself, this top-down rejection of US-CLS scholars represented an institutional decline in approval or acceptance of US-CLS at Harvard Law School. Trubek did not request a review, and returned to the University of Wisconsin Law School;[137] Dalton received a review and her tenure denial was upheld.[138]

The decision at Harvard Law School rippled through the legal academe and the broader community with the help of newspapers like the *New York Times*, which had covered the story.[139] Reading between the lines, those with an interest in the saga of US-CLS at Harvard would have seen that the movement was no longer going to wield the power it once had; however, at this stage, its actual death would not have been so easy to predict. A *New York Times* article contains a quotation from Robert Gordon, of Stanford Law School, which in hindsight is telling. Gordon gets to the heart of the competition between US-CLS and law and economics, stating that, "There's a peculiar kind of vanity or megalomania at Harvard, that the place is the soul

---

[132] "Vorenberg, Former Law School Dean, Dies at 72", *The Harvard Crimson* (online, 14 April 2000) <https://www.thecrimson.com/article/2000/4/14/vorenberg-former-law-school-dean-dies/>.

[133] Jennifer A. Kingson, "Harvard Tenure Battle Puts 'Critical Legal Studies' on Trial", *The New York Times* (online, 30 August 1987) <https://www.nytimes.com/1987/08/30/weekinreview/harvard-tenure-battle-puts-critical-legal-studies-on-trial.html>.

[134] Ibid.

[135] Hackney (n 57) 28.

[136] Kingson (n 133).

[137] Ibid.

[138] Ibid.

[139] Ibid.

of the American ruling class . . . Whoever wins in local institutional battles there thinks they will control America's cultural and institutional destiny."[140]

In 1989, two years after the denial of tenure to Trubek and Dalton, the dean of law at Harvard Law School who had overseen the prominent US-CLS years, James Vorenburg, stepped down.[141] Vorenburg was succeeded by Clark, a traditionalist with a background in corporate law,[142] whose appointment was met with dissatisfaction from the Crits.[143] Gerald Frug, a Crit and part of the six-person faculty search committee that helped shortlist the potential deans, believed the appointment of Clark was a mistake.[144] The Harvard University president, Derek Bok, however, gave his full support to Clark, overriding Frug and any similar criticisms.[145] The appointment of Clark as dean allowed a reshuffling of the faculty, separating the factions and removing more of the power Crits held in the law school.[146] The move set the tone for the start of a new decade.

In 1991 law and economics's Coase won the Nobel Prize for Economic Science.[147] With this award, Coase joined other law and economic influencers, Friedrich Hayek in 1974, and Milton Friedman in 1976.[148] The prestige of this award and the lineage behind it further legitimised the law and economics approach. Now facing a Nobel Prize–winning opponent, reflective of governments throughout the world,[149] US-CLS as the "extension of sixties activism" was being crystalised as legal whimsy. Given the nature of law and economics as reflective of a dominant political and business class, the final blow to US-CLS came in the form of corporate endowments—notably the endowments provided by John M. Olin and the Olin Foundation.[150] After giving money to the law and economics movement in the 1970s,[151] the Olin Foundation pushed for a law and economics programme at Harvard Law

---

[140] Ibid.
[141] Allan Gold, "Traditionalist Is Named as Harvard Law Dean", *The New York Times* (online, 18 February 1989) <https://www.nytimes.com/1989/02/18/us/traditionalist-is-named-as-harvard-law-dean.html>.
[142] See, e.g., Robert Clark, *Corporate Law* (Little Brown, 1986).
[143] Ibid.
[144] Ibid.
[145] Ibid.
[146] Yen, "As HLS Mulls Its Mission" (n 53).
[147] "All Prizes in Economic Sciences", *The Nobel Prize* (online, 2023) <https://www.nobelprize.org/prizes/uncategorized/all-prizes-in-economic-sciences>.
[148] Ibid.
[149] See, e.g., Harvey (n 130) 5–38.
[150] John J. Miller, Karl Zinsmeister, and Ashley May, *Agenda Setting: A Wise Giver's Guide to Influencing Public Policy* (Philanthropy Roundtable, 2015) 38.
[151] Ibid 39.

School, which was accepted by the university president, Bok.[152] Similar to Gordon's earlier observation, Steven Teles identifies Harvard Law School as a target for the Olin Foundation: "Because of its size and prestige, Harvard Law School has an outsized impact on American legal culture and the character of the legal professoriate."[153] The multiyear grant established the "John M. Olin Center for Law, Economics, and Business", which would go on to receive funding of more than $18 million from the Olin Foundation.[154]

Towards Posthumous Critical Legal Studies

The ongoing competition between US-CLS and law and economics throughout the 1980s provides some context to the question asked in Yen's 1995 article for the *Harvard Law Record*. Broadly, in the face of a changing law school, where were the Crits? Historically it can be argued that, as the unsuccessful side in a jurisprudential overhaul, the Crits had stepped out of the limelight, no longer gracing the pages of mainstream newspapers and magazines.[155] However, in Yen's specific context, within Harvard Law School, the Crits also "Remain Quiet".[156] Turning to both Kennedy and Horwitz, as well as Clark, Yen received unanimous confirmation that US-CLS was not as it once had been. Whilst there is a heavy motif of death around US-CLS in the article, there is no unified understanding of what had actually died. Each interviewee, and Yen, draws different conclusions, reflecting the complexity of the situation.

Chronologically the article presents a short quotation from Clark, who bluntly states, "I didn't kill them."[157] Given the animosity of the Crits towards Clark's appointment,[158] this short statement is telling, first about the indication that it could be his fault by proxy, and second that, even outside of the immediate community, people were aware that US-CLS was dead. Yen moves from Clark's protest-like statement to her own experience of US-CLS at Harvard Law School. Citing Kennedy, she states that US-CLS is as "dead as a doornail".[159] Having made this observation, she provides a longer quotation from Clark, in which he refers to US-CLS as entering another phase in its

---

[152] Ibid 40.
[153] Teles (n 88) 192.
[154] Ibid.
[155] See, e.g., Kingson (n 133); Gold (n 141); Louis Menand, "What is 'Critical Legal Studies': Radicalism for Yuppies" (17 March 1986) *The New Republic* 20; Marc Granetz, "Duncan the Doughnut" (March 17, 1986) *The New Republic* 22.
[156] Yen, "As HLS Mulls Its Mission" (n 53).
[157] Ibid.
[158] Gold (n 141); Yen, "As HLS Mulls Its Mission" (n 53).
[159] Yen, "As HLS Mulls Its Mission" (n 53).

lifecycle, or having changed or retired.[160] Clark's choice of words, which this time do not mention death, seem to be applicable only after something is no longer a threat—that is, as a respectful memoriam to US-CLS.

Whilst thematically similar, Yen and Clark do present different ideas of what this death means. In questioning Kennedy, however, Yen achieves a more detailed understanding from one of US-CLS's founders:

> You have to distinguish Critical Legal Studies the movement, from Critical Legal Studies the academic school . . . There isn't at Harvard Law School or nationally any CLS movement left. The movement completely collapsed several years ago. The school of thought, which is academic, is alive and well, but the school of thought doesn't have any activist component, period.[161]

Kennedy's response provides an assessment of US-CLS as living a half-life, one that is no longer able to do what it used to. Kennedy's concession is that despite not wanting to create "just another set of bibliographical headings" when US-CLS began, the current state of US-CLS was just that.[162] Horwitz follows a similar line about the state of the then-contemporary US-CLS, but optimistically argues for a resurgence once it was safe to come out again.[163] Although not referencing them directly, the implication Horwitz makes is that the situation that befell Trubek and Dalton in 1986 was still a very real concern for the younger Crits—something which Kennedy agreed with, and had addressed a year earlier.[164]

As representatives of the Crits at Harvard Law School, both Kennedy and Horwitz present a dire view of contemporary (in 1995) US-CLS, but with an overarching assumption that it would live on in one form or another. However, the hope for US-CLS to reemerge in a decade, per Horwitz,[165] or to continue as an area of academic interest, per Kennedy,[166] seems to deny, or not fully appreciate, that in the same article there is a consensus that US-CLS is dead. Given that US-CLS never reemerged and that its academic influence also waned, the optimism that Kennedy and Horwitz showed was ill-placed. Instead, what can be taken from Yen's article is that the death of US-CLS was not hyperbole, and that in 1995 US-CLS was as dead as a doornail.

Recognising US-CLS as dead, rather than on hiatus, clarifies two important areas. Firstly, in relation to Yen's article, it frames the responses to the state

---

[160] Ibid.
[161] Ibid.
[162] Yen, "Crits at HLS a Dying Breed?" (n 54).
[163] Ibid.
[164] Gerard J. Clark, "A Conversation With Duncan Kennedy", *Suffolk University Law School Journal* (1994) 24(2) 56, 58.
[165] Yen, "As HLS Mulls Its Mission" (n 53).
[166] Ibid.

of US-CLS as individual acts of mourning. For example, this can be seen in Clark's uncomfortable and jocular tone presenting a pre-emptive "not guilty", backed up with pleasantries about a once-real foe that is no longer a threat. Mourning is also evident in Horwitz and Kennedy's demonstrations of optimism that US-CLS will continue or be reborn. Even Yen's premise for the article, her line of questioning about "what happened to the Crits", becomes an act of discovery—that the once-vibrant US-CLS at Harvard Law School is dead. The second clarification is more important to Critical Legal Studies as a whole, as it creates a way to understand and interpret the narrow US-based Critical Legal Studies work that continued after 1995:

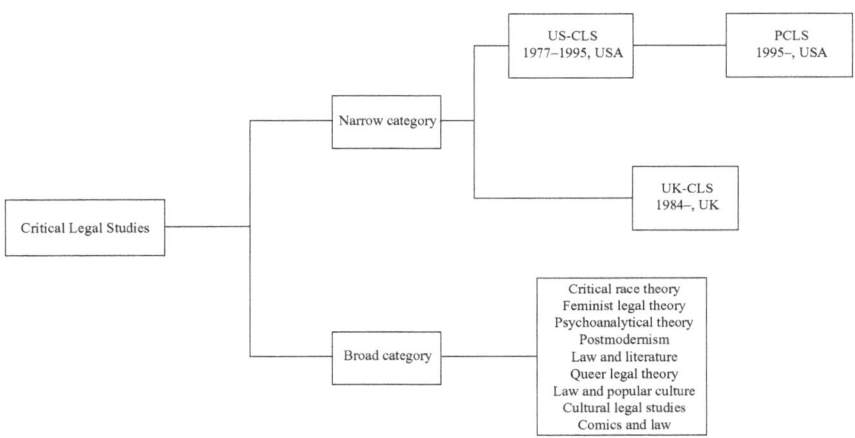

Figure 2.7 Family Tree: Complete

PCLS, beginning with the declaration of US-CLS's death in 1995 and continuing from that point, completes the Critical Legal Studies family tree. The creation of this genealogy, a refinement on both Davies's and Douzinas and Gearey's original divisions, provides a framework that aids in the overall demystification of Critical Legal Studies. The idea of the Critical Legal Studies family tree provides a system to address the questions, "What is Critical Legal Studies?" and "Which Critical Legal Studies?" Using the family tree as a flow chart or map, these questions can be answered, albeit after further measures are accounted for. Such measures include the need to identify a broad or narrow reading, whether it relates to US-based or another (most notably UK-CLS), and if it was before or after US-CLS was considered "dead as a doornail". However, the clarity created by dividing Critical Legal Studies into branches and limbs comes with its own set of related questions, primarily about the relationship between, and implications of, US-CLS and PCLS.

3

Death on the Books

O, death. Won't you spare me over 'til another year?

Traditional

From its declaration in the *Harvard Law Record*,[1] a motif of death lingers around US-CLS. However, death's place in the broader history of US-CLS is not clear. In the early 2000s, Duncan Kennedy opined that, "[C]ritical legal studies [US-CLS] as a political movement has been dead for a number of years, critical legal studies as a legal academic school of thought is very much alive".[2] He retains this stance twenty years later.[3] However, aside from Kennedy, few people have discussed the death of US-CLS. The effect of a death that is known but not discussed adds to the confusion surrounding US-CLS. First, by not acknowledging this death, there is an assumption that what continued as Critical Legal Studies post-1995—what we have called Posthumous Critical Legal Studies, or PCLS—was no different to what came before. Second, there is an uneasy relationship between any post-1995 left-wing legal critiques and US-CLS. For example, in these works there is a sense of duty to acknowledge, reify, or distance themselves from US-CLS.

Books on legal history and jurisprudence, which take a critical stance or focus on critical approaches to law, are likely to mention of the death of US-CLS. These mentions are often not in-depth, but inform their broader discussions and understandings of Critical Legal Studies. Conversely, books

---

[1] Hope Yen, "As HLS Mulls Its Mission, CLS Scholars Remain Quiet", *Harvard Law Record* (Cambridge, 1 December 1995) 2; Hope Yen, "Crits at HLS a Dying Breed?", *Harvard Law Record* (Cambridge, 1 December 1995) 4.

[2] Duncan Kennedy, "Two Globalizations of Law & Legal Thought: 1850–1968' (2003) 36(3) *Suffolk University Law Review* 631.

[3] Duncan Kennedy and Corinne Blalock, "Provocation as Strategy" (2022) 121(2) *South Atlantic Quarterly* 377, 378.

which do not take a critical approach will mention Critical Legal Studies, but are less likely to mention its death. For example, Margaret Davies, who, takes a critical, rather than abstract view, of jurisprudence,[4] has a subsection of her chapter on Critical Legal Studies titled, "Is It Dead?"[5] In this chapter, Davies draws from Kennedy's discussion in "Two Globalizations of Law & Legal Thought: 1850–1968",[6] after which Davies poses some questions about the death of US-CLS and its potential assimilation into mainstream law. However, the author offers no definitive outcome for US-CLS, instead seeing its end as coinciding with the expansion of "broad" Critical Legal Studies, such as feminist legal theory and critical race theory.[7]

In their work *Critical Jurisprudence: The Political Philosophy of Justice*,[8] Costas Douzinas and Adam Gearey dedicate a chapter to Critical Legal Studies.[9] Much like for Davies, theirs is a broad understanding Critical Legal Studies that begins with US-CLS. However, unlike Davies, Douzinas and Gearey introduce the death of US-CLS on their first page. This discussion comes after the authors present a series of questions about the way in which US-CLS can be categorised, asking in regard to its history: "Is it correct to impose a tradition on a body of thought that has set its face against tradition?"[10] Douzinas and Gearey argue that these types of difficult questions leave US-CLS with an uneasiness about itself, "an anxiety towards its own constitution".[11] Its death, the authors argue, is at once a symptom and influence of this anxiety, stating that "[i]n American CLS, the repeated announcements of its own death have marked this unique anxiety."[12]

While they do not spend a lot of time on the death of US-CLS, Davies and Douzinas and Gearey engage with it as an integral event in their analyses of Critical Legal Studies more broadly. In contrast, jurisprudential works that do not take a critical approach, are less likely to make any mention of the death of US-CLS. For example, in Denise Meyerson's *Essential Jurisprudence*, the author makes mention of US-CLS,[13] but makes no mention of the its death. Instead, she focuses primarily on the general ideas and thinkers behind

---

[4] Margaret Davies, *Asking the Law Question* (Thomson Reuters, 3rd ed, 2008) 11–12.
[5] Ibid 210.
[6] Kennedy, "Two Globalizations" (n 2).
[7] Davies (n 4) 212.
[8] Costas Douzinas and Adam Gearey, *Critical Jurisprudence: The Political Philosophy of Justice* (Hart, 2005) 229.
[9] Ibid.
[10] Ibid.
[11] Ibid.
[12] Ibid.
[13] Denise Meyerson, *Essential Jurisprudence* (Routledge Cavendish, 2008) 104.

US-CLS, taking a meta view of the movement. Meyerson's section on Critical Legal Studies is brief but thorough;[14] most interesting is the way in which she ends the section. Quoting from Alan Hunt and Peter Fitzpatrick's *Critical Legal Studies*,[15] Meyerson concludes in the present tense. The implication of this is that US-CLS did not die, and, according to Meyerson, there is still a "significant core of unity" within Critical Legal Studies.[16]

Taking a similar generalist approach to jurisprudence, Ian McLeod's *Legal Theory* makes mention of US-CLS, but not of its death.[17] Instead, McLeod ends his short section with a quotation from Neil Duxbury's *Patterns of American Jurisprudence* which positions US-CLS as continually "losing momentum" after its mid-1980s peak.[18] Interestingly, in Duxbury's original, the paragraph directly preceding this quotation grapples with the decline of US-CLS, stating that, "if not entirely dead, [US-CLS] certainly has little life left in it."[19] Duxbury's own statement relies on personal correspondence, rather than academic sources, which could account for McLeod's omittance of this necessary qualification.

The lack of recognition of the death of US-CLS in dominant generalist texts can be understood through the way in which Critical Legal Studies fits into the authors' broader jurisprudential narrative. Within Meyerson and McLeod's books, for example, Critical Legal Studies is positioned in a linear and progressive fashion—that is, legal realism begat Critical Legal Studies, Critical Legal Studies begat critical race theory, and so on. Following this linear approach, the ends of the preceding movements are positioned as logical transitions rather than deaths. Similarly, in critical approaches to jurisprudence, the works engage with the death of US-CLS, but only in a cursory manner. Davies, Douzinas and Gearey, and Duxbury all acknowledge the death of US-CLS, but do not deeply interrogate the aftereffects of the event.

Reading these texts, a unified approach to understanding Critical Legal Studies emerges. First, the death of US-CLS is something reserved for critical approaches to jurisprudence. Second, across these and other jurisprudential remembrances, US-CLS was a moment or iteration of legal critique that made way for new critical imaginations. Surely this is a logical approach, but

---

[14] Ibid 104–16.
[15] Peter Fitzpatrick and Alan Hunt (eds), *Critical Legal Studies* (Basil Blackwell, 1987).
[16] Meyerson (n 13) 105, quoting Fitzpatrick and Hunt (n 15) 2.
[17] Ian McLeod, *Legal Theory* (Palgrave Macmillan, 5th ed, 2010).
[18] See Neil Duxbury, *Patterns of American Jurisprudence* (Clarendon Press, 1995) 426; McLeod (n 17) cites this passage from Duxbury at page 115.
[19] Ibid 426.

it is one that leaves little scope for US-CLS works which have continued after the death, or the effect that the death has had upon them.

Moving away from general jurisprudence and historical accounts of US-CLS, there are two notable references that engage more substantially with the ideas of death and US-CLS. The first is a review by Richard Michael Fischl of Mark Kelman's *A Guide to Critical Legal Studies*.[20] Fischl's article centres on the death of US-CLS, proposing that the question that killed US-CLS was, "What would you put in its place?" The question is one that Fischl and other Crits identify as a common retort from critics of US-CLS when Crits advocated removing the rule of law.[21]

Fischl's article was published in 1993, and chronologically it is the first open mention of US-CLS being dead, coming two years before Hope Yen's article in the *Harvard Law Record*. However, whilst Fischl is engaged with the motif of death around US-CLS, he states that despite the difficulty of the question,[22] his title is ironic, and the piece is not a eulogy.[23] More broadly, Fischl's use of "death" can be read in a similar way to that of Kennedy and Morton Horwitz in 1995:[24] Fischl acknowledges the move of US-CLS away from the public eye, but demonstrates optimism about the continuation of Critical Legal Studies. So whilst death is central to Fischl's piece, both his stance and the context of his article as a response to a common misconception separate it from confirming the death of US-CLS.[25]

In contrast, the second article does address the death of US-CLS. In 1998, Arthur Austin published a critique of various critics of law called *The Empire Strikes Back: Outsiders and the Struggle over Legal Education*.[26] Austin's "outsiders",[27] those who target and attack the "empire", were those involved

---

[20] Richard Michael Fischl, "The Question That Killed Critical Legal Studies" (1992) 17(4) *Law & Social Inquiry* 779.
[21] Ibid 780.
[22] See especially Andrew Altman, *Critical Legal Studies: A Liberal Critique* (Princeton University Press, 1990); Richard Bauman, *Ideology and Community in the First Wave of Critical Legal Studies* (University of Toronto Press, 2000); see also Jack M. Balkin, "Critical Legal Theory Today" in Francis J. Mootz III (ed), *On Philosophy in American Law* (Cambridge University Press, 2009) 64.
[23] Fischl (n 20) 780.
[24] Yen, "As HLS Mulls Its Mission" (n 1); Yen, "Crits at HLS a Dying Breed?" (n 1).
[25] See John Henry Schlegel, "CLS Wasn't Killed by a Question" (2007) 58(5) *Alabama Law Review* 967, 968. Schlegel's response to Fischl identifies the "fading away" of US-CLS, rather than a death. This aligns both pieces as acknowledging the decline in US-CLS, but not the "death" that Duncan Kennedy and Arthur Austin focus on.
[26] Arthur D. Austin, *The Empire Strikes Back: Outsiders and the Struggle over Legal Education* (New York University Press, 1998).
[27] Ibid.

in Critical Legal Studies (both in the broad and narrow sense) but primarily US-CLS, critical race theory, and feminist legal theory.[28] In *The Empire Strikes Back*, Austin is explicit in his description of the death when discussing US-CLS, titling the chapter focused specifically on the Crits "CLS Is Dead As a Doornail".[29] Austin takes this phrase directly from Hope Yen's article, and from his vantage point in 1998, he writes about US-CLS as if he is doing so posthumously. Austin, however, did not see an emergence of PCLS, merely that US-CLS died and was no more than "an episode, not a movement—a mild hangover from . . . the 1970s",[30] distancing himself further from the understanding demonstrated by Fischl, Horwitz, and Kennedy.

Austin's analysis also discusses a theory about what killed US-CLS, centring on the posthumous discovery of Paul de Man's anti-Semitic writings in the Belgian newspaper *Le Soir*.[31] For Austin, it is de Man's fall from grace which, after causing irreparable damage to literary criticism, was in turn responsible for, or at least a key contributor to, the death of US-CLS. Austin concocts a flimsy connection between de Man and US-CLS through de Man's relationship with Jacques Derrida.[32] Although Derrida's influence on US-CLS is evident, specifically around the idea of deconstruction,[33] Austin offers little more to make this into a convincing reason why US-CLS died.

Despite the strange turn in Austin's book and the rationale behind Fischl's review, both authors strengthen the argument that US-CLS has died. Even taking into account their vastly different stances, thematically both authors acknowledge the figure of death surrounding Critical Legal Studies, with both pieces building from this position. Compared to the death of US-CLS that was confirmed in Yen's article,[34] there is nothing as blatant within the US-CLS-era

---

[28] Ibid ix. See generally Arthur Austin, "The Top Ten Politically Correct Law Review Articles" (1999) 27 *Florida State University Law Review*, 233.

[29] Ibid 83.

[30] Ibid 109.

[31] See James Atlas, "The Case of Paul de Man", *The New York Times* (online, 28 August 1988) <https://www.nytimes.com/1988/08/28/magazine/the-case-of-paul-de-man.html>; Louis Menand, "The de Man Case", *A Critic at Large*, *The New Yorker* (online, 24 March 2014) <https://www.newyorker.com/magazine/2014/03/24/the-de-man-case>; Evelyn Barish, *The Double Life of Paul de Man* (Liveright, 2014).

[32] Austin, *The Empire Strikes Back* (n 26) 83.

[33] See David L. Gregory, "A Guide To Critical Legal Studies" (1987) 1987(6) *Duke Law Journal* 1,138, 1,141–2 nn 12: "Deconstruction, always controversial, is now deeply embarrassed as well as perennially embattled." Gregory goes into great detail discussing the issues facing deconstruction after the de Man revelations. While it can be broadly related to US-CLS through their use of the term, there is no great connection to the death of US-CLS more specifically.

[34] Yen, "As HLS Mulls Its Mission" (n 1); Yen, "Crits at HLS a Dying Breed?" (n 1).

writings from other Crits or their commentators. Even Kennedy's optimistic stance sees the death as a move from the political to the academic, rather than the end of US-CLS.[35] Following the family tree, however, there are articles classified as PCLS post-1995 which discuss the disappearance of US-CLS.[36] Interestingly, these works do not discuss a death per se, but instead yearn for US-CLS and ask why it is no longer around. This questioning by PCLS scholars, and dismissal by critics of US-CLS like Austin, can also be read politically—that is, with neither side wanting to contend that there is scope for a middle ground. US-CLS is either dead and gone, or it is transformed and waiting to emerge from the shadows.

---

[35] Kennedy, "Two Globalizations" (n 2).
[36] See generally, E. Dana Neacsu, "CLS Stands for Critical Legal Studies, If Anyone Remembers' (2000) 8(2) *Journal of Law and Policy* 415.

4

Searching for Death

O sancta simplicitas! What strange simplification and falsification mankind lives in! One can never cease to marvel when one has acquired eyes for this marvel! How we have made everything around us bright and free and easy and simple! How we have known how to bestow on our senses a passport to everything superficial, on our thoughts a divine desire for wanton gambolling and false conclusions!

Friedrich Nietzsche, *Beyond Good and Evil* (1886)

There is a privileging of knowledge which ensures that certain understandings are only available to those with the right access. One might imagine a fortress, sealed with combination locks that only open with the right utterances.[1] The preceding chapter can be understood as somewhat reinforcing that privilege – its analysis drawn from the pages of books critical to and critical of jurisprudence, descriptions that are read only by those with the right kind of access. Or to put it another way, there is an analogy to high and low status. If the last chapter addressed the high remembrances and mentions of the US-CLS death, then this chapter will take the low road and look at more accessible sources.

To achieve this accessibility, an online search and an analysis of legal dictionary entries will be undertaken, both for "Critical Legal Studies". By assessing three entries from each medium, a composite picture of how US-CLS is remembered will be formed, and any mention of its death will be noted. This choice of texts relates to a "first port of call" for information—that is, if you had never heard of Critical Legal Studies, how would you find out about it? While a text like Mark Kelman's *A Guide to Critical Legal Studies*[2] is logically

---

[1] Patricia J. Williams, *The Alchemy of Race and Rights* (Harvard University Press, 1992).
[2] Mark Kelman, *A Guide to Critical Legal Studies* (Harvard University Press, 1987).

titled as a place to start reading, it is, however, unlikely to be close to hand, and stylistically it is not immediately easy to read.[3] Instead, within the law school, a legal dictionary is a logical port of call to define or understand a term. More broadly, an internet search, predominantly via Google,[4] is likely to be undertaken first.[5]

In the age of artificial intelligence (AI), this type of data is drawn upon when an AI generator is used to write about Critical Legal Studies. Without entering specific works into a generator, the free and available descriptions of US-CLS are those which will be used, in turn creating a dominant and common understanding. There is also an implication that these accessible materials will lack the emotional character of specific pro- or anti-US-CLS works. For example, Arthur Austin's assessment of US-CLS as "a failed movement, a confession that when all the Critbabble is carved away, [US-]CLS is basically antipragmatic, little more than a blend of elitism and narcissism"[6] is unlikely to be mirrored in a legal dictionary. However, the method employed to analyse these texts will still assess the content and its implications.

The method for this analysis is adapted from two existing methodologies: content analysis and critical reading. Both methodologies offer insight into how the death of US-CLS is remembered; however, neither fully achieves the necessary mix of empirical and qualitative analysis individually. Content analysis, originally a social science methodology, has been adapted for law,[7] with an apt analogy as to why this is justified: "Legal scholars [are] the mockingbirds of the academy . . . great borrowers of scholarly methods. We experiment with the tools of historians, economists, sociologists, literary theorists, moral philosophers, and others, often to great effect."[8]

Content analysis takes a series of papers "on a particular subject, and systematically reads them, recording consistent features of each and drawing inferences about their use and meaning".[9] In the current context, this approach is a useful method for assessment. However, traditionally and to a

---

[3] See generally Richard A. Posner, "Bookshelf: A Manifesto for Legal Renegades", *The Wall Street Journal* (online, 27 January 1987).
[4] Siva Vaidhyanathan, *The Googlization of Everything: (And Why We Should Worry)* (University of California Press, 2012) 51.
[5] See generally Newton Lee, "To Google or Not to Google", in Newton Lee (ed), *Google It* (Springer, 2016) 3.
[6] Arthur D. Austin, *The Empire Strikes Back: Outsiders and the Struggle over Legal Education* (New York University Press, 1998) 86.
[7] Mark A. Hall and Ronald F. Wright, "Systematic Content Analysis of Judicial Opinions" (2008) 96 *California Law Review* 63, 63.
[8] Ibid.
[9] Ibid 64.

lesser extent in its application to law, content analysis requires the coding of materials to assess them statistically,[10] and in most instances a larger sample size to draw from.[11] In both cases, the specificity of the death of US-CLS hinders the use of a larger sample and thus it does not benefit from coding and statistics. If the question was broader—for example, "How is Critical Legal Studies remembered online?"—then a greater number of search results would be required, and this method would be applicable.

Instead, fulfilling the mockingbird metaphor, a systemic reading and assessment of the inferences in the texts will be undertaken through the content analysis method.[12] This reading will be critical, not only addressing the way in which the death of US-CLS has or has not been presented, but also the format, layout, and context of the source. In addition, any mention of Critical Legal Studies as a way demystify law will be identified.

Within a legal context, this type of critical reading methodologically aligns with a US-CLS approach.[13] However, the application of a US-CLS method to non-legal texts such as websites and dictionaries is not directly transferable. In other disciplines, the critical approach to more generalist texts has been developed. For example, the philosopher Roberto Esposito identifies this type of inquiry as "philosophical reflection",[14] a way "to critically dismantle opinion, [and] to radically interrogate what is presented as immediately clear to all".[15] Similarly, in her proposed method of critical ethnography, D. Soyini Madison states it is necessary "to deconstruct and reinvent those epistemological certainties that foreclose alternative possibilities for ordering and reordering authoritative regimes of truth."[16]

Thematically, these different disciplines converge on the purpose of critical readings to question what is immediately clear, what is an epistemological certainty, and what this means for the subject more broadly. In the current context, these theorists signpost what needs to be assessed in a critical reading. For US-CLS, the focus is on a lack of acknowledgment or interaction with its death, which in turn adds to its mystification; but also that the chosen

---

[10] See generally Martin Abbott and Jennifer McKinney, *Understanding and Applying Research Design* (John Wiley & Sons, 2013) 318.
[11] Ibid.
[12] Hall and Wright (n 7) 63.
[13] See generally Alan D. Freeman, "Truth and Mystification in Legal Scholarship" (1981) 90(5) *Yale Law Journal* 1,229, 1,230–1.
[14] Roberto Esposito, "The *Dispositif* of the Person" (2012) 8(1) *Law, Culture and the Humanities* 17.
[15] Ibid.
[16] D. Soyini Madison, *Critical Ethnography: Method, Ethics, and Performance* (Sage, 2nd ed, 2012) 6.

texts demonstrate unified histories and understandings of US-CLS, which need to be engaged with. The similarities between the dictionary entries and the cross-linking of the websites create "epistemological certainties" around US-CLS,[17] which become difficult to challenge and add to the mystification of Critical Legal Studies more broadly.

Legal Dictionaries

The reviewed dictionaries are *Black's Law Dictionary*, the LexisNexis *Concise Australian Law Dictionary*, and the Oxford *Australian Law Dictionary*.[18] These dictionaries were chosen due to their prevalence in law schools, often bundled with first-year textbooks, and their inclusion of Critical Legal Studies.[19] While the dictionaries list contributing authors, they do not specify which author wrote or contributed to which entry.[20] This makes the identification and analysis of "whose" version of Critical Legal Studies is being read difficult, while adding to the anonymous authority derived from a dictionary entry.

The first dictionary assessed is *Black's Law Dictionary*:

> **Critical Legal Studies.** (1978) **1.** A school of thought advancing the idea that the legal system perpetuates the status quo in terms of economics, race and gender by using manipulable concepts and creating an imaginary world of social harmony regulated by law. The Marxist wing of this school focuses on socioeconomic issues. Fem-crits emphasize gender hierarchy, whereas critical race theorists focus on racial subordination. See *fem-crit* under CRIT; CRITICAL RACE THEORY. **2.** The body of work produced by adherents to this school of thought.—Abbr. CLS.[21]

The entry in *Black's* is short, to the point, and offers no divisions, associated texts or theorists. The entry begins with the year 1978, positioning this Critical Legal Studies as US-CLS, albeit a year after the first Conference on Critical Legal Studies (CCLS).[22] It is important to note that despite the start date, there is no end date presented, and no mention of a death or similar in the definition. The lack of an endpoint is compounded by the tense used,

---

[17] Ibid.
[18] Bryan A. Garner (ed), *Black's Law Dictionary* (Thomas West, 9th ed, 2014); Trischa Mann (ed), *Australian Law Dictionary* (Oxford, 2010); Peter Butt (ed), *Concise Australian Dictionary* (LexisNexis Butterworths, 4th ed, 2011).
[19] For example, *West's Encyclopedia of American Law* gives one brief sentence on CLS; the *Oxford Dictionary of Law* does not include CLS.
[20] These dictionaries list a general editor, before a sizeable list of contributors to the edition.
[21] Garner (n 18) 432.
[22] Duncan Kennedy, *Legal Education and the Reproduction of Hierarchy: A Polemic Against the System* (New York University Press, 2004) 204.

presenting Critical Legal Studies as still active. The entry is not restricted by types of Critical Legal Studies, mentioning both fem-crits and critical race theory. It can be inferred from this inclusion (and since both fem-crits and critical race theory have their own definitions listed) that the entry uses Critical Legal Studies as an umbrella term.

In the Oxford *Australian Law Dictionary*, Critical Legal Studies is listed as

> **critical legal studies (CLS)** A left-leaning movement, critical of *legal liberalism*, which was especially strong in the USA in the 1980s. It draws variously on Marxism, feminism, *postmodernism* and even American *legal realism* to criticise and deconstruct ("trash") *legal positivism*, *legal formalism*, rights and modernist epistemologies. Leading "Crits" include Duncan Kennedy and Roberto Unger.[23]

This entry is brief and focuses only on US-CLS, with no mention of variants of Critical Legal Studies. Whilst not addressing the broad/narrow divide, other geographic locations are implied with the phrasing that Critical Legal Studies "was especially strong in the USA". Unlike in *Black's*, the italicised terms linked to Critical Legal Studies are not from the broad category, but instead situate US-CLS in its broader jurisprudential setting. The entry identifies the politically left stance of US-CLS, its primary target of liberalism, and its timeframe.

The phrasing surrounding the timeframe is relevant in the current context as it states that US-CLS "was especially strong . . . in the 1980s." Whilst arguably true, this statement allows the entry to ignore the CCLS and other 1970s milestones, as well as any question of why it became less strong, or weaker, from the 1980s onwards. By focusing only on the 1980s, this entry stays neutral on whether US-CLS did or did not die. This stance also means there is no engagement with what happened to US-CLS after this time, aside from the implication that it got weaker.

In the LexisNexis *Concise Australian Legal Dictionary*, the Critical Legal Studies entry provides article citations, making it longer than the previous entries:

> **critical legal studies** *Abbr*—**CLS** A movement which began in the United States in the 1970s, according to which there is no universal foundation for law amenable to rational deduction. Critical legal studies is opposed to positivist jurisprudence, and rights-based theories (such as those proposed by Ronald Dworkin and John Rawls). It is most strongly opposed to liberal

---

[23] Mann (n 18) 156–7. Italics added to replace the different font in the original text for other terms covered within the dictionary.

legal theory, claiming that it conceals the power structures underlying legal systems. In this sense CLS shares a common position with Marxist critiques of legal systems in liberal-democratic societies. Leading proponents of the school are Roberto Unger, author of *The Critical Legal Studies Movement* (1986), and Duncan Kennedy, author of "The Stages of Decline of the Public-private Distinction" (1982) 6 *U Pennsylvania LR* 1349. See also **Dworkin, Ronald; Marx Karl, positivism; Rawls, John**.[24]

The LexisNexis entry is roughly double the length of those in *Black's* and the Oxford Dictionary. In spite of this increase, it covers similar ground. Again, there is no broad/narrow approach, nor is there mention of any Critical Legal Studies variants. The geography is the same, with this entry also focusing purely on the US and US-CLS. Similarly to the *Black's* entry, LexisNexis provides a starting date. However, it is less precise, referencing the whole of the 1970s. Despite this being the only direct reference to a date, there is still a correlation with the Oxford entry: the prominence of US-CLS in the 1980s implied through the publication dates of the works referenced. Once again, opposition to liberalism and US-CLS's similarities with Marxism appear. Unlike the Oxford entry, the LexisNexis one does not include any Crit jargon. Instead it goes further, taking a quasi-US-CLS tone to open the entry. The latter part of the opening sentence states that "there is no universal foundation for law amenable to rational deduction." The statement, which does not appear to be a quotation from a Crit, takes a simple message about US-CLS critiquing the rule of law and conveys it in an overly complicated way. For those familiar with US-CLS works,[25] this approach is fitting or even amusing; however, for the purpose of accessibility, this entry struggles.

The LexisNexis entry had the length and potential to discuss the intricacies of Critical Legal Studies. However, whilst expanding on it slightly compared to *Black's* and Oxford, it covered similar ground. In line with the other entries, there is no explicit mention of US-CLS terms like demystification,

---

[24] Butt (n 18) 147.
[25] See, e.g., Peter Gabel and Duncan Kennedy, "Roll Over Beethoven" (1984) 36(1/2) *Stanford Law Review* 1, 3:

> Okay, the unalienated relatedness which is immanent in our current alienated situation. What I'm saying is, that that does not sound to me like an evocation which can fulfill the legitimate functions of communication, of language and knowledge, because it's abstract bullshit, whereas what we need is small-scale, microphenomenological evocation of real experiences in complex contextualized ways in which one makes it into doing it.

This article exemplifies the heavily wordy nature associated with US-CLS.

but there are allusions to it with LexisNexis discussing the "concealment" of power structures, similarly, Oxford conflates trashing and deconstruction, and *Black's* presents Critical Legal Studies rallying against an "imaginary world".

The LexisNexis entry also follows *Black's* and Oxford by not discussing the end of US-CLS. All three entries position Critical Legal Studies in the present tense, which neither confirms nor denies its death. However, where *Black's* includes broad Critical Legal Studies variants and Oxford discusses a strong point of US-CLSt, the LexisNexis entry avoids making mention either of US-CLS continuing in different forms, or of its influence waning. With its singular focus and present tense, the LexisNexis entry implies that US-CLS has continued uninterrupted from the 1970s to the present.

The death of US-CLS is not a feature in these three legal dictionaries and, by extension, it is unlikely to feature in any mainstream legal dictionary.[26] Similarly, the broad theme of demystification can be read into some, but not all, and is not expressly mentioned in any of the entries. They do, however, share quite similar information. There are differences, but these are subtle and nuanced, whereas the similarities are blatant, leaving a reader of all three entries with a specific view of Critical Legal Studies and creating an authoritative regime of truth.[27]

Online Sources

The second area to be assessed is online, specifically through the search engine Google. Google has established its place as a frequent first port of call for those seeking information online, superseding other available search engines.[28] Using the same logic applied to the legal dictionaries, the full name "Critical Legal Studies" was searched. It is important to note that despite many results from a term searched (usually within the millions), the first few listings on the first page of results are the most clicked on, and subsequently accepted (rightly or wrongly) as the most important.[29]

When "Critical Legal Studies" is searched via Google, the first three results are listed in order as: *Wikipedia*; Cornell University's *Wex*, which provides free legal information; and Harvard University's *The Bridge*, which is similar to *Wex*.[30] Interestingly, each of these sites follows an encyclopedic approach to

---

[26] See those in n 19. It is unlikely that it features in any other mainstream legal dictionary either.
[27] Madison (n 16).
[28] Vaidhyanathan (n 4).
[29] Ibid.
[30] Depending on the user's algorithm, these results may vary. However, these free web-based encyclopedias are likely to be a user's choice over journal articles which also appear on the first page.

the subject, which, like the dictionary entries, makes identifying an author difficult. However, the association to known entities *Wikipedia*, Cornell, and Harvard implies some level of authority to the websites.

Wikipedia

The first result for the search criteria entered is a link to the *Wikipedia* article on Critical Legal Studies. *Wikipedia* is a free and collaboratively written encyclopedia, which "allows basically anybody to produce and edit content".[31] This must be noted when comparing it with the other sources available, as there is an expectation of expert or peer-reviewed work forming the entries of more traditional encyclopedias. However, as *Wikipedia* itself states, it is "written largely by amateurs".[32]

In spite of these factors, or perhaps because of them, it is not surprising that the first search result is *Wikipedia*. As Thomas Leitch describes in his book *Wikipedia U*, "Wikipedia is the source everyone uses but no one is supposed to use or admits using",[33] and at least some part of this usage is because "[s]earch engines rank their pages near the top".[34] As such, it is likely that a more obscure term such as "Critical Legal Studies" should return the *Wikipedia* entry in the top results. Given this status, the information is likely to be reflective of the dictionaries but may also display interest in a pro- or anti-US-CLS stance.

The format of the *Wikipedia* entry is segmented, divided into a series of subsections. These subsections begin with a brief overview of Critical Legal Studies, before addressing its influence, its history, the relationship between Critical Legal Studies and American legal realism, Critical Legal Studies as a literature and a network, the intellectual and political context of Critical Legal Studies, its themes, and its continued influence, with the remainder of the headings offering external links and references cited. The brief overview section begins by providing a short statement, similar to the Oxford *Dictionary* entry, focusing on legal power structures. As per the dictionary entries, the overview section only addresses US-CLS, with no mention of either narrow or broad Critical Legal Studies.

---

[31] René König, "WIKIPEDIA: Between Lay Participation and Elite Knowledge Representation" (2013) 16(2) *Information, Communication and Society* 160, 161.
[32] Wikipedia, *Wikipedia Contributors* (Web Page) <https://en.wikipedia.org/wiki/Wikipedia:About#Wikipedia_contributors>.
[33] Thomas Leitch, *Wikipedia U: Knowledge, Authority, and Liberal Education in the Digital Age* (Johns Hopkins University Press, 2014) 4.
[34] Ibid 57.

As the overview continues, it makes a claim that there is a general consensus on the "key goals" of US-CLS. This claim is footnoted, and the hyperlinked footnote offers both the second and third search results as authority, citing Cornell's *Wex* and Harvard's *The Bridge* entries on Critical Legal Studies. The issue of cross-referencing from another website as a cited authority will be addressed when comparing all three entries; however, what is currently pertinent are the stated "key goals" of US-CLS. This type of list was avoided in US-CLS, given its non-doctrinal approach and the wide range of topics it covered.[35] Any goals, let alone "key goals"—which implies a separation from other types of goals—are problematic. The overview lists the goals as bullet points, which gives a sense of authority in descending order:

- to demonstrate the ambiguity and possible preferential outcomes of supposedly impartial and rigid legal doctrines.
- to publicize historical, social, economic and psychological results of legal decisions.
- to demystify legal analysis and legal culture in order to impose transparency on legal processes so that they earn the general support of socially responsible citizens.[36]

So far this is the first reference to demystification, and from its position as the last goal of US-CLS it can be read as falling behind legal impartiality and publicising the influence of other academic fields on legal decisions. However, as they are presented, both points one and two fall under the broad understanding of legal demystification. This is strengthened further when the last point on demystification seems to confuse the matter by stating that this demystification is "so that they earn the general support of socially responsible citizens". This presumably is meant to lead back to the preceding sentence, which states that, "Despite wide variation in the opinions of critical legal scholars around the world there is general consensus regarding the key goals of Critical Legal Studies." In this reading, the aim of Critical Legal scholars worldwide is to "earn the general support" of citizens who are socially responsible. In short, the key goals stated in the *Wikipedia* entry are nonsensical. The phrases and wording used are reminiscent of US-CLS, and general areas of critical legal thought can be picked out of them, such as demystification; however, as a grouping, they offer no clarity or further understanding.

---

[35] See generally Chapter 2.
[36] Wikipedia, *Critical Legal Studies* (Web Page) <https://en.wikipedia.org/wiki/Critical_legal_studies>.

As the entry continues, the issues that arose in the overview section also continue. Given the propensity for online research and the likelihood of people using *Wikipedia* on which to base their assumptions and understandings, this entry is problematic. Further issues are caused by the stylistic nature of the site: it reads in a disinterested, encyclopedic way, and cites a number of primary sources. For example, the *Wikipedia* page draws upon big name sources like Roberto Unger's reissued *The Critical Legal Studies Movement*,[37] but also more obscure papers like a 1984 paper on Unger and rights.[38] This mixture of sources allows those with some knowledge of US-CLS, including the contributors to the page, to justify the content—that is, they indicate that it provides more than a surface-level understanding. However, taken at face value by someone unfamiliar with US-CLS, the entry is misleading and is less clear than the dictionary entries.

Under the other headings, the *Wikipedia* entry makes allusions to geographic divisions in Critical Legal Studies, referencing Costas Douzinas and Colin Perrin's 2011 *Critical Legal Theory* series[39] to illuminate the development of broad Critical Legal Studies. This lack of subcategorisation under the banner of Critical Legal Studies is consistent throughout, with reference to the *Australian Feminist Law Journal* and Birkbeck College as continuing Critical Legal Studies. There are some rather obscure mentions to Karl Popper and Immanuel Kant, without a great deal of context, that read as though the author or authors of the page have made connections to existing philosophical work on critique and feel they warrant inclusion. Overall this typifies the entry, which, for an initial understanding of Critical Legal Studies, misses the mark.

Wex

The second result is from Cornell University Law School's Legal Information Institute (LII). The not-for-profit institute provides free legal information online; however, unlike *Wikipedia*, its contributors are selected for their knowledge in the field.[40] *Wex* is the LII's "legal dictionary and legal encyclopedia", which is contributed to by "legal experts".[41] It should be noted that, despite

---

[37] Roberto Mangabeira Unger, *The Critical Legal Studies Movement: Another Time, a Greater Task* (Verso, 2015).
[38] Allan C. Hutchinson and Patrick J. Monahan, "The 'Rights' Stuff: Roberto Unger and Beyond" (1984) 62(8) *Texas Law Review* 1,477.
[39] Costas Douzinas and Colin Perrin (eds), *Critical Legal Theory* (Routledge, 2012).
[40] Legal Information Institute, *Who We Are* (Web Page) <https://www.law.cornell.edu/lii/about/who_we_are>.
[41] Ibid.

the search parameters, the page title is "Critical Legal Theory": a broader, but sometimes interchangeable, title for the narrow understanding of Critical Legal Studies, with Critical Legal Studies as the subject matter throughout the entry.[42] This structure implies a certain understanding of Critical Legal Studies in a similar way to the broad and narrow description, except here the broad term is "Critical Legal Theory" and the narrow is "Critical Legal Studies". Interestingly, the final paragraph of the entry does discuss subgroups which would fit within the broad categorisation, which it frames as having "fundamentally different, even contradictory, views", specifically highlighting critical race theory, feminist legal theory, and postmodernism.

The layout of the entry follows a more traditional encyclopedia style, with four paragraphs and no subheadings. Despite the lack of subheadings, each paragraph stands alone, addressing different aspects of Critical Legal Studies. The first paragraph deals with the intent and nature of Critical Legal Studies, discussing social hierarchies and the idea of law as politics. The second discusses its history and key thinkers. As well as Duncan Kennedy and Roberto Unger, the list also includes Robert Gordon. The third paragraph looks at the academic influences on Critical Legal Studies, citing the Frankfurt School, Karl Marx, Antonio Gramsci, as well as Michel Foucault and Max Weber. The final paragraph, as addressed above, covers the Critical Legal Studies subgroups.

Within the structure of the *Wex* article, it is the second paragraph that should thematically address the issues pertinent to the death of US-CLS. However, there is no explicit discussion about this or subsequent PCLS work. What the second paragraph does make explicit is the geographic location associated with what is presented as Critical Legal Studies. For the *Wex* article, Critical Legal Studies is only concerned with US-CLS, referring to its starting point at the 1977 CCLS in Wisconsin. This is continued with the opening line to the third paragraph, stating that "CLS has been largely contained within the United States". The entry dates the roots of US-CLS as beginning with social activism around American civil rights and the Vietnam War, also highlighting the breadth of fields that Critical Legal Studies borrowed from. Whilst there is no mention of the death of US-CLS or any posthumous work, there is an implication of demystification with the third paragraph's reference to legal realism and its attention to the social context of law.

---

[42] Legal Information Institute, *Critical Legal Theory* (Web Page, August 2022) <https://www.law.cornell.edu/wex/critical_legal_theory>; but see Ofer Raban, *Modern Legal Theory and Judicial Impartiality* (Glasshouse Press, 2003) 59 on Ronald Dworkin's different application of the term "critical legal theory"; see also, Ian Ward, Introduction to Critical Legal Theory (Routledge Cavendish, 2nd ed, 2004).

After all the Critical Legal Studies–specific content is addressed, the *Wex* entry offers further reading on Critical Legal Studies, linking to a 2007 *Harvard Law Review* article. However, the linked article, while interesting, is seemingly random. The article, "Critical Legal Consciousness in Action" by Scott Cummings,[43] is one of two short responses to a full-length article by Orly Lobel.[44] Lobel's original article is a PCLS piece, and by extension Cummings's response falls into this same category. This ten-page response does not expand on anything within the *Wex* entry, and does not engage with Critical Legal Studies more broadly—as it is a response to a specific paper and argument, which is not linked.

In spite of this, the *Wex* entry on Critical Legal Studies offers a concise and seemingly more focused analysis than *Wikipedia*, with its layout more akin to the dictionary entries. Although *Wex* makes no mention of the death of US-CLS, work that came after 1995 (PCLS) specifically, or demystification, it offers a more comprehensive reading of Critical Legal Studies than the other online entries or dictionaries so far.

The Bridge

The third result comes from Harvard Law School's *The Bridge*. The page's purpose is not too dissimilar from that of Cornell's *Wex*: it is a database for law school students, providing information on American legal theory and legal reasoning.[45] The page layout, however, is more closely aligned with *Wikipedia*, presenting key Critical Legal Studies ideas under a number of headings. The entry offers a tiered page title, beginning with "Legal Theory: Critical Theory", sitting just above the much larger "Critical Legal Studies Movement". The page on the CLS movement itself is then broken up into six parts, beginning with a broad but detailed introduction and then five key areas under separate headings. These are: "Indeterminacy", "Law's Contribution to Group Inequality (or 'Tilt')", "Mystification and Legitimation", "New Visions", and "Opposition".[46]

---

[43] Scott L. Cummings, "Critical Legal Consciousness in Action" (2007) 120 *Harvard Law Review* 62.
[44] Orly Lobel, "The Paradox of Extralegal Activism: Critical Legal Consciousness and Transformative Politics" (2007) 120 *Harvard Law Review* 937. See also, Robert C. Fellmeth, "State-Lovers, State-Haters, and Orly Lobel" (2007) 120 *Harvard Law Review* 36.
[45] Berkman Klein Center for Internet and Society at Harvard University, *The Bridge* (Web Page, 1 March 2023) <https://cyber.harvard.edu/research/bridge>.
[46] Berkman Klein Center for Internet and Society at Harvard University, "Critical Legal Studies Movement", *The Bridge* (Web Page, 23 October 2023) <https://cyber.harvard.edu/bridge/CriticalTheory/critical2.htm>.

Immediately there are several points of note: first, the use of "Mystification" as a subheading, the first reference to the mystified nature of law within the online sources. Secondly, as mentioned previously, the *Wikipedia* entry cites *The Bridge* as a source that it has drawn from. Reviewing *The Bridge* itself, it appears that the information has been paraphrased, leading to a lack of clarity in the *Wikipedia* entry. As such, the critical review of *The Bridge* will still address the entry as a whole, but focus will be given to the effect of *The Bridge* as a source for other websites and then its specific use of mystification.

The Bridge entry starts by presenting Critical Legal Studies as beginning in 1977 with the CCLS. There is no mention of other jurisdictions or the broad/narrow divide, keeping the entry firmly focused on US-CLS. Despite this narrow US-CLS focus, *The Bridge* goes through an overview of Critical Legal Studies more comprehensively than the other entries, addressing prevalent themes such as law as politics, hierarchies and the masking of power, and the alleged neutrality of legal language. Amongst these points, the entry also states that annual US-CLS conferences and workshops were held between "1977 and 1992", a statement which is not expanded or touched on again. This is not an explicit mention of the death of US-CLS; however, the entry highlights that US-CLS changed soon after 1992. Still, it is frustrating, given the depth *The Bridge* goes into, that there is no discussion of Critical Legal Studies post-1992, or any explanation of why the conferences and workshops ceased.

The Bridge does not list notable Crits, but instead details key authors' positions within the relevant subheadings. For example, under the subheading "New Visions", the focus is entirely on Unger, discussing concepts from *The Critical Legal Studies Movement*,[47] including super-liberalism and the deviationist doctrine, but without reference to the original text. These posts have a hyperlink reference to where the concepts are taken from, but none on the page seems to work. This is problematic, as in the Unger example, the phrases are not common or easily searchable without knowing the primary text.[48] Other sections of the site follow this approach and focus separately on prominent Crits Kennedy and Kelman, with Horwitz and Joseph Singer discussed together in relation to law's contribution to inequality. This method provides summaries of some of the big US-CLS ideas, without getting bogged down in their nuances and intricacies. Instead of being left with a list of names and no context, *The Bridge* notes the authors briefly but concentrates on differentiating their approaches to US-CLS.

---

[47] Roberto Mangabeira Unger, *The Critical Legal Studies Movement* (Harvard University Press, 1983).
[48] See, e.g., ibid 41–2 for "Super-liberalism".

Notably, *The Bridge* also identifies opposition to Critical Legal Studies. Given the tumultuous reception US-CLS received from the American academe, it is interesting that the raft of opposition or attacks on it were not discussed in the other entries. Following the same format as the other sections on the page, *The Bridge* dedicates a short paragraph to the criticism. The critics named individually are Owen Fiss and Paul Carrington, with Daniel Farber and Suzanna Sherry addressed together. A brief highlight of each critique is mentioned with the authors, but no detail about where and how their critique took place is included. It is possible to deduce from what is stated that Fiss is referred to for his 1986 critique of US-CLS.[49] Likewise, Carrington's mention can be presumed to be his famous critique of US-CLS that same year in the *Journal of Legal Education*.[50] As a timeline, these two critiques focus on US-CLS at its prime, aligning with *The Bridge*'s earlier implication that CLS operated between 1977 and 1992.

The critique by Farber and Sherry is likely to come from their 1997 book, *Beyond All Reason: The Radical Assault on Truth in American Law*.[51] The timing of the book's publication puts it out of step with the earlier critiques, and with *The Bridge*'s own description of the Critical Legal Studies timeline. Stylistically, the book moves away from the nuanced engagement of Fiss,[52] and instead focuses on "extremists" who share "an abandonment of moderation and a death of common sense".[53]

Beyond All Reason can be aligned with the work of authors like Austin, focusing on the "battle" over legal education and offering only a limited understanding of Critical Legal Studies. The difference in the calibre of critique can be seen when the authors introduce Critical Legal Studies and state that, "Much of CLS scholarship was aimed at deconstructing legal doctrine to show its indeterminacy."[54] Factually this is an accurate statement, but it is undeveloped: the statement is taken at face value without any attempt to codify or clarify what it actually means.[55] As the book progresses, Critical Legal Studies is lumped together with critical race theory and feminist legal

---

[49] Owen M. Fiss, "Death of the Law" (1986) 72(1) *Cornell Law Review* 1. Note that this article does not aid the discussion of the death of US-CLS.
[50] Paul D. Carrington, "Of Law and the River" (1984) 34 *Journal of Legal Education* 222.
[51] Daniel A. Farber and Suzanna Sherry, *Beyond All Reason: The Radical Assault on Truth in American Law* (Oxford University Press, 1997).
[52] Fiss (n 49) 12.
[53] Farber and Sherry, *Beyond All Reason* (n 51) 3.
[54] Ibid 20.
[55] The authors offer an endnote that provides a reference to their definition. See Lawrence B. Solum, "On the Indeterminacy Crisis: Critiquing Critical Dogma" (1987) 54 *Chicago Law Review* 462.

theory, which are used collectively as precursors and influencers of the book's real target of "radical multiculturalists".

The inclusion of Farber and Sherry's book, without any more context than "treat[ing] critical legal studies as a simplistic and failed assault on liberal principles and Enlightenment notions of truth",[56] is one of the best examples of why *The Bridge*—as well as *Wikipedia* and *Wex*—is problematic. The inclusion of critiques and opposition to Critical Legal Studies is a necessary part of knowing what it did or did not do; however, the choice of critique or opposition matters.

Ostensibly, the book does discuss US-CLS and its attack on liberalism, but the inclusion of *Beyond All Reason* as one of only three critiques of Critical Legal Studies cited by *The Bridge* is conducive to confusion and mystification, especially given the availability of more detailed and coherent pieces.[57] This is a key issue with the way Critical Legal Studies has been remembered online, with each website offering a similar story that embellishes or removes issues through a sporadic and random approach, with no justification. US-CLS is presented as a coherent and consistent story, one that is settled and not in need of revision. In fact, these online sources create a feedback loop, distorting the original subject matter. This can be seen through the ways in which *Wikipedia* cites *The Bridge*; notably, in the *Wikipedia* entry, *The Bridge* is used as an authority for the key goals of Critical Legal Studies:

- to demonstrate the ambiguity and possible preferential outcomes of supposedly impartial and rigid legal doctrines.
- to publicize historical, social, economic and psychological results of legal decisions.
- to demystify legal analysis and legal culture in order to impose transparency on legal processes so that they earn the general support of socially responsible citizens.[58]

Given the structure of the website and its limitations in hyperlinking pinpoint references, the key goals appear to come from *The Bridge*'s introduction to Critical Legal Studies. In its original context, *The Bridge* lists four common areas addressed by US-CLS scholars to conclude its overview and introduction to the subject. These are stated as:

1. seek[ing] to demonstrate the indeterminacy of legal doctrine and show how any given set of legal principles can be used to yield competing or contradictory results;

---

[56] *The Bridge* (n 46).
[57] See, e.g., Solum (n 55), which is far more engaged with US-CLS than Farber and Sherry.
[58] Wikipedia, *Critical Legal Studies* (n 36).

2. undertak[ing] historical, socioeconomic and psychological analyses to identify how particular groups and institutions benefit from legal decisions despite the indeterminacy of legal doctrines;
3. expos[ing] how legal analysis and legal culture mystify outsiders and work to make legal results seem legitimate; and
4. elucidate[ing] new or previously disfavored social visions and argu[ing] for their realization in legal and political practices in part by making them part of legal strategies.[59]

Aside from addressing one extra feature, *The Bridge* presents these concluding points as a logical refinement of the broad topics addressed by US-CLS scholars. This summary is made after a much more detailed five-paragraph introduction that provides a clear summary of US-CLS; at no point are these common areas considered to be the primary aims or goals of the movement. Conversely, *Wikipedia* presents its key Critical Legal Studies "goals" after three introductory sentences. The paraphrased and reduced approach taken by *Wikipedia* does not appear to have been undertaken maliciously, or to be intentionally deceptive; instead it is likely that the paraphrasing was a way of positioning Critical Legal Studies in a more accessible way than that of *The Bridge*. However, given *Wikipedia*'s prominence as the number one search result for Critical Legal Studies, this reduction—which changes commonalities to goals and lacks any real context—aids the mystification of Critical Legal Studies, especially in terms of how it is remembered or learned by those both in and outside the academe.

The final element raised in *The Bridge* is the inclusion of the term "mystification". Although the *Wikipedia* goals include the term "demystify", there is no explanation of how this may apply. Conversely, *The Bridge* lists that Critical Legal Studies sought to expose how legal culture mystified outsiders, and then presents a subheading titled "Mystification and Legitimation". Under this heading, *The Bridge* asks how law "can . . . appear fair and objective and nonetheless predictably tend to perpetuate the power of the powerful". This simple question gets to the heart of the complex issue US-CLS identifies through law's mystification. However, the format and sources used in response to it limit the impact of this question. Following the theme throughout *The Bridge*, the work of only one Crit is used to answer the question—in this case, it is Kelman.

The response to the question is focused on Kelman's work in psychology and law, specifically in regard to the concept of denial.[60] However, this is only

---

[59] *The Bridge* (n 46).
[60] Kelman, *A Guide to Critical Legal Studies* (n 2) 286.

dealt with in one sentence, which, given the complexity of such a concept, leaves it underexplained and lacking in impact. Further, the paragraph as a whole contains references, but as mentioned above, the links are dead, making any additional context difficult to find. It can be assumed that *The Bridge* is referring to Kelman's use of denial in the final chapter of *A Guide to Critical Legal Studies*, "Toward a Cognitive Theory". However, if this is correct, the issue of context is compounded, as this chapter concludes Kelman's book which itself is a very detailed assessment of Critical Legal Studies.

As the reference to Kelman ends, some space is given to an example of mystification in employment law, before addressing how mystification can be used to separate the Crits from the legal realists. The last point offers an important distinction, discussing US-CLS's move away from its realist roots, viewing law as a hindrance to, rather than a tool of, change. While the position taken by *The Bridge* addresses some forms of what may be considered mystification, there is very little that relates clearly to the demystification identified in the article's introduction.

Summation

The information contained within the dictionaries and websites is ostensibly correct, in the sense that it is not quite wrong. It is, however, reductive and incomplete. The short entries and larger issue of self-referencing eschew any differences in their histories. The death of US-CLS, the broad-narrow divide, and other geographic iterations are lost amongst a homogenised narrative. The power of this misinformation is an identifiable thread running through all six sources, and it is cause for concern. Given the accessibility of these sources compared to those in works of jurisprudence, this simple and reinforced narrative shapes how Critical Legal Studies is remembered and interacted with— leading to inaccurate epistemological certainties and regimes of truth.[61]

The effect of this can already be seen in a 2018 online article by Andrew Kelman.[62] The article was published by *Quillette*, a modestly read,[63] self-proclaimed platform for "free thought".[64] Whilst it does not label itself as such, the professionally presented blog focuses this free thought on the conservative

---

[61] Madison (n 16).
[62] Andrew Kelman, "Beyond All Warnings: The Radical Assault on Truth in the Law", *Quillette* (online, 2 April 2018) <http://quillette.com/2018/04/02/beyond-warnings-radical-assault-truth-law>. Andrew Kelman does not appear to be related to Crit Mark Kelman.
[63] The site displays a Facebook fan number of 52,000 (1 March 2023).
[64] Quillette, *What is Quillette?* (Web Page, accessed 6 November 2022) <https://quillette.com/about>.

end of liberalism,⁶⁵ although it does offer more centrist articles in response to earlier writings.⁶⁶

Kelman's article, "Beyond All Warnings: The Radical Assault on Truth in the Law", is an unabashed nod to Farber and Sherry's *Beyond All Reason* and their follow-up journal article, "Beyond All Criticism".⁶⁷ The roughly three-thousand-word piece opens with a quotation from conservative Canadian psychologist, Jordan Peterson, stating that both law and law schools are corrupt.⁶⁸ The quotation comes from an earlier interview Kelman conducted with Peterson,⁶⁹ where Kelman discusses *Beyond All Reason* as a text that faced similar criticism to Peterson's own work.⁷⁰ Kelman's article, "Beyond All Warnings", builds on this perceived connection to address radicals in the law school.

Kelman approaches the issue of left-wing radicalism in law school through the lens created by Farber and Sherry, leading him to tackle Critical Legal Studies. This approach presents two related issues: first, that Critical Legal Studies is only a catalyst for what is important in Kelman's article, and second, that Kelman does not look too far beyond Farber and Sherry's understanding of Critical Legal Studies. The limits of this approach are immediately clear when Critical Legal Studies is introduced. Kelman states: "*Critical Legal Theory* has its roots in the 1970s, when postmodern neo-Marxist radicals began challenging and overturning accepted norms and standards."⁷¹ With some minor adjustments, Kelman's description is dreadfully similar to the opening line of another website entry on US-CLS, that of *Encyclopedia.Com*,

---

⁶⁵ See, e.g., Avel Ivanov, "The Student's Dilemma: Conformity or Education", *Quillette* (online, 15 May 2018) <https://quillette.com/2018/05/15/students-dilemma-conformity-education>; Katie Kelaidis, "The Enlightenment's Cynical Critics", *Quillette* (online, 15 June 2018) <https://quillette.com/2018/06/15/the-enlightenments-cynical-critics>. Respectively, these articles are about left-wing bias in higher education, and a distinction between the Enlightenment and slavery.

⁶⁶ See, e.g., the response to Kelman's article: Matt McManus, "In Defence of Critical Legal Theory: A Reply to Andrew Kelman", *Quillette* (online, 14 April 2018) <https://quillette.com/2018/04/14/defence-critical-legal-theory-reply-andrew-kelman>.

⁶⁷ Daniel A. Farber and Suzanna Sherry, "Beyond All Criticism" (1999) 83 *Minnesota Law Review* 1,735.

⁶⁸ Kelman, "Beyond All Warnings" (n 62).

⁶⁹ Andrew Kelman, "Walking the Tightrope Between Chaos and Order—An Interview with Jordan B. Peterson", *Quillette* (online, 27 January 2018) <https://quillette.com/2018/01/27/walking-tightrope-chaos-order-interview-jordan-b-peterson>.

⁷⁰ See, e.g., Pankaj Mishra, "Jordan Peterson & Fascist Mysticism", *The New York Review of Books* (online, 19 March 2018) <https://www.nybooks.com/daily/2018/03/19/jordan-peterson-and-fascist-mysticism>.

⁷¹ Kelman, "Beyond All Warnings" (n 62).

which states that it is "[a] movement that challenges and seeks to overturn accepted norms and standards in legal theory and practice."[72]

As the article continues, so does Kelman's reliance on Google to inform his understanding of Critical Legal Studies. Wikipedia is not directly cited, but when discussing Critical law schools and academics, the examples chosen mirror the lists given on that site. At one point, Kelman does cite the *Wex* entry on Critical Legal Studies, but only in relation to a minor comment about Critical Legal Studies changing the landscape of legal theory. Neither *The Bridge* nor *Wikipedia* is mentioned or linked to within the article.

Kelman's article serves as an example of the direct effect *Wikipedia*, *Wex*, and *The Bridge* have had on Critical Legal Studies. Whilst Kelman's article could not be considered indicative of all the work developed from a Google search for Critical Legal Studies, it is a prominent piece that displays the negative aspects of such an approach: by drawing from mystified understandings of Critical Legal Studies, it perpetuates this mystification.

---

[72] Encyclopedia.Com, *Critical Legal Studies* (Web Page, November 2023) <https://www.encyclopedia.com/law/encyclopedias-almanacs-transcripts-and-maps/critical-legal-studies>.

5

Theoretical Ghosts and Spectres

Oh He gives to us his joy,
That our grief He may destroy:
Till our grief is fled an gone
He doth sit by us and moan.

William Blake, "On Another's Sorrow" (1789)

The death of US-CLS is unexplored. As we have seen, there are a handful of statements here or there by key Crits and their immediate rivals. Some easier-to-access sources briefly nod towards things changing in the 1990s, and in selected texts a death is discussed. But beyond this collection of minor utterances, the death of US-CLS goes unacknowledged.

An argument can be made that an event warranting such little time in existing explorations and discussions on CLS is therefore unimportant—or, even if not unimportant to the overall history of CLS, the event adds nothing new. In contrast to the identifiable tools and spaces created by US-CLS, the question inevitably becomes, "Why focus on its death?"

This curiosity extends beyond the morbid, to the real effects of a pronounced death in a field of legal theory. As the family tree presented, the acknowledgment of the death of US-CLS creates a new branch: Posthumous Critical Legal Studies (PCLS). If the death is underrepresented in the literature, then the works that came after this event (post-1995) scarcely make a mention. For Duncan Kennedy, the death of CLS was not totalising, but an act of reduction, finalising only its activist and political side. Kennedy balanced the finality of its demise while referring to its continuation as "very much alive" and "alive and well".[1]

---

[1] Duncan Kennedy, "Two Globalizations Of Law & Legal Thought: 1850–1968" (2003) 36(3) *Suffolk University Law Review* 631.

However, in the decades since this statement was made, US-CLS cannot be considered alive or well. Instead, the US-CLS work that has come after the declaration of its death, the resulting "PCLS", operates in a greatly reduced capacity, unable to offer insights or analysis comparable to its predecessor. A theme in PCLS works by those not directly involved in US-CLS is the repeated questioning of what happened to US-CLS or the Crits themselves.[2] This new wave of PCLS Crits are constrained, restricted, or—in line with the image of death—haunted by US-CLS.

The type of haunting proposed is one unique to the relationship between US-CLS and PCLS. It draws from the specific language used when Kennedy exclaimed that US-CLS was "dead as a doornail",[3] a phrase which has since been used as an epitaph for US-CLS.[4] The phrase itself is relatively common, but does come with specific connotations. To explore the relationship between US-CLS and PCLS, a literary analogy is drawn through the etymology of "dead as a doornail". Primarily, this analysis comes from a close reading of Charles Dickens's *A Christmas Carol*,[5] a story that provides a clear discussion on what it means to be dead as a doornail and how this type of death invites hauntings and ghosts. However, unlike Dickens, who draws from William Shakespeare's *Hamlet*,[6] no ghost of CLS appears, and as such we are left with a continually "passively" haunted subject, in contrast to those actively haunted, that is, Scrooge or Hamlet.

This novel concept of US-CLS passively haunting PCLS is unique. However, ideas of haunting and literary analogies to ghosts are not unique within analysis more broadly.[7] A notable example is Jacques Derrida's "hauntology" in *Specters of Marx*.[8] Derrida's work, a direct response to Francis

---

[2] E. Dana Neacsu, "CLS Stands for Critical Legal Studies, If Anyone Remembers" (2000) 8(2) *Journal of Law and Policy* 415.
[3] Hope Yen, "As HLS Mulls Its Mission, CLS Scholars Remain Quiet", *Harvard Law Record* (Cambridge, 1 December 1995) 2.
[4] See generally, Arthur D. Austin, *The Empire Strikes Back: Outsiders and the Struggle over Legal Education* (New York University Press, 1998) 83.
[5] Charles Dickens, *A Christmas Carol and Other Christmas Writings* (Penguin, 2003).
[6] William Shakespeare, *Hamlet*, ed. Bernard Lott (Longman, 1997).
[7] See generally Margaret Thornton, "Gothic Horror in the Legal Academy" (2005) 14(2) *Social & Legal Studies* 267; Noël Carroll, *The Philosophy of Horror or Paradoxes of the Heart* (Routledge, 1990); Eugene Thacker, *In the Dust of This Planet: Horror of Philosophy* (Zero, 2011) vol 1. These sources are quite disparate in their approaches, but demonstrate the broad application and impact of horror.
[8] Jacques Derrida, *Specters of Marx: The State of the Debt, the Work of Mourning and the New International*, tr. Peggy Kamuf (Routledge, 1994) [trans of: *Spectres de Marx* (1993)].

Fukuyama's *The End of History and the Last Man*,[9] utilises spectres and hauntings to counter the idea of an "end" of history, and also draws from *Hamlet*.[10]

Given Derrida's influence on Critical Legal Studies, the similarities between the terms relating to the two hauntings, and the time at which *Specters of Marx* was published (a few years before the death of US-CLS), it would be remiss not to acknowledge this connection. However, aside from the similarities in terminology, the concept of a passive haunting and Derrida's hauntology do not share a direct relationship. Instead, through a discussion of *Specters of Marx* and Fukuyama's original "End of History?" article,[11] historical context is given to the climate surrounding competing theories, an understanding of why death was lingering in the air, and why the image of a passive haunting aids the understanding of US-CLS.

Ghosts and the End of History

To talk of the death of Critical Legal Studies in a serious manner and to draw from this the idea of US-CLS haunting PCLS seems at first farfetched and fanciful. This fancy is then compounded when the proposed legitimacy is offered through the literary interpretation of the phrase "dead as a doornail". However, at the time US-CLS was dying, the idea of its death was not farfetched or fanciful; in fact, it was not even particularly unusual.[12] To understand where this motif was expounded, it is necessary to look at Derrida's creation of "hauntology".

Hauntology was coined by Derrida in *Specters of Marx*, as a response to Fukuyama's book, *The End of History and the Last Man*.[13] Broadly, Derrida proposes the image of a haunting and the return of a spectre in response to Fukuyama's premise of a final stage of history. Somewhat simply, Derrida states, "one can never distinguish between the future-to-come and the

---

[9] Francis Fukuyama, *The End of History and the Last Man* (Free Press, 1992).
[10] Derrida is not alone in his use of *Hamlet* as an allegorical or metaphorical text, with a number of interpretations being derived from it. See especially Anselm Haverkamp, "The Ghost of History: Hamlet and the Politics of Paternity" (2006) 18(2) *Law and Literature* 171. For psychoanalytic readings, see Peter Alexander, *Hamlet: Father and Son* (Oxford University Press, 1955); Avi Erlich, *Hamlet's Absent Father* (Princeton University Press, 1977); Peter Buse and Andrew Stott (eds), *Ghosts: Deconstruction, Psychoanalysis, History* (Macmillan, 1999). See also Bonnie Honig, *Antigone, Interrupted* (Cambridge University Press, 2013) 147–50, on Carl Schmitt's use of "Hamletization"; Victoria Kahn, "Hamlet or Hecuba: Carl Schmitt's Decision" (2003) 83(1) *Representations* 67, 80–7.
[11] Francis Fukuyama, "The End Of History?" (1989) 16 *National Interest* 3.
[12] See generally Samuel Moyn, *The Last Utopia* (Belknap Press, 2010) 5.
[13] Derrida, *Specters of Marx* (n 8) 13.

coming-back of a specter".[14] For Derrida, Fukuyama's definite "end of history" is problematic, as the future is always littered with ghosts from the past.

To appreciate the importance of Derrida's hauntology, as well as its similarities and differences to the proposed passive haunting of PCLS, it is beneficial to begin with the assertion that led to hauntology, Fukuyama's suggestion of the "end of history". Although this term was popularised in his 1992 book, the idea was originally published in an article in the late 1980s.[15] It is this original article which offers a raw insight into Derrida's "hauntological" response, as well as the motif of death that Fukuyama help promulgate.

In 1989, Fukuyama published "The End of History?" in the *National Interest*. Thematically, the article is an attempt by the author to reclaim G. W. F. Hegel's concept of the end of history. Fukuyama proposes his renewed Hegelian interpretation by positioning himself in opposition to Karl Marx's existing inversion of Hegel.[16] Tellingly, Fukuyama's opposition to Marx does not engage with critiques of Marx's reading of Hegel,[17] nor the complexity of their relationship.[18] Instead, Fukuyama is primarily focused on rejecting Marx's proposed "communist utopia" as the end of history.[19] Within the article, Marx is used as a straw man, an icon of communism against whom Fukuyama, at the end of the Cold War, can present his alternative: Western liberal democracy.[20] The author states that, for "the end of history as such: that is, the end point of mankind's ideological evolution and the universalization of Western liberal democracy as the final form of human government."[21]

Fukuyama legitimises his right-wing Hegelian approach by drawing from Alexandre Kojève's interpretation of Hegel, specifically his reading of a "universal homogenous state" as the end of history.[22] Fukuyama makes the somewhat obvious claim that Kojève's interpretation is more truthful to Hegel than Marx's inversion,[23] with Kojève following Hegel's direct identification

---

[14] Ibid 46.
[15] Fukuyama, *The End of History and the Last Man* (n 9) 17.
[16] See, e.g., J. J. Clarke, "'The End of History': A Reappraisal of Marx's Views on Alienation and Human Emancipation" (1971) 4(3) *Canadian Journal of Political Science* 367.
[17] See generally Norman Levine, *Marx's Discourse with Hegel* (Palgrave Macmillan, 2012).
[18] Carl Schmitt, "Hegel and Marx" (2014) 22(3–4) *Historical Materialism* 388, 389.
[19] Fukuyama, *The End of History and the Last Man* (n 9) 2.
[20] See generally Louis Menand, "Francis Fukuyama Postpones the End of History", *The New Yorker* (online, 3 September 2018) <https://www.newyorker.com/magazine/2018/09/03/francis-fukuyama-postpones-the-end-of-history>. Menand reads Fukuyama's "The End of History?" as luckily well-timed, preceding events which initially strengthened his proposal.
[21] Fukuyama, *The End of History and the Last Man* (n 9) 1.
[22] Ibid 3.
[23] Clarke (n 16), 367.

of the year 1806 as the end of history.[24] For Hegel and Kojève, 1806 and the defeat of the Fourth Coalition by Napoléon Bonaparte at the Battle of Jena–Auerstedt established the basis for the homogenous state.

Fukuyama builds on the work of Hegel and Kojève, and argues that whilst 1806 was not a contemporary vision of the Western liberal democracy, it enshrined its basic principles:

> While there was considerable work to be done after 1806—abolishing slavery and the slave trade, extending the franchise to workers, women, blacks, and other racial minorities, etc.—the basic principles of the liberal democratic state could not be improved upon.[25]

As the article progresses, Fukuyama's central argument on the benefits of liberal democracy is expanded. Fukuyama presents the increase in liberal democratic states after the Second World War as testament to the political ideology's rightful place at the end of the history. Following this train of thought, Fukuyama argues that the world wars aided this outcome, stating: "If we admit for the moment that the fascist and communist challenges to liberalism are dead, are there any other ideological competitors left?"[26] The rhetorical question, which presents all reasonable competition as dead, leaves the reader with Fukuyama's vision of Western liberal democracy as the "final form" of human government.

Fukuyama sees this final form as exemplified by the United States,[27] even going so far as to suggest that Marx's initial inversion has also been satisfied, and positioning the US as a classless society:

> Kojève (among others) noted, the egalitarianism of modern America represents the essential achievement of the classless society envisioned by Marx. This is not to say that there are not rich people and poor people in the United States, or that the gap between them has not grown in recent years.[28]

Fukuyama then proposes that the status of rich and poor Americans is separate from the egalitarian nature of liberalism, tying residual inequality to "premodern" factors: "black poverty in the United States is not the inherent

---

[24] Fukuyama, *The End of History and the Last Man* (n 9) 3.
[25] Ibid.
[26] Ibid 13.
[27] See Menand (n 20), who believes it reads more as exemplified by Europe than America, a point Fukuyama also makes in this *Guardian* article: Francis Fukuyama, "The History at the End of History', *The Guardian* (online, 3 April 2007) <https://www.theguardian.com/commentisfree/2007/apr/03/thehistoryattheendofhist>.
[28] Fukuyama, *The End of History and the Last Man* (n 9) 8.

product of liberalism, but is rather the 'legacy of slavery and racism' which persisted long after the formal abolition of slavery."[29]

Fukuyama's article is full of such broad and unironic analysis which draws from Marx or Kojève, but does not engage with them in a meaningful way. However, in the current context, what is important is that despite these flaws in Fukuyama's work, its impact normalised the discussion of death in relation to movements and ideologies—highlighted through the author's statement that alternatives to liberalism are dead.[30] As Fukuyama phrased it, this is an unquestionable fact, and something that needs to be admitted to by those who see historical alternatives (fascism or communism) as anything but lifeless.

The deaths Fukuyama talks of were seen in other progressive and leftwing fields, with Samuel Moyn highlighting that the rise of human rights relied on its utopian vision,[31] and its survival as "the god that did not fail while other political ideologies did".[32] Similarly, Corinne Blalock saw this trend broadly as well as affecting US-CLS directly:

> [US-CLS] is seen as another casualty of the more general death of metatheory in the postmodern era . . . a historical crisis of the leftist political imaginary at the end of the twentieth century. After the fall of communism, the story goes, the left was incapable of imagining an alternative to the model of democratic market-capitalism that had been the object of the crits' critique. This inability to imagine an alternative—experienced by the left as a cessation of progress and as an inability to escape the realities of the present moment—is oftentimes referred to as the "end of history."[33]

"The End of History?" is not law-specific; however, its argument that ideologies outside of Western liberal democracy are dead, as well as its reinvigoration of "the end of history", fits into the broader narrative that has surrounded left-versus-right politics. As Moyn and Blalock identify, this climate affected a number of left-wing ideologies, including US-CLS.[34] It is worth noting that

---

[29] Ibid.
[30] Ibid 13.
[31] Moyn (n 12) 4.
[32] Ibid 5.
[33] Corinne Blalock, "Neoliberalism and the Crisis of Legal Theory" (2014) 77 *Law and Contemporary Problems* 71, 78–9.
[34] There is no direct engagement with Fukuyama from the Crits or US-CLS, or vice versa. However, the implications of Fukuyama's thesis, the "end of history", was broadly opposed by Duncan Kennedy in 1981: "The left doesn't need a counter-theory that *ends* with rights. We need utopian thinking, but the short-term, practical and creative manner, rather than in the form of rationalist 'end-of-history' deductions of the ideal state of mankind."

despite Fukuyama not interacting directly with US-CLS, his original lecture, which spawned his article and book, was requested by law and economics's corporate donors, the Olin Foundation.[35] Fukuyama has continued to receive criticism of his proposed end of history, and in recent years has distanced himself from his thesis.[36] However, the impact of his book, *The End of History and the Last Man*, was felt broadly and presented the end of history argument to a much wider audience.

The End of History continues and expands on the same themes and approach as "The End of History?". Fukuyama reinforces his pro-liberal (read: neoliberal) stance through Hegel and Kojève, introducing Immanuel Kant to bolster ideas of individualism and competition leading to a more egalitarian society.[37] Fukuyama reiterates that, "[a]t the end of history, there are no serious ideological competitors left to liberal democracy".[38] While some argue that the book is not just the article on steroids,[39] there is little compelling in the much-expanded argument. The real benefit of Fukuyama's theory in book rather than article form is its broader accessibility and the reactions to it—in particular, Derrida's.

Derrida's 1993 book, *Specters of Marx*, draws its ghoulish title thematically from the opening line of Marx and Friedrich Engels's *The Communist Manifesto*, which stated that "[a] spectre is haunting Europe – a spectre of Communism".[40] Despite the appearance of this spectre in *The Communist Manifesto*, neither it, nor hauntings, features again. Instead the spectre is symbolic for what the authors believe is an impending revolution in Germany.[41] However, in *Specters of Marx*, Derrida develops the titular symbolism further, bringing ghosts, spectres, and hauntings from modes of fiction to modes of interpretation.

Initially, Derrida's themes of death and haunting are a direct response to the ideas presented by Fukuyama in *The End of History*. Derrida presents the

---

See Duncan Kennedy, "Critical Labor Law Theory: A Comment" (1981) 4 *Industrial Relations Law Journal* 503, 506 (emphasis in original).

[35] In both the article and the book, Fukuyama identifies that his initial talk on the end of history was given at the John M. Olin Center at the University of Chicago.

[36] Fukuyama, *The End of History and the Last Man* (n 9); see also Eliane Glaser, "Bring Back Ideology: Fukuyama's 'End of History' 25 Years On", *The Guardian* (online, 21 March 2014) <https://www.theguardian.com/books/2014/mar/21/bring-back-ideology-fukuyama-end-history-25-years-on>.

[37] Fukuyama, *The End of History and the Last Man* (n 9) 58–9.

[38] Ibid 211.

[39] Menand (n 20).

[40] Karl Marx and Friedrich Engels, *The Communist Manifesto* (Penguin Classics, 2002) 218.

[41] Ibid 258.

idea of the "specter" as a way of playing with ideas and concepts that have been prefaced with "the end"—like Fukuyama's idea of the end of history—and balancing them against 1950s concepts relating to "ends of man . . . [and] ends of philosophy".[42] Derrida's effect here is twofold. First, there is the immediate reduction in both the relevance and seriousness of Fukuyama's claims, with the argument that they are no more than a "tiresome anachronism".[43] The second is Derrida's response that Fukuyama's argument is flawed when it proposes that there has been a clear-cut death of liberalism's rivals.

Derrida uses a homophone in his argument, drawing on the term "ontology" to create "hauntology".[44] His term offers a related but different sense of being: something that has been disavowed but which continues.[45] Derrida provides an example of hauntology in the attempted installation of neocapitalism and neoliberalism (Fukuyama's Western liberal democracy), which cannot rid themselves of certain ghosts of Marx and Marxist thought.[46]

However, it is the justification Derrida gives for the scholastic rather than the fantastic use of ghosts and spectres, which is pertinent here:

> There has never been a scholar who really, and as a scholar, deals with ghosts. A traditional scholar does not believe in ghosts—nor in all that could be called the virtual space of spectrality. There has never been a scholar who, as such, does not believe in the sharp distinction between the real and the unreal, the actual and the inactual, the living and the non-living, being and non-being.[47]

Derrida's justification for his methodology is also part of his critique of Fukuyama as a "traditional scholar": Fukuyama could not conceive of ghosts which might prevent the end of history. Derrida's justification grounds the worth and usefulness of his methodology in his application of spectres and hauntings. A methodology which has been utilised by scholars taking hauntology as "the idea that there is something from the past which is always present in the present; and, also, that this something is waiting for its return in a future to come"[48] provides an alternative to teleological understandings

---

[42] Derrida, *Specters of Marx* (n 8) 16.
[43] Ibid.
[44] Ibid.
[45] Ibid 46.
[46] Ibid.
[47] Ibid 12. However, see especially Colin Davis, "Hauntology, Spectres and Phantoms" (2005) 59(3) *French Studies* 373, 376. Davis addresses the overlooked contribution made to this field by Nicolas Abraham and Maria Torok.
[48] Chris Hughes, "Dialogue between Fukuyama's Account of the End of History and Derrida's Hauntology" (2012) 7(18) *Journal of Philosophy: A Cross-Disciplinary Inquiry* 13, 15.

of history. This re-conception has led to a thread amongst those who use hauntology as a way to address non-linear modes of time.[49]

This focus on hauntology as a tool,[50] isolated from the argument against Fukuyama or other concepts presented in *Specters of Marx*, does not reduce its scope or application. In fact, it follows a similar path to Derrida's earlier influential method of deconstruction, with Peter Goodrich arguing that it was the idea of "deconstruction" rather than the text *Of Grammatology* that was seized upon in the United States.[51] Wendy Brown, however, situates the importance of hauntology, and its place alongside concepts by Michel Foucault and Friedrich Nietzsche, as revolutionising historical consciousness, stating in *Politics Out of History* that

> Derrida endeavors to reconceive the press of history on the present, an endeavor that may break even more radically with progressive historiography than does genealogy as formulated by Nietzsche and Foucault. In his porous schema of spectrality that includes ghosts, haunting, and conjuration, Derrida experiments with a mode of historical consciousness that does not resort to discredited narratives of systematicity, periodicity, laws of development, or a bounded, coherent past and present.[52]

Brown's positioning of hauntology gives rise to a logical argument for viewing Critical Legal Studies, itself unbound and incoherent, through the lens of hauntology. However, while useful, a strict Derridean approach would not be as effective in understanding the relationship between US-CLS and PCLS, a primary issue in the demystification of Critical Legal Studies. Instead, what can be taken from Derrida's response to Fukuyama's "end of the world" thesis is the very real theme of death in the late 1980s and early 1990s, affecting related areas of law and academia.

It would not be an overstatement to conclude that this theme's prominence existed to such an extent that Kennedy's act of declaring US-CLS dead was no more than an *en-vogue* cultural statement. It should also be understood that the established influence of haunting and hauntology moves the

---

[49] See e.g., Martin Hägglund, *Radical Atheism: Derrida and the Time of Life* (Stanford University Press, 2008); Mark Fisher, "What Is Hauntology?" (2012) 66(1) *Film Quarterly* 16; Hughes (n 48).

[50] Contra, Peter Goodrich, "Europe in America: Grammatology, Legal Studies, and the Politics of Transmission" (2001) 101(8) *Columbia Law Review* 2,033, 2,038.

[51] Ibid. In his article, Goodrich proposes that this separation led to the misinterpretation of deconstruction. However, unlike deconstruction, hauntology benefits from its separation and broader application. The original context of hauntology relies on continued and dated reference to Fukuyama, who has now distanced himself from the "end of history" thesis.

[52] Wendy Brown, *Politics Out of History* (Princeton University Press, 2001) 143.

idea of PCLS being passively haunted from being farfetched and fanciful to a relevant and appropriate way of addressing the schism in US-based Critical Legal Studies.

A Haunting Framework

In Kennedy's statement in the *Harvard Law Record* and Arthur Austin's *Empire Strikes Back*, itself drawing from Kennedy, the term as "dead as a doornail" is used to describe US-CLS. The proposed importance of this phrase is easily overlooked, as initially it merely reinforces the motif of death around US-CLS and nothing more. However, this specific language describes a particular type of death, offering a way to understand what it meant and continues to mean. Intentionally or not, the choice of words used by Kennedy comes attached with certain etymological roots, which illuminate this understanding of death.

Originating in the late fourteenth century, the phrase "dead as a doornail" has been used to mean something that is completely or certainly dead,[53] employed as a simile to give a totalising effect. The history of this phrase, especially where it has been used and questioned, shapes the type of death it is associated with. Within the current context, the relevance of being "dead as a doornail" is the competing issues of declaring US-CLS as completely or certainly dead, whilst PCLS continues. The phrase is used and discussed within Dickens's *A Christmas Carol*.[54]

Culturally, *A Christmas Carol* is famous for its use of ghosts representing visions to the protagonist, Ebenezer Scrooge. A key trope presented within the book is that of ghosts both representing and displaying the past, present, and future to Scrooge. This aspect of *A Christmas Carol* is one that has been picked up and used in a multitude of other stories;[55] as such, it is often these ghosts who are a synecdoche for the story as a whole. However, the concept of a haunting that relates to the phrase "dead as a doornail"—and is therefore relevant to the relationship between US-CLS and PCLS—is the haunting of Scrooge by his former business partner, Jacob Marley, the first ghost to appear in the story.

As a text, *A Christmas Carol* is broken up into staves, rather than chapters, with the first stave, "Marley's Ghost", beginning with the eponymous line, "Marley was dead: to begin with." This juxtaposition summarises the oxymoron of death as both a finality and a beginning, as in context it pre-empts the return of Marley in his spectral form. The opening paragraph ends with the

---

[53] *Oxford English Dictionary*, under "dead" section 32B "dead as a doornail".
[54] Dickens, *A Christmas Carol* (n 5) 33.
[55] See, e.g., *It's a Wonderful Life*, dir. Frank Capra (Liberty Films, 1946), as well a large number of television shows that use this trope—unsurprisingly, around Christmas.

standalone sentence: "Old Marley was as dead as a door-nail." In and of itself, the mere use of this phrase would not be significant given its commonness.[56] However, in *A Christmas Carol*, its use precedes a discussion the narrator has with himself about the use of this specific simile and its relation to death:

> Mind! I don't mean to say that I know, of my own knowledge, what there is particularly dead about a door-nail. I might have been inclined, myself, to regard a coffin-nail as the deadest piece of ironmongery in the trade. But the wisdom of our ancestors is in the simile; and my unhallowed hands shall not disturb it, or the Country's done for. You will therefore permit me to repeat, emphatically, that Marley was as dead as a door-nail.[57]

In context, the narrator repeats *ad nauseam* that Marley truly was dead, and that the most emphatic way of stating this is through the phrase "dead as a doornail". This repetition is important, as the stave's title depicts, because Marley will soon return to the mortal world. However, the analysis given by the narrator can also be read as a way to understand that "dead as a doornail" means dead, but not fully gone. As the narrator knows Marley will return as a ghost, their initial confusion and deference to holier and wiser ancestors can be understood as signifying that this choice of words symbolises a different type of death, one in which a revenant returns, or a haunting will occur. Following this logic, the use of a different simile for death—for example, "as dead as a coffin nail"—would have a different outcome for Marley himself. Applying this understanding to the declaration that US-CLS was as dead as a doornail provides a way for US-CLS and PCLS to be explored from the same position.

What this haunting means for PCLS can be further explained by addressing the relationship between Scrooge and Marley. It should be noted that Scrooge and Marley are not allegories for US-CLS and PCLS; rather, their relationship gives a way to discuss the effect of a haunting on two parties: the one who haunts, and the haunted subject. The concept of a haunted subject can be understood through the importance of Marley's death. As outlined in the first sentence of *A Christmas Carol*, Marley was dead, but only to begin with. This premise paired with the stave's title foretells Marley's return, which by the end of the first page is joined by a reference to *Hamlet*, making it even clearer that Marley was dead, but would return as a ghost. Flagging this for the reader, the narrator states:

> If we were not perfectly convinced that Hamlet's Father died before the play began, there would be nothing more remarkable in his taking a stroll at

---

[56] See, e.g., William Shakespeare, *Henry VI*, Part 2, Act 4, Scene 10.
[57] Dickens, *A Christmas Carol* (n 5) 33.

night, in an easterly wind, upon his own ramparts, than there would be in any other middle-aged gentleman rashly turning out after dark in a breezy spot—say Saint Paul's Churchyard for instance—literally to astonish his son's weak mind.[58]

To appreciate the return of Marley (or the dead King Hamlet), the reader must first be convinced that Marley was truly dead. So, whilst this stave introduces Scrooge as the protagonist, it is set up in such a way that once the reader is convinced Marley did in fact die, they are waiting for his reappearance. The effect this has on the first stave is that only the appearance of an undead Marley will begin the story proper. As such, any discussion of Marley's death and Scrooge's life pre–Marley's ghost are there only to set the scene.

The common purpose of the period between acknowledging Marley's death and Marley's ghost visiting Scrooge is perhaps most logically understood as also introducing other prominent characters to the story, such as Scrooge's nephew, Fred, and his clerk, Bob Cratchit. Reference to Marley in this section is scarce: he is only mentioned in passing when Scrooge is asked to donate to a charity, with the reader learning from this that Marley died seven years ago to the day, on Christmas Eve.

It is worth noting that both the original story and its adaptions have followed a similar glossing over of Scrooge's existence prior to Marley's spectral return. In the 1984 film adaptation, *A Christmas Carol*,[59] the importance of the phrase "dead as a doornail" is stated. The narrator follows this description of Marley with: "This must be distinctly understood. If not, nothing wonderful can come of this story I am going to relate."[60] Whilst this contraction of the novel's opening page has the same gist as the original text, the film skips over any further mention of Marley until he appears to Scrooge as a ghost. Within the text and its adaptations, this period for Scrooge can be seen as merely a precursor. However, it is this period that develops the haunting framework.

The form of haunting found in the relationship between Scrooge and Marley can be broken up into two distinct categories: passive and active. The passive haunting is Scrooge's life after Marley's death and before Marley's return as a ghost, and the active haunting is Scrooge's life after he is visited by Marley's ghost. This division between passive and active haunting is not unique to *A Christmas Carol*, but is perhaps best exemplified by it. For example, Dickens's reference to *Hamlet* is both a tell for the reader that Scrooge is about to be visited by a ghost, but also an existing and famous example of the

---

[58] Ibid 33–4.
[59] *A Christmas Carol*, dir. Clive Donner (Entertainment Partners, 1984). This version was chosen for its release date in the midst of US-CLS.
[60] Ibid 00:00:29–00:00:40.

trope of transformative haunting. In both texts, the arrival of a ghost transforms the protagonist's direction, acting as a mechanism to allow the narrative to transpire—that is, but for Hamlet's father, or but for Marley, neither Hamlet nor Scrooge would have embarked upon the stories that make up *Hamlet* and *A Christmas Carol* respectively. However, the transition achieved through the arrival of the ghost demonstrates that before this event, both Hamlet and Scrooge are passively haunted.

For PCLS, this distinction is vital, as there has been no spectre or ghost of US-CLS which has appeared and created a transition to an actively haunted PCLS. The effect of the death of US-CLS, and the argument that this has caused PCLS to be comparatively regressive and constricted, therefore relies on passive haunting. This unique way of thinking about haunting as operating in an active and passive way relates to the dominant understanding of haunting as occurring when a ghost or spiritual being visits a subject. However, to say that this is an exhaustive use of the term "haunting" would be misleading.

In terms of definitions, the verb "haunt" also means "[t]o visit frequently and habitually with manifestations of their [ghosts or spirits] influence and presence".[61] Whilst the dominant premise of a haunting relies on the supernatural, the associated ideas of influence and presence after death can be understood as occurring before the arrival of a ghost. For example, in both *A Christmas Carol* and *Hamlet*, the influence of Marley or King Hamlet is still felt before either ghost arrives. Commonly these pre-haunting periods may be conflated with mourning or bereavement; however, there is an expectation within dominant religious practice, and broader society, that these periods are somewhat structured and eventually end.[62] As such the idea of a passive haunting can vary, continuing past the mourning or bereavement of a death and into the reality of a continual or permanent "influence" or "presence" of the deceased. In this way, the subject is haunted without a ghost manifesting—that is, they are passively haunted, potentially unaware of the influence and presence of the deceased in a very different way to when a ghost appears and the subject is actively haunted.

The key issue in the division between passive and active hauntings rests on the non-appearance of a ghost and, subsequently, whether this process can justifiably be called a haunting. Although the argument can be made that in *A Christmas Carol* and *Hamlet* both passive and active hauntings take place, in each text the two kinds are dependent on each other. The idea of establishing

---

[61] *Oxford English Dictionary*, "Haunt".
[62] Within the Abrahamic religions, for example, the practice of Shiva in Judaism lasts a week; in Islam, Iddah lasts four months and ten days; and in Catholicism, depending on the relationship, mourning will last between thirty days and six months.

a passive haunting as an independent occurrence is therefore problematic. Despite the non-existence of ghosts as they are portrayed in fiction, an active haunting—the dominant understanding of a haunting—requires a ghost to exist in this manner. Meanwhile, the concept of passive haunting requires only the effect of death and its continued influence or presence, rather than a ghost per se. The lack of a supernatural element required in a passive haunting removes it from the position of an allegorical fiction, and makes it an applicable lens for viewing subjects that have experienced death or finality in an unsatisfactory manner.

The acceptance of two types of haunting, rather than one unified understanding of the term, does however come with some immediate problems. The most obvious issue that arises is that if no ghost appears and everyone experiences death—either their own or witnessing someone else's—then is it justifiable to consider it a passive haunting, or, conversely, does everyone suffer from it? With regard to the latter issue and the universal experience of death, it can be argued that in the specific texts relied upon, not all characters are haunted, either passively or actively. In *A Christmas Carol*, it is only Scrooge who is, to the reader's knowledge, visited by Marley and the other ghosts. Similarly, in *Hamlet*, despite a number of characters seeing and interacting with the King's ghost, it is only Hamlet himself who is passively then actively haunted. Neither text denies the broad experiences of death—perhaps exemplified most in the final scene of *Hamlet*[63]—but not all deaths result in either form of haunting. Whilst differences can be highlighted between Scrooge and Hamlet, and those who are not haunted, there is no perfect schema or model that can delineate why this is.

It is possible to turn to another work of fiction and rely on the definition of "un-dead" created by Bram Stoker to describe the affliction facing the namesake in *Dracula*.[64] Stoker's now commonplace description relates to something clinically dead, but not yet at rest.[65] If the subject, either Marley or US-CLS, were not at rest, their un-dead status could lead to the passive haunting of Scrooge or PCLS. However, within the overall aim of demystifying Critical Legal Studies, drawing upon further works of fiction—which requires the blending of supernatural beings such as ghosts and vampires—may be counterproductive. Instead, what can be understood is that only some subjects will be passively haunted, and that this affliction should be discernible from the facts presented.

---

[63] Shakespeare, *Hamlet*, (n 6) 205–25.
[64] Bram Stoker, *Dracula* (Penguin Classics, 2003).
[65] In the *Oxford English Dictionary*, the adjective "un-dead" is attributed to Stoker in *Dracula* (1897).

As discussed above, the first stave of *A Christmas Carol* is purposefully introductory, and a dominant reading would reflect this. However, in isolation, away from the broader context of Marley's actual ghost, there are minor images and statements about Scrooge's life after Marley's death that demonstrate a passively haunted subject. This passive haunting ends when Marley appears and Scrooge is exposed to the other ghosts in the story. However, for US-CLS and PCLS, there is no end, with this relationship demonstrating the effect of a passively haunted subject.

In the opening page of *A Christmas Carol*, the narrator outlines that upon Marley's death, "Scrooge was his [Marley's] sole executor, his sole administrator, his sole assign, his sole residuary legatee, his sole friend and sole mourner."[66] The narrator then discloses that despite a relationship that had lasted "I don't know how many years",[67] Scrooge did not attend Marley's funeral: "And even Scrooge was not dreadfully cut up by the sad event, but that he was an excellent man of business on the very day of the funeral, and solemnised it with an undoubted bargain."[68] The initial effect is apparently to affirm Scrooge's miserly and uncaring ways. However, this position can be challenged with the narrator's statement that Scrooge was at once the sole mourner and not dreadfully cut up by the death. Whilst these seem like somewhat oppositional stances to take, there is a similar sentiment in Kennedy's reaction to the death of US-CLS: "I think that while [US]CLS is dead as a doornail, there is still a very significant public interest movement, which I for one strongly support."[69]

For both Scrooge and US-CLS, it is reasonable to assume that their respective deaths were acknowledged, but that the significance of them was either downplayed or not fully appreciated.[70] However, as time progressed, the impact of the deaths became more apparent, and the elements of a passive haunting can be drawn out. For Scrooge, this appears on the second page of *A Christmas Carol*, where the narrator states:

> Scrooge never painted out Old Marley's name. There it stood, years afterwards, above the warehouse door: Scrooge and Marley. The firm was known

---

[66] Dickens, *A Christmas Carol* (n 5) 33; A parallel between the friendship of Marley and Scrooge and its correlation to US-CLS and PCLS could be drawn here; however, this would add a necessary element to PCLS that the PCLS authors be *known* to their US-CLS "friends"—which would limit the effect of the haunting. Furthermore, the definition of friendship from which to differentiate this relationship is a rather detailed point in itself: see, e.g., Giorgio Agamben, "Friendship" (2004) 5 *Contretemps* 1, 6.
[67] Dickens, *A Christmas Carol* (n 5) 33.
[68] Ibid.
[69] Yen, "As HLS Mulls Its Mission" (n 3).
[70] See, e.g., Ernest Becker, *The Denial of Death* (Free Press Paperback, 1997).

as Scrooge and Marley. Sometimes people new to the business called Scrooge Scrooge, and sometimes Marley, but he answered to both names: it was all the same to him.[71]

This excerpt presents the static nature of the passively haunted subject. The progression of time leads new users to the business; in turn, Scrooge's choice to retain Marley's name above the warehouse door leads to the assumption, seen with the use of either name, that Marley's death changed nothing. Whilst relatively minor, the direct effect of Scrooge being referred to as his dead partner keeps the "presence" and "influence" of Marley with him at all times. This effect is then compounded when the narrator outlines Scrooge's living arrangements: "He lived in chambers which had once belonged to his deceased partner. They were a gloomy suite of rooms . . . It was old enough now, and dreary enough, for nobody lived in it but Scrooge."[72] In both excerpts, Scrooge is presented as taking on significant elements of Marley's life: his name and his home. The direct effect of this is to keep Scrooge in some sort of stasis, where he is still living but not progressing—or, to put it another way, that Marley's passive haunting of Scrooge means that he is regressive and constricted. For PCLS, the passive haunting of US-CLS can be seen in a similar way. First, there is the issue of names. Whilst PCLS has been designated as such to clarify which Critical Legal Studies is which, the more common approach is for the posthumous version of Critical Legal Studies to just be called "Critical Legal Studies".

Second is the issue of a home. For PCLS, the idea of a shared home is less specific than the image of a single particular location that Laura Kalman provided in *Yale Law School and the Sixties*,[73] and instead refers to the position that Critical Legal Studies has in legal academia. However, at this point Critical Legal Studies and *A Christmas Carol* diverge. Shortly after Scrooge returns to his dreary abode, Marley's ghost appears and Scrooge experiences an active haunting. For PCLS, no such ghost has appeared and, as will be argued, no such ghost of US-CLS will emerge. Instead, PCLS remains in stasis, crippled by the regressive and constricting nature of a passive haunting.

Posthumous Critical Legal Studies: Regressive and Constricted

The ability defiantly to state that PCLS will remain passively haunted and will not experience the relief of an active haunting comes from the reissuing of two

---

[71] Dickens, *A Christmas Carol* (n 5) 34.
[72] Ibid 41.
[73] Laura Kalman, *Yale Law School and the Sixties: Revolt and Reverberations* (University of North Carolina Press, 2005) 7.

germane US-CLS texts during the PCLS period. In 2004, Kennedy's *Legal Education and the Reproduction of Hierarchy: A Polemic against the System* was reissued,[74] with Roberto Unger's *The Critical Legal Studies Movement* (with a new subheading, *Another Time, a Greater Task*) reissued in 2015.[75] Both original texts set the tone for two distinct approaches to US-CLS, and as reissues, rather than reprints,[76] they included additional materials. However, whilst both texts included addenda, these took the form of retrospective insights, rather than a way forward or a call to arms.

In *Legal Education and the Reproduction of Hierarchy*, Kennedy gives a brief introduction to the new edition, but provides a longer assessment in his afterword.[77] Within the afterword, Kennedy provides some thoughts on the end of US-CLS, touching on a range of different factors that affected its death. Kennedy affirms the timeline for US-CLS's decline, identifying that in 1992 the writing was on the wall, with Mark Tushnet stating that the US-CLS conference was "just another academic conference":[78] what had made US-CLS unique was no longer possible. Kennedy does try to restore some optimism by outlining the US-CLS's influence on most areas of law, stating that "the sun never sets on Critical Legal Studies".[79] He also gives some reasons for why US-CLS ended,[80] but these follow the author's earlier statements.[81] Kennedy's continued optimism offers a new critical approach to law, but one that is not US-CLS, and one that he does not have to found:

> There is a lot of radical legal scholarship and scholarly activity still around for the student who is willing to look for it, even if there is not the sense of an all-inclusive open movement to join or rebel against. It's time for something new here, too.[82]

---

[74] Duncan Kennedy, *Legal Education and the Reproduction of Hierarchy: A Polemic Against the System* (New York University Press, 2004).

[75] Roberto Mangabeira Unger, *The Critical Legal Studies Movement: Another Time, a Greater Task* (Verso, 2015).

[76] Contra, Peter Goodrich, "Duncan Kennedy as I Imagine Him: The Man, the Work, His Scholarship, and the Polity" (2001) 22 *Cardozo Law Review* 971, 976. Goodrich highlights an argument about both reissues and reprints of Kennedy's *Sexy Dressing, Etc*: "I . . . said that it was unfortunate that the book consisted entirely of papers that had already been published and that he had not had anything new to say." See further discussion at 978–81. However, the addenda in these reissues had scope to alleviate the passively haunted state.

[77] Kennedy, *Legal Education and the Reproduction of Hierarchy* (n 74) 202.

[78] Ibid 219.

[79] Ibid 221.

[80] Ibid 219–20.

[81] See Kennedy, "Two Globalizations" (n 1); Yen, "As HLS Mulls Its Mission" (n 3).

[82] Kennedy, *Legal Education and the Reproduction of Hierarchy* (n 74) 221.

Where Kennedy's tone is encouraging but without direction, Unger is far more blunt. Although he addresses US-CLS in great detail across an additional two chapters, Unger succinctly states that, "Critical legal studies was never intended to generate a permanent genre of legal writing, or to take its place among a standing cast of schools of legal theory. It was a disruptive engagement in a particular circumstance".[83]

The authors' approaches are stylistically different and are taken several years apart; however, both Unger and Kennedy can be read as agreeing that US-CLS is dead, and neither has an interest in returning to it or revitalising it. With this unified approach, these founders of US-CLS extinguish any chance of an active haunting relieving the passively haunted PCLS. The definitive nature of this statement can be understood through a return to Derrida's concept of hauntology, which relies exclusively on the appearance of a ghost. Drawing from *Hamlet*, Derrida positions the effect of hauntology before the return of the ghost, in the passive haunting phase. In this state, Derrida describes the apprehension and sense of excitement that surrounds the possibility of the ghost's return:

> As in *Hamlet*, the Prince of a rotten State, everything begins by the apparition of a specter. More precisely by the *waiting* for this apparition. The anticipation is at once impatient, anxious, and fascinated: this, the thing ("this thing") will end up coming. The *revenant* is going to come. It won't be long. But how long it is taking. Still more precisely, everything begins in the imminence of a re-apparition, but a reapparition of the specter as apparition *for the first time in the play.* The spirit of the father is going to come back and will soon say to him "I am thy father's Spirit" (I, iv), but here, at the beginning of the play, he comes back, so to speak, for the first time. It is a first, the first time on stage.[84]

In *Hamlet*, Hamlet's excitement is due to the sighting of the ghost by Bernardo, Marcellus, and Horatio.[85] In *A Christmas Carol*, Marley serves a similar purpose, warning or foretelling Scrooge that spectres will come to visit him. For PCLS, a return would be in the form of Kennedy or Unger, ghosts of US-CLS, exciting the passively haunted PCLS to a state where the "anticipation is at once impatient, anxious, and fascinated: this, the thing ('this thing') will end up coming. The *revenant* is going to come. It won't be long."[86] However, in reissuing their texts, a forum where this might have been

---

[83] Unger (n 75) 4.
[84] Derrida, *Specters of Marx* (n 8) 2 (emphasis in original).
[85] Shakespeare, *Hamlet* (n 6) 3.
[86] Derrida, *Specters of Marx* (n 8) 2 (emphasis in original).

possible, both authors are adamantly not creating this type of anticipation. Instead, their tone aligns with T. S. Eliot's sentiments on death, that US-CLS ends not with a bang, but with a whimper.[87]

---

[87] T. S. Eliot, *Collected Poems 1909–1962* (Harcourt Brace Jovanovich, 1991) 77.

6

The Haunting of Critical Legal Studies

Nothing is so painful to the human mind as a great and sudden change.
Mary Shelley, *Frankenstein* (1818)

Declarations of hauntings, much like declarations of deaths, do not lead to clarity without exposition. The argument that PCLS (Posthumous Critical Legal Studies) exists and suffers through a passive haunting by US-CLS may provide an explanation for why Critical Legal Studies is not the same today as it was in 1984. However, if this was its only purpose then it would be a rather convoluted route to arrive at the same argument as: theories evolve, theorists change their minds, we live in different times, et cetera. Instead, the purpose of this reimagining of PCLS as haunted is to move past the more obvious issues of why CLS ground to a halt, and to think about why it has struggled to re-emerge.

For this purpose, the relationship between old and new CLS (that is, US-CLS and PCLS) is the focal point. The death of US-CLS has ensured that all US-based Critical Legal Studies have been affected to some degree by the resultant haunting. Only by understanding this relationship and seeing its effect is it possible for the remaining CLS to move past its haunted state.

A demonstration of the effect of passive haunting can be undertaken through the analysis of two Critical Legal Studies articles, one from the US-CLS limb and one from PCLS. However, if the argument is that the death of US-CLS led to the passive haunting of PCLS, which in turn has resulted in the latter's constricted and regressive nature, then this presents an issue about whether equal papers can be chosen from US-CLS and PCLS. If the argument is correct, the PCLS paper will always be comparatively constricted and regressive.

Still, knowing there is a power imbalance does not mean the analysis cannot be undertaken, it just means that the papers chosen must have more connections than merely being from US-CLS and PCLS authors. As such,

Peter Gabel and Duncan Kennedy's 1984 article, "Roll Over Beethoven",[1] has been selected to be analysed alongside Jerry Anderson's 2004 article, "Law School Enters the Matrix: Teaching Critical Legal Studies".[2]

Both "Roll Over Beethoven" and "Law School Enters the Matrix" use popular culture to discuss Critical Legal Studies. The titles of both articles reference this connection, with "Roll Over Beethoven" drawing on a Chuck Berry song, and "Law School Enters the Matrix" referencing the film, *The Matrix*.[3] The popular-culture link is strengthened further in "Roll Over Beethoven", when Gabel and Kennedy dispense with musical references and turn to the film *Invasion of the Body Snatchers* as an allegorical text.[4] The dystopian science-fiction themes anchor both papers and the relationships US-CLS and PCLS have with the non-Critical world.

The publication date of "Law School Enters the Matrix" places it squarely as a PCLS paper. Anderson's article was published in 2004, nearly ten years after Kennedy's declaration that US-CLS was "dead as a doornail". "Law School Enters the Matrix" follows a thematic trend amongst a number of PCLS articles published around the turn of the millennium that question what happened to US-CLS.[5] After "Law School Enters the Matrix", the closest contender for a comparative PCLS text is E. Dana Neacsu's "CLS Stands for Critical Legal Studies, if Anyone Remembers".[6]

Neacsu's paper has a similar theme to "Law School Enters the Matrix", with an emphatic call to remember and return to US-CLS. Where Anderson approaches this through a practical pedagogical approach, Neacsu focuses on what could be salvaged from Kennedy's *Legal Education and the Reproduction of Hierarchy: A Polemic Against the System*. Despite the different approaches in their calls for a return or remembrance of US-CLS, both papers exemplify this theme of yearning for its return.

There is a pragmatic hope in these articles that US-CLS, dead or otherwise, may be able to be resuscitated—a stance exemplified by another PCLS

---

[1] Peter Gabel and Duncan Kennedy, "Roll Over Beethoven" (1984) 36(1/2) *Stanford Law Review* 1.
[2] Jerry L. Anderson, "Law School Enters the Matrix: Teaching Critical Legal Studies' (2004) 54(2) *Journal of Legal Education* 201.
[3] *The Matrix*, dir. the Wachowskis (Warner Brothers, 1999).
[4] *Invasion of the Body Snatchers*, dir. Don Siegel (Walter Wanger Productions, 1956).
[5] See, e.g., the 2001 CLS Symposium in (2000–2001) 22 *Cardozo Law Review*; see also, Jack M. Balkin, "Critical Legal Theory Today", in Francis J. Mootz III (ed), *On Philosophy in American Law* (Cambridge University Press, 2009) 64.
[6] E. Dana Neacsu, "CLS Stands for Critical Legal Studies, If Anyone Remembers" (2000) 8(2) *Journal of Law and Policy* 415.

paper, Jeremy Paul's introductory article to the "2001 CLS Symposium".[7] Paul's article concludes by arguing: "for the [US-]CLS project to prosper, we must look to push each other hard, to talk to rather than at each other, to ask hard questions, and to think hard about why we aren't yet getting through."[8]

Arguably, any of these papers could represent this dominant theme in PCLS. However, only Anderson's article outlines a practical way for the reintroduction of US-CLS to transpire. Despite Neacsu presenting a similar resuscitation of US-CLS through a popular-culture lens, she uses a more tenuous analogy. Neacsu presents a way to return to US-CLS through the animated series *South Park*,[9] and specifically the ever-dying character Kenny McCormick.

Neacsu pairs Kenny's ability to die and be resurrected with US-CLS, hoping that a similar fate might occur if people are reminded of the movement's benefits. She finishes framing US-CLS as following the path of Kenny by referring to the TV show's feature-length film:[10] "just as Kenny found his post-mortem voice and purpose in *South Park: Bigger, Longer, & Uncut*, [US-]CLS also might rediscover its own."[11] The timing and popular-culture basis for the article, as well as the acknowledgement that US-CLS did in fact die, is compelling. However, the *South Park* analogy, whilst novel, lacks the applicability of Anderson's "Law School Enters the Matrix".

> Like Kenny, who is an outsider and who speaks a language unintelligible to all except, astonishingly, his classmates, [US-]CLS no longer seems to possess a voice comprehensible to anyone outside its own small circle. Kenny, unlike all other cartoon figures, dies in every episode. Significantly, often Kenny's death has been self-inflicted – though not necessarily intentional – when, for instance, he ignores warnings of imminent danger. Like Kenny, [US-]CLS has suffered many often self-inflicted injuries. Like South Park, generally, [US-]CLS is certainly colorful, but often little more than that and, as in the cartoon, except for the certainty of Kenny's death and later resurrection, there seems more flash than substance in its existence. We are left to guess whether [US-]CLS will prove to be as resilient after apparent death, as Kenny.[12]

---

[7] Jeremy Paul, "CLS 2001" (2001) 22 *Cardozo Law Review* 701.
[8] Ibid 720.
[9] *South Park*, dir. Trey Parker (Comedy Central, 1997).
[10] *South Park: Bigger, Longer & Uncut*, dir. Trey Parker (Scott Rudin Productions, 1999).
[11] Neacsu (n 6) 416.
[12] Ibid.

Comparatively, Anderson's use of *The Matrix* synergises better with US-CLS as a whole. Anderson states:

> Consider, for example, that the main thrust of [US-]CLS is that the entire legal system is merely an apparatus designed to appease the masses, fooling them into thinking that their needs may be addressed, while in fact its purpose is merely to keep them docile while perpetuating the hierarchy that provides the upper class with its advantages. Instead of pods filled with bodies attached to the power plant, just substitute workers stuck in cubicles in a high-rise office building, all working to feed the vast machine that lines the pockets of the CEO. If I were to try to create a metaphorical vision of [US-]CLS, it would look a lot like *The Matrix*.[13]

Reading Anderson's analogy in conjunction with the below excerpt from "Roll Over Beethoven" shows a continuity in theme that is not present in Neacsu's work:

> So there's this conflict, which is, on the one hand, you want to get the best one you can; you want to be lucid; you want to be explicit; you want to get clear. But unfortunately the body snatchers are always nearby, and you wake up and they're all pods. The whole conceptual structure has been turned into a cluster of pods.[14]

Amongst a cohort of similarly themed articles, "Law School Enters the Matrix" takes PCLS's yearning for US-CLS and makes a practical claim for how it can be presented to students in an accessible and beneficial way. Through his use of *The Matrix*, Anderson taps into the popular-culture roots of US-CLS and offers a way to reinvigorate interest in it through film and the allegorical connections to the vast illusion of law.

In doing this, Anderson connects with the themes that underpin "Roll over Beethoven". Anderson even makes reference to the article; however, he does not draw on the popular-culture connection himself, a failing which will be addressed in the reading of his article. However, articulated by Anderson or not, the connection is there, and it links the two papers under discussion, in turn demonstrating the passively haunted state of PCLS.

***

Comparatively, there are more US-CLS articles than PCLS ones, which stands to reason given the "posthumous" nature of PCLS. Having a greater pool of articles to choose from comes with a similar but distinct set of criteria to the selection of

---

[13] Anderson (n 2) 211–21.
[14] Gabel and Kennedy (n 1) 7.

"Law School Enters the Matrix". For US-CLS, the criteria relate to the article's themes and time, but also to the authors, the article's prominence, and how much the article exemplifies US-CLS. Not only is "Roll Over Beethoven" a US-CLS piece in terms of time and content, but through its unusual structure within a prestigious journal, it also acts as a demonstration of US-CLS.

"Roll over Beethoven" was published in 1984, in volume one of the *Stanford Law Review*. The two-volume edition was a "US-CLS edition", hosting a collection of articles presented as part of the Critical Legal Studies Symposium. It was alleged to be the "largest-selling single law review issue in history".[15] As Hendrik Hartog remembered, "its appearance was, for many in legal education at the time, an event."[16] The year 1984 is important to US-CLS more broadly;[17] unbeknownst to those at the time, it sits almost at the midway point of US-CLS's existence, which began with the hiring of Unger, Horwitz, and Kennedy by Harvard Law School in 1973 and the first Conference on Critical Legal Studies in 1977. Following this timeline, the 1984 *Stanford Law Review* sits several years before the decline US-CLS, prior to the tenure denials in 1987, and long before the finality of Hope Yen's article in 1995.[18] An argument can be made that in 1984, US-CLS was at its prime.

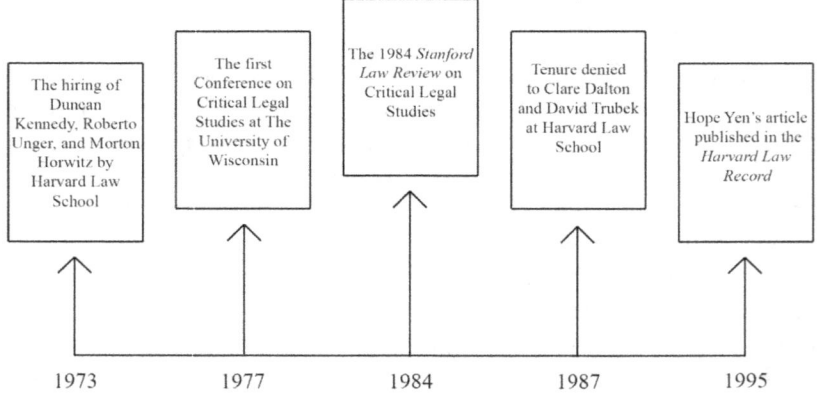

Figure 6.1 The US-CLS Timeline

[15] David Luban, "Legal Modernism" (1986) 84(8) *Michigan Law Review* 1,656.
[16] Hendrik Hartog, "Introduction to Symposium on 'Critical Legal Histories': Robert W. Gordon. 1984. Critical Legal Histories. *Stanford Law Review* 36:57–125" (2012) 37(1) *Law & Social Inquiry* 147, 147.
[17] See Steven M. Teles, *The Rise of the Conservative Legal Movement: The Battle for Control of the Law* (Princeton University Press, 2008) 193–4.
[18] Hope Yen, "Crits at HLS a Dying Breed?", *Harvard Law Record* (online, 1 December 1995); Hope Yen, "As HLS Mulls Its Mission, CLS Scholars Remain Quiet", *Harvard Law Record* (online, 1 December 1995) 2.

The *Stanford Law Review* was not the only major CLS publication in 1984, with Kennedy and Karl Klare's "A Bibliography of Critical Legal Studies" also published that year.[19] While this article contained a more comprehensive list of US-CLS works, it acted as a point of reference, not a repository of accessible articles. The "Bibliography" provides an alphabetical list of selected US-CLS authors and their respective works, relisting pieces if there are multiple authors. The article was written to provide "many people, including lawyers, teachers, students, and researchers in a variety of fields"[20] a substantive but self-proclaimed incomplete list of US-CLS works.[21]

When addressing US-CLS, this bibliography is a good place to start. Kennedy and Klare state: "The idea was to provide in a readily accessible form a document that tells people where they can go to read [US]CLS-type works, not to establish a research clearinghouse."[22] The 1984 *Stanford Law Review* houses a collection of US-CLS material from its prime, rather than publishing a list of references during this same period. The journal itself also adds prominence to "Roll over Beethoven": the *Stanford Law Review* has constantly been the third most-cited US law journal, only behind Harvard and Yale.[23] Whilst these types of measure do not ensure the calibre of the articles published, they are a useable metric to estimate readership and visibility.

In its original format as a two-volume hard-copy journal, the first article in the 1984 *Stanford Law Review* is "Roll Over Beethoven".[24] The article's demonstration of US-CLS through its style and content is initially evidenced through its juxtaposition to the journal itself. In a pre-digital age, "Roll Over Beethoven" was the first article, but not the first page of the journal. Instead, within the physical copy of the *Law Review*, there are a number of introductory and preliminary pages. These pages lead up to the article itself and play into the juxtaposition that it presented.

Following the title page, and in place of the more traditional colophon, is a visual hierarchy of the Stanford University School of Law and *Law Review* editorial board.[25] The verso categorically lists, in order of importance, the

---

[19] Duncan Kennedy and Karl E. Klare, "A Bibliography Of Critical Legal Studies" (1984) 94(461) *Yale Law Journal* 461.
[20] Ibid 461.
[21] Ibid 462.
[22] Ibid.
[23] See Fred R. Shapiro and Michelle Pearse, "The Most-Cited Law Review Articles of All Time" (2012) 110(8) *Michigan Law Review* 1,483, 1,502. This article shows the *Stanford Law Review* as the constant third most-cited journal, behind the *Yale Law Journal* and the *Harvard Law Review*.
[24] Gabel and Kennedy (n 1) 1.
[25] These would be pages ii–iii; they are not numbered in the journal.

administrative officers, emeritus faculty, current faculty, and lastly the lecturers in law. Each name is followed by the individual's abbreviated qualifications, and any named positions they hold. The recto moves away from the list style and uses a structure more akin to a family tree for the editorial board of the *Stanford Law Review*, descending from the president to other roles. These two introductory pages are followed by twenty-two pages of detailed, indexed notes and references to the articles and reviews in the edition. As these pages conclude, a reader is greeted by page one of the journal proper.

On page one, there is a marked change, not only from the preceding formality of the journal's introduction, but also from what may be considered a "standard" or "normal" law review article. "Roll Over Beethoven" enforces its primacy, not only with this position, but the names of its authors. Despite Kennedy's dominance in US-CLS, he takes second place to Peter Gabel. The article itself does not seem to favour one author's opinion over another and, given its layout, there seems to be an equal contribution from both parties. The piece opens with a statement from "Duncan", and there is some record of Kennedy presenting this paper, with no direct mention of Gabel.[26] As this journal places the articles alphabetically by first author's surname, it could be hypothesised that Kennedy taking the position of second author was to ensure that "Roll Over Beethoven" was the first article a reader would encounter.

If the authors' names had not been in this order, a reader of the 1984 *Stanford Law Review* would have been greeted by Robert Gordon's "Critical Legal Histories", an important, but less radically presented, text. Gordon focuses on a critique of evolutionary functionalism,[27] challenging this dominant historical form and providing "a brief account of the impulses that have prompted the Critical scholars to their chosen ways of writing history (or rather histories, since the Movement has actually spawned several different historiographical practices)."[28] "Critical Legal Histories" was also an important piece of work, and was revisited with a symposium in 2012. However, while it makes a convincing argument to explain US-CLS's position, it does not "perform" in the same way as "Roll over Beethoven".

From the title's nod to Chuck Berry, to its unconventional structure, "Roll Over Beethoven" can be read as the myth of US-CLS come to life.

---

[26] Gary Minda, *Postmodern Legal Movements: Law and Jurisprudence at Century's End* (New York University Press, 1995) 46.

[27] Robert W. Gordon, "Critical Legal Histories" (1984) 36 *Stanford Law Review* 57; Robert W. Gordon, "'Critical Legal Histories Revisited': A Response" (2012) 37(1) *Law & Social Inquiry* 200.

[28] Gordon, "Critical Legal Histories" (n 27) 57.

The authors are the "white male heavies"[29] from privileged backgrounds[30] that led to some of the *ad hominem* critiques of US-CLS as a whole.[31] The article, within a prestigious journal, is immediately juxtaposed with the introductory text and seems to demonstrate the fears of the liberal class that US-CLS had infiltrated the law school and presented a viable threat. The article is a US-CLS version of US-CLS, a performative piece with content that addresses issues it faced, but approached in a US-CLS way: "Roll over Beethoven" is metonymic of US-CLS. The article is confrontational, jargonised, critical, flippant, and written from a position of privilege,[32] and it is for these reasons that it works so well for comparison to PCLS.

Ian Ward takes on the difficult task of reducing the article to a concise few lines.[33] For Ward, "Roll Over Beethoven"

> provided a vivid illustration of the rival positions which emerged within [US-]CLS and which remain largely unresolved, perhaps by definition unresolvable. Gabel and Kennedy assumed these very different, indeed polar, positions within [US-]CLS scholarship: whilst Gabel advocated some form of reconstructive enterprise, Kennedy maintained a more radical and uncompromising position determined to concentrate on "trashing" liberal legalism.[34]

---

[29] David M. Trubek, "Foundational Events, Foundational Myths, and the Creation of Critical Race Theory, or How To Get Along with a Little Help from Your Friends" (2011) 43(5) *Connecticut Law Review* 1,503, 1,506.

[30] Aside from their educational connection at Harvard, both Gabel and Kennedy were educated privately at two highly ranked private schools: Gabel at Deerfield Academy (Deerfield Academy, "Peter Gabel '64", *Alumni* (Web Page, 5 June 2015) <https://deerfield.edu/alumni/class-notes/2015/06/peter-gabel-64/10223689>), and Kennedy at Phillips Academy Andover. See Tor Krever, Carl Lisberger, and Max Utzschneider, "Law on the Left: A Conversation with Duncan Kennedy" (2015) 10(1) *Unbound* 1, 3. Note that both schools are part of the Eight Schools Association, although this grouping occurred after Gabel and Kennedy had graduated.

[31] See generally James D. Gordon III, "Law Review and the Modern Mind" (1991) 33(2) *Arizona Law Review* 265, 268–9.

[32] See generally Richard D. Kahlenberg, *Broken Contract: A Memoir of Harvard Law School* (University of Massachusetts Press, 1992) 83–5. See also reviews of Kahlenberg's book by Robert Gordon and Arthur Austin: Robert W. Gordon, "Bargaining with the Devil" (1992) 105(8) *Harvard Law Review* 2,041; Arthur D. Austin, "Life at Harvard Law School: 'Sometimes It's Tough to Get Out of Bed When You're Wearing Silk Pajamas'" (1993) 78 *Iowa Law Review* 427.

[33] Ian Ward, *Introduction to Critical Legal Theory* (Routledge Cavendish, 2nd ed, 2004).

[34] Ibid 146.

Ward builds on Kennedy's approach in the first eight pages of "Roll Over Beethoven", summarising Kennedy's tone for the article as a whole:

> Whilst approving the appeal to political action, Duncan Kennedy dismissed all this talk about "experienced reality" and "intersubjective zap" as "abstract bullshit". Philosophy does not provide the answer to the real political problems experienced by modern men and women. Rather, it turns people into "pods", incapable of thinking for themselves, and merely the voicepieces of someone else's ideology. Instead of philosophy, Kennedy suggested that critical lawyers must operate through more familiar media, such as "soap opera, pop culture, all that kind of stuff". Such an approach, Kennedy alleged, was intellectually and appropriately ironic. Critical lawyers must proceed by being ironic, and will operate more effectively by "communicating" with "jokes" than they ever will with "abstract formulation".[35]

Whether this method worked for Kennedy is not clear, given that his proceeding works did not shy away from philosophy.[36] However, Ward's summary positions "Roll Over Beethoven" as the coming together of two voices in US-CLS, the articulation of their differences, and the instigator of some changes to how US-CLS was practiced. Similarly, Gary Minda identifies "Roll Over Beethoven" as a significant point of change for US-CLS, as Kennedy "recanted his own theory of 'fundamental contradiction'",[37] something which Neil Duxbury also addresses as a significant part of the movement's history.[38]

However, more broad than any transformations to US-CLS itself was the visceral impact of "Roll Over Beethoven", seen through readers' reactions to the piece which Minda collates:

> The political significance of *Roll Over Beethoven* can be judged by the effect it had on its audience. It has been reported that one "well-known professor was so upset when Kennedy presented *Roll Over Beethoven* at the Columbia Legal Theory Workshop, that he totaled his car on the way home." Another law professor, David Luban of the University of Maryland School of Law, admitted that his "initial reaction" to the piece was that it was a "pile of crap".

---

[35] Ibid 147; See also Peter Goodrich, "Satirical Legal Studies: From the Legists to the Lizard" (2004) 103(3) *Michigan Law Review* 397.

[36] See, e.g., Duncan Kennedy, *A Critique of Adjudication (fin de siècle)* (Harvard University Press, 1998); Peter Goodrich, "Duncan Kennedy as I Imagine Him: The Man, the Work, His Scholarship, and the Polity" (2001) 22 *Cardozo Law Review* 971.

[37] Minda (n 26) 122.

[38] Neil Duxbury, *Patterns of American Jurisprudence* (Clarendon Press, 1995) 462–3.

These reactions illustrate how the second generation of CLS scholarship is now perceived as even more radical and dangerous than the first.[39]

Here, Minda refers to a 1986 article by David Luban, which positions US-CLS as the legal equivalent of modernist art: "The thesis that I want to explore here is roughly this: [US-]CLS is to legal theory as modernist art was to traditional art. [US-]CLS is legal modernism."[40] Luban's in-depth analysis of "Roll Over Beethoven" continues, with the author stating that "the one [US-]CLS piece I know of that is through-and-through modernist, Peter Gabel and Duncan Kennedy's 'article' Roll Over Beethoven."[41] Luban's overview is less methodical than Ward's; however, it still conveys a relatable position: "It is exhausting to read—fifty-four pages of transcript that often sounds like a pair of old acid-heads chewing over a passage in Sartre."[42] Luban articulates the complexity of "Roll Over Beethoven" through an allusion to modern art, a lens which he uses to assess and reassess the piece:

> My own initial reaction to *Roll Over Beethoven* was that it was a pile of crap. How dare they waste my time with a self-indulgent rap session! I was able to read only the first half of the article—it *is* tiring—then dipped into a few more pages to assure myself that it was all of a piece, then made fun of it to everyone within earshot. It's boring. It's rude. If Duncan Kennedy weren't notorious (and from Harvard), no journal would touch it without using tongs. Gabel ought to burn his library of phenomenology and take a cold shower. Anyone can turn on a tape-recorder and reel off a lot of pretentious pickle-smoke. You recognize a classic reaction to modernism. Anyone can do a drip-painting. Anyone can make random percussion sounds. It isn't real art, or music, or legal theory, or philosophy, or, or, or . . .[43]

In his final line, Luban starts to recognise what he comes to term a "courageous article", moving through stages of how and why "Roll Over Beethoven" has so many different layers.[44] But what is the effect of these layers, and how can we understand them? Given the unusual format of the piece, there are

---

[39] Minda (n 26) 122.
[40] Luban (n 15) 1,656.
[41] Ibid 1,672.
[42] Ibid 1,671.
[43] Ibid 1,672; (emphasis in original). Arthur Austin makes a similar claim in "The Top Ten Politically Correct Law Review Articles" (1999) 27 *Florida State University Law Review* 233, 253: "After reflection, I concluded that *Roll Over* anticipated Live Painting, in which artists covered themselves with car paint and hang for hours on hooks, talking or staring at onlookers."
[44] Luban (n 15) 1,672.

three plausible readings of "Roll Over Beethoven". By reading the article in these three different ways, a composite view is formed that highlights the article's depth and layers.

Reading "Roll Over Beethoven": Verbatim

Visual

The text of "Roll Over Beethoven" is dense, with each of the fifty-five pages that make up the article offering insight into US-CLS. This insight includes the relationship between Gabel and Kennedy, the ideas each author represents, and this epoch in US-CLS's history. To focus the analysis, a close reading of page one is undertaken. Given the nontraditional structure of the article, its first page is a useful example of the piece as a whole, rather than being a more conventional abstract and introductory page.

The first reading is as a transcript of a real conversation; that "Roll Over Beethoven" is a verbatim transcription of speech-to-text. This dominant reading of the text is supported by the article's visual style, which stands in stark contrast to traditional academic articles, including others within the same edition of the *Stanford Law Review*. The combination of visual presentation and the text within this structure is characteristic of a typed conversation.

Visually, the article begins with a centred title, not italicised or with punctuation: "Roll Over Beethoven" is not a citation, but a new use for a phrase previously popularised by a song. Semiotically, the title is likely to denote the Berry song of the same name, perhaps even as far as creating a musical memory for those who know the song. However, for those not familiar with it, the connotative understanding is about the need for a long-dead composer to move out of the way, which still offers a similar effect to the dominant understanding. Strengthening the connection to the song, the authors include four lines of lyrics after their names, and before the body of text:

> Roll over Beethoven
> Tell Tchaikovsky the news
> I got the rockin' pneumonia
> Need a shot of rhythm and blues[45]

The lyrics are laid out as they would be in the liner notes on a record, with each sentence representing a bar of the song. The first two lines finish a verse, before the next two lines start a new one. In this verbatim reading, it is hypothesised that the placement of this excerpt and the title of the article were chosen after the conversation was transcribed. This proposal is based on

---

[45] Gabel and Kennedy (n 1) 1.

the fact that there is no reference to the song in the body of the text, despite other popular culture references throughout.

Due to this lack of reference, it seems unlikely that Gabel or Kennedy decided to discuss their views on US-CLS with this specific song in mind or with any direct relation to it. As a postscript, however, the title and the lyrics guide the reader in pre-empting what the article is about: the need for new ideas as a cure to classical ailments, and for a changing of the guard.

The song sets a tone for the article, but perhaps more so for US-CLS as a movement. In a literal sense, the song *Roll Over Beethoven* is about a rebellious, new wave of rock 'n' roll, taking over from established and revered classical composers Ludwig van Beethoven and Pyotr Ilyich Tchaikovsky. The allusion between rock versus classical music and US-CLS versus a liberal or formalist approach to law can be drawn from this. In both the song and the early works of US-CLS, the critique goes beyond an immediate predecessor, instead tackling more foundational elements of their respective media. For example, in the song, Berry doesn't deride jazz or country; instead he challenges a dominant understanding of what "proper" music should be. In US-CLS, this type of critique is evident in Kennedy's "The Structure of Blackstone's Commentaries",[46] challenging Blackstone's foundational eighteenth-century tome.

After this lyrical subheading, the transcribed conversation begins. The first page of the article contains four blocks of text, each assigned to a speaker, either Duncan or Peter. The language is punctuated in a conversational style, with short sentences that give a sense that the conversation was already underway when somebody decided to hit "record". Duncan's opening line, "You are betraying our programme by conceptualizing it", enforces this point.[47] Despite being a fully-formed sentence it bears little resemblance to a standard introductory line. Given the lyrical flow of the preceding subheading, Duncan's sentence is a jarring introduction to the piece. However, despite this juxtaposition, the opening line introduces the reader to a dominant theme within the article: the play between doing US-CLS and conceptualising it. The difference between these is seen throughout as Duncan and Peter toy with how and if US-CLS could or should be conceptualised.

The appearance of the article, and specifically the opening page, set expectations for what is being presented. The authors do not declare a reason for their stylistic choice, but there are certain possible or plausible reasons that can be inferred from it. In his framing of US-CLS as modern art, Luban offers a very in-depth analysis of "Roll Over Beethoven". Addressing

---

[46] Duncan Kennedy, "The Structure of Blackstone's Commentaries" (1979) 28 *Buffalo Law Review* 209.
[47] Ibid.

the article's style, he simply asks the reader, "But why do it that way?"[48] While Luban then gives six points on his understanding of "Roll Over Beethoven", he deliberately does not answer this question. Instead Luban finishes his section on the article by stating that "[i]t keeps working on you after you have set it aside."[49]

The breadth Luban identifies is one of the challenges of thinking through the appearance of "Roll Over Beethoven", to which any number of meanings could be ascribed. For example, one could take a Derridean approach and argue that, in presenting speech as text, the authors are engaging with Jacques Derrida's logocentric bias, which contextually privileges certain ideas over another.[50] In this case, a law journal is a written rather than spoken text, and the speech-to-text nature of "Roll Over Beethoven" challenges this established hierarchy.[51] If the authors were taking this approach, it would also play into Derrida's preference for speech over text in *Of Grammatology*.[52] However, any such connection is made by the reader rather than explicitly by the authors, and whilst a Derridean reading of this style could be applicable, it is unlikely to be the first thing that springs to every reader's mind.

Alternatively, a verbatim reading, as the dominant approach to "Roll Over Beethoven", focuses on how the use of transcription aligns the article with other critical works of the time, which also included transcriptions of interviews and lectures.[53] Whether this alignment was deliberate or not is not something that can be discovered from the text itself. However, it can be argued through the authors' connections to other works and approaches.

Understanding "Roll Over Beethoven" as a transcription implies that it can be categorised with other philosophical and theoretical works that use transcriptions of lectures and interviews—particularly the works of US-CLS influencers Claude Lévi-Strauss and Michel Foucault. Through Kennedy's work specifically, there is a connection to both authors, which aids the argument that "Roll Over Beethoven" deliberately mirrored this format. In 1994, reminiscing about his early influences, Kennedy states that he "liked to go to coffee houses and listen to Joan Baez and Bob Dylan type stuff. Then I got interested in structuralism, particularly in people like Lévi-Strauss and

---

[48] Luban (n 15) 1,672.
[49] Ibid 1,675.
[50] Minda (n 26) 118.
[51] Ibid.
[52] Ibid 117. See Jacques Derrida, *Of Grammatology*, tr. Gayatri Chakravorty Spivak (Johns Hopkins University Press, 1976) [trans of: *De la Grammatologie* (1967)] 97–316.
[53] See, e.g., Jacques Lacan, Écrits: The First Complete Edition in English, tr. Bruce Fink (W. W. Norton, 2006).

Piaget."⁵⁴ Lévi-Strauss in particular appears throughout Kennedy's work, notably in "The Structure of Blackstone's Commentaries" and *A Critique of Adjudication (fin de siècle)*.⁵⁵ Lévi-Strauss's work appears in a similarly transcribed format: for example, *Myth and Meaning*, a compilation of lectures given as part of the CBC radio series *Ideas*.⁵⁶

Moving from transcribed lectures to transcribed interviews, this same speech-to-text style is found within Foucault's *Power/Knowledge*.⁵⁷ Most notably there is a similarity between "Roll Over Beethoven" and a conversation with Foucault and others titled "Confessions of the Flesh",⁵⁸ led by Alain Grosrichard. Although it came several years later, Kennedy utilised this same collection for his 1991 article, "The Stakes of Law, or Hale and Foucault!"⁵⁹ In both "Roll Over Beethoven" and "Confessions of the Flesh", the texts appear to offer an insight into other works of the authors, providing insider access or acting as addendums to the texts in question. For Foucault, this is his use of the term *dispositif* in his first volume of *The History of Sexuality*.⁶⁰ For Gabel and Kennedy, it is US-CLS as a whole, or at least US-CLS at its current point in time.

However, despite the similarities between the structures of "Confessions of the Flesh" and "Roll Over Beethoven", the texts differ greatly in terms of who leads the discussion and the resulting content. In "Confessions of the Flesh", Foucault is being asked by Grosrichard et al. about certain aspects of his work, and elaborating on or defending them. In contrast, "Roll Over Beethoven" is a conversation between two colleagues, a discussion rather than an interview. Stylistically, approaching "Roll Over Beethoven" as a transcribed conversation, or what Luban calls a "rap session", there is an assumption that the informality of a conversation between colleagues is more relaxed and inviting than a traditional article would be. However, this is immediately rebutted by the content and direction of the "conversation".

---

54 Gerard J. Clark, "A Conversation with Duncan Kennedy" (1994) 24(2) *Suffolk University Law School Journal* 56.
55 Kennedy, *A Critique of Adjudication* (n 36) 133 nn 2.
56 Claude Lévi-Strauss, *Myth and Meaning* (Routledge, 1989) v.
57 Michel Foucault, *Power/Knowledge*, ed. Colin Gordon, tr. Colin Gordon et al. (Harvester Press, 1980).
58 Conversation with Alain Grosrichard et al., ibid 194.
59 Duncan Kennedy, "The Stakes of Law, or Hale and Foucault!" (1991) 15(4) *Legal Studies Forum* 327; see also Ben Golder, "The Distribution of Death: Notes Towards a Bio-Political Theory of Criminal Law" in Matthew Stone, Illan rua Wall, and Costas Douzinas (eds), *New Critical Thinking: Law and the Political* (Routledge, 2012) 91.
60 Michel Foucault, *The History of Sexuality: Volume One and Introduction*, tr. Robert Hurley (Pantheon Books, 1978).

With this interpretation, there is an uneasiness to the text, as it sits someway between the recording of a public discussion and a curated article. The reader is left not knowing if they are reading a natural discussion on US-CLS, or what Gabel and Kennedy want to be read on US-CLS. Whilst this combination of visual structure and rhetoric manipulates the reader, it also demonstrates that there is a great deal of depth to the points being made. On a practical level, the format still allows the insights of an addendum or companion text: for example, Peter addresses the issue of rights:

> Exactly what people don't need is their *rights*. What they need are the actual forms of social life that have to be created through the building of movements that can overcome illusions about the nature of what is political, like the illusion that there is an entity called the state, that people possess rights.[61]

This statement gets to the heart of a controversial approach taken by US-CLS towards rights, but is not bound by the conventions of a traditional article. Instead, Peter can clearly articulate a position without the necessary formality required in a traditional journal article, such as citations or signposts leading to the statement. The downside to this approach is that such a clear statement critiquing rights is buried two-thirds of the way through the article. An issue that can be understood through further analysis is the conflict between the simplistic layout and the complexity of the text.

Textual

The complexity of "Roll Over Beethoven" is evident from Duncan's utterance in the opening line: "You are betraying our program by conceptualizing it." The statement's audience is ambiguous; if this were a private conversation, then the statement would be addressed to Duncan's counterpart, Peter. However, if this were a traditionally written paper, the opening line would be more likely to be a response to whomever asked for US-CLS to be conceptualised. Alternatively, Duncan's audience could be anyone with an interest in US-CLS who has asked, "What is Critical Legal Studies?"

The following lines offer little in the way of clarification. Still addressing the anonymous "you" from the opening line, Duncan rejects the associated idea that US-CLS's "goal is to return to the unalienated situation". In response, Peter states simply that it's "[n]ot that", before he reasons with Duncan that the Crits need to realise that there is an "unalienated relatedness that is immanent within our alienated situation". This reply does little to clarify whether or not it was Peter who asked for a conceptualisation of US-CLS, or if he is merely clarifying the issues in Duncan's original statement.

---

[61] Gabel and Kennedy (n 1) 33 (emphasis in original).

Similarly to the different readings of the article's image, the text itself is open to different interpretations. The one constant across a variety of possible readings is that the reader is always an observer of the conversation taking place.[62] Even if they are the "you" referred to within Duncan's opening line, they are acknowledged but not engaged with directly, privy to this intimate US-CLS discussion only as a voyeur. This voyeuristic position is strengthened with the familiarity in tone between Peter and Duncan, which further distances the reader and adds to a mix of formality and informality throughout.

Through this mixed approached, "Roll Over Beethoven" demonstrates the complexity and associated issues that come with "a relatively large, loosely organized theory group".[63] From the use of the author's full names at the top of the page, to their first names only designating who has said what, to the old pop song and terms like "intersubjective zap",[64] the article makes a deliberate demonstration not only of the difficulty of conceptualising US-CLS, but also of US-CLS as a whole. In doing this Peter and Duncan articulate the difficulties they and other Crits face tackling other questions, including the biggest question that US-CLS faced:

> I've been asked a million times why CLS "failed," but it seems a more interesting question how such an overtly leftist, anti-mainstream academic movement, with no outside funding of any kind, could take off, expand so quickly, and last for about fifteen years as a highly visible factor in legal academia (of all places).[65]

Richard Michael Fischl restates the question most succinctly in the way it was put to him: "The problem with critical legal studies is that it didn't offer any alternative program. Now I'm no great defender of the rule of law, but what would you put in its place?"[66] In Fischl's article, this question is not answered.

Leaving aside the ramifications that would come from providing a specific plan or map to a nondoctrinal mode of thought, "Roll Over Beethoven" gives not only a reason why this didn't occur, but a glimpse at the mess in trying to formulate an answer. When Peter and Duncan address the conceptualisation of US-CLS, a related but significantly smaller question, they display

---

[62] Contra, Luban (n 15) 1,671, who states that certain devices "attempt explicitly to acknowledge the very problematic relationship between book and reader (beholder), by forcing the reader out of the voyeuristic mode in which we customarily appropriate scholarship."
[63] Jeff Manza, "Critical Legal Studies" (1990) 35 *Berkeley Journal of Sociology* 137, 137.
[64] Gabel and Kennedy (n 1) 4.
[65] Duncan Kennedy, *Legal Education and the Reproduction of Hierarchy: A Polemic Against the System* (New York University Press, 2004) 204.
[66] Richard Michael Fischl, "The Question that Killed Critical Legal Studies" (1992) 17(4) *Law & Social Inquiry* 779, 780.

the jargonised, drawn-out, and generally futile nature of trying to answer the much bigger question: what do you replace the rule of law with?

As the article continues with some natural stream-of-conscious banter, it always returns to the same "idea" of US-CLS: now that it exists, how does it continue without being further co-opted? The conversation remains reflective, addressing US-CLS retreats, important terminology, and the fears (primarily from Duncan) associated with creating something without being able to control it. As each term and topic is addressed, the language of both Peter and Duncan is progressive, examining how US-CLS might or should continue. The verbatim reading of the text allows the reader to experience a candid account of an organic and lively field of critique and jurisprudence, bearing witness to the intricacies and difficulties experienced by those partially responsible for it. Although the article deals with a number of issues that eventually led to the end of US-CLS, the authors tackle these with optimism, rather than harking back to earlier US-CLS for guidance.

Reading "Roll Over Beethoven": Scripted

If "Roll Over Beethoven" were not published in a law journal, its style would suggest it was a script as much as a transcription. Given the discussion of the visual power of the article, its presentation as a script adds yet another layer to the article's depth. There are several scripting conventions within the article—most notably the repetition of a symbol, which appears throughout: a trefoil, looking like a black club with a line a through it. Symbolically this breaks up the conversation—perhaps where the tape was stopped or passages were edited from the verbatim reading. However, it can also be read as signifying a change of scene.[67] Finally there are the separate voices of Peter and Duncan, who maintain their individual character and direction throughout, even when agreeing or discussing the same theme.

The use of "Roll Over Beethoven" as the title of the script aligns the piece with other plays that use metaphorical titles. From a theatrical perspective, "Roll Over Beethoven" can be matched with plays like Henrik Ibsen's *A Doll's House*,[68] or Tennessee Williams's *The Glass Menagerie*,[69] which are, respectively, not about doll's houses or glass cages for animals. Instead these titles are metaphors for the themes of the plays, in the same way that "Roll Over Beethoven" conjures lyrical imagery about a cultural revolution, rather than the physical movement of classical composers. The titles represent their script's content figuratively. Whilst this is implied in the verbatim reading, the lineage of

---

[67] Gabel and Kennedy (n 1) 14, 26, 36, 44.
[68] Henrik Ibsen, *A Doll's House* (CreateSpace, 2013).
[69] Tennessee Williams, *The Glass Menagerie* (Penguin, 2009).

metaphoric titles is more closely aligned with fictional or allegorical tales than with traditional academic articles, allowing for clarity and a stronger purpose in a scripted reading. The metaphorical title also sets up the reader to wonder what is real, what is fictional, and what is metaphorical within the body of the text.

An excerpt from Berry's lyrics follows the title, which in a scripted understanding would not be read or spoken; instead, these would be heard by the audience as the song plays. There are two dominant ways for songs and sound to be incorporated into a performance: as either diegetic or non-diegetic sound. Diegetic sound is the sound coming from within the script, that is, Peter or Duncan speaking. Non-diegetic sound is heard by the audience only, for example the shark's leitmotif in *Jaws*.[70] The characters do not hear this ominous music; instead the audience is given an auditory clue that the shark is coming closer. The excerpt of music that begins "Roll Over Beethoven" could therefore be either diegetic, so that Peter and Duncan could hear it, or non-diegetic and for the audience only. The non-diegetic use of the song would have a similar effect to the lyrics being stated in the verbatim reading, framing the content for the audience only. However, a diegetic use would expand the effect. If the song were heard by the characters, then there might be an effect on the direction of the conversation on revolutionary ideas and popular culture, influenced on some level by hearing that song.

As a script, "Roll Over Beethoven" lacks any stage direction. This does not remove it from the realms of being a script; stage directions may be left to the imposition of a director. A scene description is normally set before a scene begins; in "Roll Over Beethoven" this would appear under the title and before the excerpt of music. This description is, as with any directions in a script, usually fairly idiosyncratic,[71] but some basic elements tend to be included. For "Roll Over Beethoven" these would be the location, the set, and the characters.

Given the jargon-heavy and dense text of "Roll Over Beethoven", it would be best paired with an informal setting. Such direction juxtaposes preconceptions of Harvard Law School, the celebrity of Gabel and Kennedy within US-CLS, and the content of the text—perhaps by placing them visually within an American diner. The traditional Americana implied by the

---

[70] *Jaws*, dir. Steven Spielberg (Universal Studios, 1975).

[71] See, e.g., Arthur Miller's emphasis on specific character direction in *Death of a Salesman*; conversely see the more reserved direction in August Strindberg's *The Father*. Arthur Miller, *Death of a Salesman: Certain Private Conversations in Two Acts and a Requiem* (Penguin, 2000); August Strindberg, *Three Plays*, tr. Peter Watts (Penguin, 1975).

diner sits at odds with the Ivy League scholars and their critics' assumptions about their lifestyles.[72]

This proposed image borrows from the directorial eye of Jim Jarmusch, who has previously created similar juxtapositions: specifically here, *Coffee and Cigarettes*,[73] a collection of vignettes, centred on scripted interactions between people over coffee and cigarettes. Directly, an allusion can be drawn to a famous vignette with Tom Waits and Iggy Pop.[74] The Cannes *Palme d'Or*–winning short film shows the interaction between two stars of alternative music meeting in a traditional diner. The dated décor, from the chequered table to the wood panels and lighting, sits at odds with the perception of glamour and celebrity, as well as with the expected, or perceived, alternative lifestyles of the musicians. This image challenges the perceptions and preconceptions of Waits and Pop, and could be used in a similar way with the perceptions and preconceptions of Peter and Duncan. In *Coffee and Cigarettes*, the fly-on-the-wall approach is presented on screen; however, it could easily be transposed to stage as a two-man, one-set play.

In spite of its dense nature, the text of "Roll Over Beethoven" is conversational. Stage direction should play up to this style, not requiring much direction for the characters themselves: they are talking at a table. A casual setting provides a balance between the informal image and the nature of the text. This interpretation provides a way to understand this presentation of US-CLS as "fascinating", in its traditional sense of bewitching or casting a spell over the viewer. The approach plays into the voyeuristic qualities seen in both the verbatim and scripted readings, as well as offering insights into the reactions of those who found the premise of US-CLS fascinating but who felt let down by those behind it.[75]

The scripted reading of "Roll Over Beethoven" allows this fascination to be fed, offering the reader (viewer or audience) a layered glimpse of the inner workings of US-CLS, leaving them to wonder how much of the interaction is based on fact. The informal image of Peter and Duncan at a diner gives scope for a more in-depth analysis, as it allows the viewer visual access to the

---

[72] Gordon, "Law Review and the Modern Mind" (n 31) 269.
[73] *Coffee and Cigarettes*, dir. Jim Jarmusch (Asmik Ace Entertainment, 2003).
[74] Although *Coffee and Cigarettes* came out in 2003, the scene with Tom Waits and Iggy Pop was released as a short film in 1993: *Coffee and Cigarettes: Somewhere in California*, also known as *Coffee and Cigarettes III*, dir. Jim Jarmusch (Cinesthesia Productions, 1993).
[75] Patricia J. Williams, "Alchemical Notes: Reconstructing Ideals from Deconstructed Rights" (1987) 22 *Harvard Civil Rights–Civil Liberties Law Review* 401, 401–2; Goodrich, "Duncan Kennedy as I Imagine Him" (n 36).

private workings of US-CLS, while the complexity of the text still holds them at arm's length.

Reading "Roll Over Beethoven": Performance

Building on the two readings already provided, there is another way to understand "Roll Over Beethoven". Taking its cues from the scripted reading, this final analysis understands the publication of "Roll Over Beethoven" as an act of "Performance".[76] To conceive of "Roll Over Beethoven" as a performance, it is necessary to move past the imaginary Peter and Duncan in a diner, toward an avant-garde understanding of a performance as "performance art".

Sally Banes's account of Performance may be adapted to clarify how the term can be applied to nontraditional performances.[77] Her account presents performance as separate from, and not bound by, a theatre or stage: "The 'mediumless genre' of Performance is too heterogeneous to be captured by 'essential definitions'."[78] This capitalisation of the proper noun "Performance" denotes the mediumlessness of this term, in contrast to the common use of the noun, "performance".

Simon Shepherd and Mick Wallis investigate the idea of Performance as art and its ties to the 1960s desire to "break down barriers".[79] Drawing on the work of Antonin Artaud and Noël Carroll, the authors argue that, through this lens, Performance is used to emphasise spectacle and was seen in the 1960s in "Happenings and Living Theatre".[80] For US-CLS, there are strong thematic crossovers with theatre, postmodernism, and its countercultural roots. As Kimberlé Crenshaw remembers in a 2011 reflection on US-CLS: "[US-]CLS conferences were a mix of heavy theory, whimsical aspiration, dramatic performances, and other remnants of 1960s counter-culturalism."[81] Similar to Luban's analysis of "Roll Over Beethoven" as modern art is the idea of "Roll Over Beethoven" as a "spectacle".[82]

Positioning "Roll Over Beethoven" as Performance provides the article with the power to say things that verbatim or scripted readings cannot—a subtext that is not immediately visible, or that gains greater impact through performance. There is a theatrical history to this new power, seen within

---

[76] Simon Shepherd and Mick Wallis, *Drama/Theatre/Performance* (Routledge, 2004) 82.
[77] Ibid.
[78] Ibid.
[79] Ibid 83.
[80] Ibid.
[81] Kimberlé Williams Crenshaw, "Twenty Years of Critical Race Theory: Looking Back to Move Forward" (2011) 43(5) *Connecticut Law Review* 1,253, 1,288.
[82] Luban (n 15) 1671–7.

Hamlet and the *Murder of Gonzago* (the famous "play within a play"),[83] or *The Crucible*[84] and its critique of McCarthyism through a Salem-based allegory. However, given the radical political nature of "Roll Over Beethoven", as well as the philosophical influences on US-CLS, a closer ally for analysis is Bertolt Brecht's Epic Theatre.[85] With the influence of the Frankfurt School and Karl Marx on both Brecht and US-CLS,[86] it is possible to analyse "Roll Over Beethoven" using this Brechtian method.

Epic Theatre addresses or ventilates problems[87] through "[i]ts expository character and its emphasis on virtuosity".[88] These aspects of Epic Theatre can be seen in "Roll Over Beethoven", with its expository character seen via the self-reflective US-CLS critique of US-CLS, literally exposing its inner workings. The virtuosity of "Roll Over Beethoven" is more subjective but can arguably be identified in the time and effort spent by Peter and Duncan on minor issues, evidencing their concern with the trajectory of US-CLS and with how to critique without crystallisation. Whilst these identifications can be made, "Roll Over Beethoven" lacks one tenet of Epic Theatre: alienation.

In his development of Epic Theatre, Brecht focused on the emotional alienation of the audience, who knew they were watching a play:[89]

> The integration of experience into teaching means not only that knowledge is not solely derived from the outside—as if the students simply had to be made to see, their false consciousness stripped away as if removing a blindfold—but that it includes the experience of alienation: the relation between what is and what ought to be, between real and ideal, between ideology and the everyday. For Brecht, the goal was for a collective to examine its own conditions and to chart the parameters of its possibilities for change.[90]

---

[83] William Shakespeare, *Hamlet*, ed. Bernard Lott (Longman, 1997) 105–28.
[84] Miller (n 71).
[85] W. B. Worthen, *The Wadsworth Anthology of Drama* (Thomson Wadsworth, 4th ed, 2004) 919–22; see also Phyllis Hartnoll, *A Concise History of the Theatre* (Thames and Hudson, 1978) 252–6.
[86] The connection to Brecht is more clear. See, e.g., Philip Glahn, "Work, Class and the Struggle with Marxism, 1929–33", in Philip Glahn, *Bertolt Brecht* (Reaktion Books, 2014) 93; Mark Tushnet, "Critical Legal Studies: A Political History" (1991) 100(5) *Yale Law Journal* 1,515, 1,525; see generally Akbar Rasulov, "CLS and Marxism: A History of an Affair" (2014) 5(4) *Transnational Legal Theory* 622.
[87] Worthen (n 85).
[88] Ibid.
[89] Ibid.
[90] Glahn (n 86) 100.

"Roll Over Beethoven" makes numerous mentions of alienation and "alienating their audience",[91] which demonstrates a potential alignment with the Brechtian criteria. However, in his description of Brecht's alienation, Philip Glahn continues that the examination undertaken by the collective was "an active, participatory process: 'The *Lehrstück* [Brecht's Epic Theatre] teaches by being played, not by being seen'."[92] Given the dominant view of "Roll Over Beethoven" as a transcript, which is read or seen, it is difficult to consider it Epic Theatre. However, "Roll Over Beethoven" is not far off this definition and whilst it is not strictly Epic Theatre, as Performance "Roll Over Beethoven" can still be understood through this radical approach.

Following the historical development of radical theatre, "Roll Over Beethoven" aligns more closely with a follower and critic of Brecht's, the creator of "Invisible Theatre", Augusto Boal.[93] Boal's developments of radical theatre critique Brecht's idea of alienation and the audience viewing the Performance.[94] In Invisible Theatre, Boal situates theatrical performances within nontraditional spaces,[95] presenting issues to people who do not know they are watching something rehearsed. In this method, Boal describes the newly awakened audience as "spect-actors",[96] arguing that this guerrilla approach is a true form of theatre from its earliest origins.[97] In Boal's Invisible Theatre, there is a way to highlight issues through performance with an unknowing audience.

> The chosen subject must be an issue of burning importance, something known to be a matter of profound and genuine concern for the future spect-actors. From that starting point, a small play is constructed. The actors must play their parts as if they were playing in a traditional theatre,

---

[91] See, e.g., Gabel and Kennedy (n 1) 1 for "alienate" and p. 3 for "alienation". Both terms are then used throughout the article.
[92] Glahn (n 86) 100–1.
[93] Augusto Boal, *Theatre of the Oppressed*, tr. Charles A. McBride (Theatre Communications Group, 1993) 83.
[94] See Worthen (n 85) 922.
[95] See generally Yasco Horsman, *Theaters of Justice: Judging, Staging, and Working Through in Arendt, Brecht, and Delbo* (Stanford University Press, 2011) 91–2. In this chapter, Horsman addresses the relationship between Brecht and Sergej Tretiakov, and their desire to restructure the theatrical stage, changing the perception between audience and stage. Whilst Brecht did this, it was pushed further still by Augusto Boal and his Invisible Theatre. See also Jacques Rancière, *The Emancipated Spectator*, tr. Gregory Elliott (Verso, 2011) 2–3.
[96] Augusto Boal, *Games for Actors and Non-Actors*, tr. Adrian Jackson (Routledge, 1999) xxx.
[97] Ibid xxvi. See also Rancière (n 95) 4: "What is required is a theatre without spectators, where those in attendance learn from as opposed to being seduced by images: where they become active participants as opposed to passive voyeurs."

for a traditional audience. However, when the play is ready, it will be performed in a place which is not a theatre and for an audience which is not an audience.[98]

Boal's last line portrays the reader of the 1984 *Stanford Law Review* as "an audience which is not an audience".[99] Those who picked up the journal were there to read articles, not witness an act of theatre, and as such those who read "Roll Over Beethoven" reacted more strongly than if it had been a "standard" article[100]—reacting to "Roll Over Beethoven" not as readers, but as spect-actors.

As a radical piece of Invisible Theatre, the audience is central to the author's mind; as Boal articulated, the topic must be a genuine concern for the spect-actors.[101] In "Roll Over Beethoven" the topic is US-CLS, a genuine concern for the audience. The audience is likely to be made up from Crit fellow travellers and those with an interest in US-CLS, a sizeable proportion of whom would be concerned about the spread and perceived negative influence of US-CLS.[102] This latter category of reader can be lumped together as critics of US-CLS: generally, liberals and conservatives (amongst others) who would read the *Stanford Law Review*. With this audience in mind, the subtext in "Roll Over Beethoven" taunts and targets these critics of US-CLS.

In both the verbatim and scripted readings there are jabs woven within the text, subtly responding to the common critiques and questions launched at US-CLS. These jabs can be seen more clearly within the Performance analysis through the idea that "plays are not meaningful in themselves", but that the context in which they are read or performed creates their meaning.[103] For example, the impact felt within *Hamlet* by the performance of the *Murder of Gonzago* would not have comparable if the royal family had not been in attendance. Similarly, *The Crucible* needs to be contextualised with reference to McCarthyism for it to move beyond a story of witch-hunts in Massachusetts. For "Roll Over Beethoven" its references to popular culture operate as cultural artefacts, which insult the critics of US-CLS.

One of the notably strange but seemingly overlooked issues with "Roll Over Beethoven" is that, despite being published in 1984, it uses a song title from 1956. The use of this song could be justified if nothing with similar revolutionary themes had come out in the twenty-eight years since its

---

[98] Boal, *Games for Actors* (n 96) 6: "wereplaying" [sic] in original.
[99] Ibid.
[100] See, e.g., Minda (n 26).
[101] Boal, *Games for Actors* (n 96) 6.
[102] See generally Teles (n 17).
[103] Worthen (n 85) 7.

release—however, the musical revolution of the 1960s had occurred, and had directly affected broader society. Robert Albrecht articulates this impact, describing the music of the 1960s as "an essential motivating force—not just a sonic wallpaper—behind the rebellions of the period".[104]

Moving closer to 1984, the rise of US-CLS can also be seen as parallel to the initial rise of punk, with seminal British and US punk bands forming and releasing albums in the mid-1970s to the mid-1980s. Releases during this time included the Ramones' *Rocket to Russia* in 1977, the Sex Pistols' *Never Mind The Bollocks* in 1977, the Clash's *London Calling* in 1979, and Dead Kennedys' *Plastic Surgery Disasters* in 1982—any of which contained songs with similar allegorical, revolutionary titles.

While readers of the *Stanford Law Review* may not have been as familiar with Dead Kennedys as they were with Chuck Berry, there was a litany of terminology within the 1984 *Stanford Law Review* that they would have been equally unfamiliar with. Instead, the use of *Roll Over Beethoven* was due to its familiarity—not to aid the reader, but to taunt and position those who opposed to US-CLS.

The idea of *Roll Over Beethoven* as a cultural artefact included to taunt readers is strengthened with the use of a second pop-culture reference, the "pods" from *Invasion of the Body Snatchers*, which was also released in 1956.[105] In both *Roll Over Beethoven* and *Invasion of the Body Snatchers* there is a clear divide of characters, broadly seen as the establishment versus the rebels; and in both, the narrative presents the rebels as the heroes or the "right" side to be on. For *Roll Over Beethoven*, its importance was discussed above, as a title, a lyrical reference point, and potentially a diegetic sound. However, the use of *Invasion of the Body Snatchers* follows and strengthens this analysis. The film is first referenced by Duncan several pages into "Roll Over Beethoven", where he alludes to both "body snatchers" and "pods".[106] Their mention comes in the context of the likely usurpation of US-CLS ideas by non-Crits.[107]

In the endnotes, the journal editors[108] explain that "[t]he reference illustrates the manner in which one's ideas and expressions can be appropriated

---

[104] Robert Albrecht, "'In My Life': The Transformative Power of Music and Media during the Rebellions of the 1960s" in Brian Cogan and Thom Gencarelli (eds), *Baby Boomers and Popular Culture: An Inquiry into America's Most Powerful Generation* (Praeger, 2015) 191.
[105] *Invasion of the Body Snatchers* (n 4).
[106] Gabel and Kennedy (n 1) 7.
[107] Ibid.
[108] Luban (n 15) 1,673. Luban makes the claim that it is the editors who entered the notes, rather than Gabel or Kennedy: "And it is too, too perfect that the editors of the Stanford Law Review added their own footnotes to try to tame." Luban is referring to the fourteen endnotes that conclude "Roll Over Beethoven" (n 1) 54–5.

by others for their own purposes".[109] This telling quotation summarises most of the explicit arguments put forward in "Roll Over Beethoven" about the delicate and dangerous nature of defining and inevitably crystallising an idea. However, what is more important to the current argument is the identification of the "others" and who this moniker applies to.

The premise of *Invasion of the Body Snatchers* is that aliens arrive on Earth and, after finding a sleeping body, they replicate the form, killing the original and using the duplicate body for their own alien purpose. The analogy to the appropriation of ideas is clear, but this description is also a classic cinematic trope: aliens versus humans, or more universally, good versus evil. In the film, the alien invasion is only thwarted by those who rebel against this new seemingly serene, but non-human (alien) existence. Those who accept or don't fight the invasion are soon turned into "pods" before being born again as conformists to the new regime. *Invasion of the Body Snatchers* echoes *Roll Over Beethoven*, with both works designating those with an interest in US-CLS as either cool and heroic Chuck Berry rock 'n' rollers, fighting to stop an alien invasion, or as stuffy, evil gatekeepers who welcome an unthinking alien existence.

Framed in this way, the specific use of both *Roll Over Beethoven* and *Invasion of the Body Snatchers* starts to make more sense than any contemporary critical film or song. This is compounded by the fact that both artefacts had been rereleased, either as cover songs,[110] or as remakes in the years since their release.[111] The film and the song were originally released in the childhoods of Peter and Duncan, and by extension those of a large part of their audience. The repetitions of each artefact, with both being remade in the 1960s and 1970s, serve as constant reminders about the divisions they draw.

The impact of this exploitation by Peter and Duncan can be understood further through Daniel Marcus's exploration of cultural nostalgia and its influence on the present. Marcus argues that, "For those alive in the 1950s and/or the 1960s, media imagery mixed with personal memories . . . form the subject material for personal historical interpretation"[112]—that is, those listening to *Roll Over Beethoven* or watching *Invasion of the Body Snatchers* were likely to position themselves as part of the "good guys", those who fought against the aliens, or those who supported the rise of rock 'n' roll. By laying claim to these cultural touchpoints, Gabel and Kennedy create a dichotomy that

---

[109] Gabel and Kennedy (n 1) 55.
[110] The Beatles in 1963; Electric Light Orchestra in 1973.
[111] In 1978 and after "Roll Over Beethoven" in 1993 and 2007.
[112] Daniel Marcus, *Happy Days and Wonder Years: The Fifties and the Sixties in Contemporary Cultural Politics* (Rutgers University Press, 2004) 92.

plays into the audience's cultural memory and individual identity.[113] US-CLS are now the protagonists and the rebels; conversely those wanting to co-opt or remove the existence of US-CLS are the bad guys, tinging any argument against US-CLS with this realisation.

From *Invasion of the Body Snatchers* to *The Matrix*

Unlike the depth and breadth seen in these three different readings of "Roll Over Beethoven", there is only one plausible reading of Jerry Anderson's "Law School Enters the Matrix: Teaching Critical Legal Studies". This does not mean that the article is not good, merely that it is comparatively regressive and constricted, a victim of its passively haunted state.

"Law School Enters the Matrix" was published in the *Journal of Legal Education*, a location which aids the understanding of Anderson's argument. Broadly, "Law School Enters the Matrix" tries to convince its readers that US-CLS is more than a subversive, Marxist movement of the 1980s. As such, Anderson does not offer a call to arms for a full-blown resurgence of US-CLS. Instead, he asks for US-CLS to be considered as a mechanism for teaching law students about legal critique. Anderson calls for a reimagination of sorts, positioning a new US-CLS to be considered in law schools, asking the question: "Is it possible to separate the analytical tools of CLS from the ideological baggage the movement brings with it?"[114] Anderson's reimagination is focused strongly on the image of US-CLS, how it is and was perceived, and how this can safely be challenged to provide a valuable teaching tool. Due to the context, subject matter, and Anderson's perceived audience of "Law School Enters the Matrix", his proposal is for a safe and legitimate US-CLS to be used as way to both engage and benefit law students.

Anderson's perspective on US-CLS may have been shaped by his own graduation from Stanford Law School in 1984,[115] the same year the *Stanford Law Review* ran its US-CLS edition. He witnessed US-CLS first hand, as a student, and then as a professor of law. Anderson posits his reimagination of US-CLS as a teaching tool through the use of popular culture—specifically the film, *The Matrix*. Anderson's analogy draws comparisons between the characters awakening to the "real" in the film, and the awakening that students like himself received when US-CLS was alive. *The Matrix* is used to offer students a contemporary way of learning about or understanding the broad premise of US-CLS without the jargon-heavy original texts—a

---

[113] Ibid 95.
[114] Ibid 205.
[115] Drake Law School, "Jerry Anderson Profile", *Faculty and Staff* (Web Page, 2023) <http://www.drake.edu/law/facstaff/directory/jerry-anderson>.

potentially approachable way to replace Roberto Unger or Mark Kelman's more complex summary works:[116]

> [T]here is no question that if you start students off with [US-]CLS jargon, such as the old "unalienated relatedness/fundamental contradiction" mumbo jumbo, you might get a few blank stares and some downright rude scoffs, especially from those who didn't major in philosophy. But if you say, "you know, like *The Matrix*," all of a sudden the lights go on and they may get it.[117]

The premise of Anderson's analogy to *The Matrix* is good, and clear lines can be drawn to US-CLS. However, beyond the simple recognition of similar themes, Anderson does not offer much depth to his analysis of either US-CLS or *The Matrix*. Anderson begins his paper with a clarification of two differing Critical Legal Studies, both of which are under the broad banner of this book's designator, US-CLS. Anderson refers to them as the "movement" and a "method of legal analysis",[118] a division reminiscent of Kennedy's approach to the death of US-CLS.[119] Anderson expressly states that the method of legal analysis is the focus of his paper. This division and Anderson's focus highlights an issue in PCLS writing, wherein it tries to strip back the imperfect whole of US-CLS and refine it to what Kennedy cynically calls a set of "bibliographical headings".[120]

In making this distinction, Anderson makes no mention the death of US-CLS, instead proposing that its disappearance was due its classification (wrongly) as passé or discredited. Although "Law School Enters the Matrix" argues why these assumptions were wrong, ironically the US-CLS Anderson is vouching for is itself passé, shaped to fit into the mould of a law-school mission statement that requires students to engage "critically". Given Anderson's preferred type of US-CLS, "Law School Enters the Matrix" does not advocate for a return to US-CLS, but is a PCLS paper advocating for and engaging with a discussion on PCLS—following a similar understanding of "Roll Over Beethoven" as a US-CLS paper engaging with US-CLS.

---

[116] Roberto Mangabeira Unger, *The Critical Legal Studies Movement* (Harvard University Press, 1983); Mark Kelman, *A Guide to Critical Legal Studies* (Harvard University Press, 1987).
[117] Anderson (n 2) 214 (emphasis in original).
[118] Ibid 201.
[119] Hope Yen, "As HLS Mulls Its Mission" (n 18); Yen, "Crits at HLS a Dying Breed?" (n 18); Duncan Kennedy, "Two Globalizations of Law & Legal Thought: 1850–1968' (2003) 36(3) *Suffolk University Law Review* 631.
[120] Yen, "As HLS Mulls Its Mission" (n 18).

Stylistically, "Law School Enters the Matrix" is well presented through Anderson's deliberate rhetoric. Instead of positioning himself as a Crit or an ardent fan of US-CLS, Anderson is positioned as a moderate (read: liberal) offering others within the same category the opportunity to (re)look at a moderate new US-CLS (PCLS). From this position, Anderson wastes no time addressing the likely fears of his fellow moderate, focusing on the dominant critiques of US-CLS: its language, its relation to radical thought, and its associated progressive subversion of law schools. He then mitigates any further broad concerns moderates might have, avoiding any subtleties or nuances that may be present:

> [S]ome argue that the theory does not add anything to the insights provided by legal realism and that, to the extent it goes beyond legal realism to attack the perpetuation of hierarchy, it basically preaches communism or anarchy, which most of us have no interest in promoting. The Marxists lost the Cold War, after all, and continuing to teach [US-]CLS is riding a dead horse ... Nevertheless, I hope to demonstrate in the next section that, even for those who do not accept the CLS theory wholeheartedly, the use of CLS analysis provides students insights beyond those of legal realism.[121]

By pre-emptively mitigating the fears that fellow moderates might have, Anderson is free to position PCLS as a lens for analysing law: a teaching tool. He demonstrates this teaching tool through an application of PCLS to classroom-type examples of questions on property and nuisance law, giving scenarios that are at once expanded in scope and considered through the PCLS lens.[122] The examples Anderson uses are effective in showing the broader ability one may gain by using a PCLS technique, both as a student and as an educator. However, the posthumous nature of the technique is evident with the focus on awareness of judicial ramifications and causes, rather than addressing or questioning the systems that perpetuate them. The simplicity in this method is easy to demonstrate, and arguably offers a way of critiquing existing judgments, but Anderson provides no way of returning to a US-CLS method.

The justification for Anderson's simplistic approach is that this new CLS gives law students a grasp of legal critique, as well educators who may have been baffled by US-CLS. Anderson puts himself in this category, a "merely mortal professor who will quite frankly admit that he doesn't quite understand everything Crits have written and isn't quite sure he agrees with it all",[123]

---

[121] Anderson (n 2) 202, 205–6.
[122] Anderson (n 2) 206–10: "Property Ownership Through a CLS Lens".
[123] Ibid 206 (quotation marks omitted for continuity).

concluding that "I suspect there are quite a few of us in this category".[124] The relief Anderson finds in this new simplicity is highlighted throughout the paper, focusing on the original impasse in the Crits' use of language and their accepted codes. However, in spite of Anderson's justifications for the approach he advocates, his argument reflects that in 2004, there was no other US-CLS than PCLS. The PCLS Anderson presents is both regressive, harking back to US-CLS and its original theorists, but also constricted, presenting a narrow approach under the guise of the safer and more simplistic PCLS.

"Law School Enters the Matrix": its approach to *The Matrix*

To understand PCLS, Anderson uses *The Matrix* as an analogy and teaching tool. However, the simplicity employed in his demonstration of PCLS continues with his analysis of *The Matrix*.[125] Anderson introduces the film with a similar mitigating approach to his introduction of PCLS, prefacing the first mention of *The Matrix* by "only half whimsically" using the film as an analogy. However, this whimsy appears to apply to Anderson's audience's perceptions, rather than his own thoughts on the film's usefulness as a teaching tool.

The author's caution may be better understood in context. Returning to the Critical Legal Studies family tree, the "broad" CLS of law and popular culture only emerged at a similar time to "Law School Enters the Matrix". For example, it wasn't until 2007 that William MacNeil's *Lex Populi* was published,[126] compiling articles on *Buffy the Vampire Slayer* from 2003,[127] and *The Lord of the Rings* (both the films from 2001–2004, and the books).[128] As a dominant voice in law and popular culture, MacNeil's development of this broad Critical Legal Studies can be seen as a benchmark for its emergence more generally.

In this era of development, Anderson's cautious approach can be better appreciated. As well, it helps categorise "Law School Enters the Matrix" less as law and popular culture and more as a link to US-CLS's use of popular culture and cultural artefacts, including the science fiction in "Roll Over Beethoven".

---

[124] Ibid 206 (quotation marks omitted for continuity).
[125] Ibid 202.
[126] William P. MacNeil, *Lex Populi: The Jurisprudence of Popular Culture* (Stanford University Press, 2007); See also Austin Sarat, Lawrence Douglas, and Martha Merrill Umphrey (eds), *Law on the Screen* (Stanford University Press, 2005). This book predates *Lex Populi*, drawing from a conference at Amherst in 2003; however, it does not tackle popular culture in the same way.
[127] William P. MacNeil, "'You Slay Me!': Buffy as Jurisprude of Desire", (2003) 24(6) *Cardozo Law Review* 2,421.
[128] Ibid 61. William P. MacNeil, "One *Recht* to Rule Them All! Law's Empire in the Age of *Empire*" in Andrew T. Kenyon and Peter D. Rush (ed), *An Aesthetics of Law and Culture: Text, Images, Screens (Studies in Law, Politics, and Society)* (JAI Press, 2004) 279.

Anderson makes this link explicit by citing "Roll Over Beethoven", after stating that, "Duncan Kennedy himself could have given the creators of *The Matrix* the idea for the movie in a conversation with Peter Gabel back in 1984."[129] The analysis Anderson provides compares the plight of US-CLS, especially via "Roll Over Beethoven", with the plot of *The Matrix*:

> [T]he main thrust of [US-]CLS is that the entire legal system is merely an apparatus designed to appease the masses, fooling them into thinking that their needs may be addressed, while in fact its purpose is merely to keep them docile while perpetuating the hierarchy that provides the upper class with its advantages. Instead of pods filled with bodies attached to the power plant, just substitute workers stuck in cubicles in a high-rise office building, all working to feed the vast machine that lines the pockets of the CEO.[130]

However, Anderson's analysis does not go further than this. There is scope for this connection to be more in-depth, especially with the benefit of a "standard" article format. For example, the significance of the pod people in "Roll Over Beethoven" is assumed rather than made explicit, brought to the reader's attention by the editor's endnotes.[131] In Anderson's paper, the initial analysis and connection builds a foundation that could tackle the theme of pods and hierarchies twenty years later. Instead, Anderson focuses on the power of popular culture as a teaching tool. He states that *The Matrix* and, more broadly, popular culture as a whole can be beneficial for "modern students". He does not elaborate much further on why this is the case,[132] but a fair reading of his approach is that it is due to the accessibility and prevalence of popular cultural knowledge. Although Anderson does not mention it, this was the same pedagogical reasoning given by John Denvir in *Legal Reelism* several years earlier.[133]

Anderson frames "Law School Enters the Matrix" as "simple" and an "entrée into [US-]CLS theory", and both of these are achieved. In addition, the terms signal the goal of the paper to help break down the exclusivity and inaccessibility of US-CLS: "CLS tools will never be widely accepted if they remain the province only of those who speak in the accepted code", rather

---

[129] Anderson (n 2) 213.
[130] Ibid 211–12.
[131] Gabel and Kennedy (n 1) 54–5; Luban (n 15) 1,673.
[132] Anderson (n 2). Despite discussing the specific instances of the films *Titanic* and *Body Heat*, the article is not concerned with detailing the intricacies of using popular culture as a teaching tool—just that in Anderson's experience it has been successful.
[133] This technique is discussed at length by Denvir in John Denvir (ed), *Legal Reelism: Movies as Legal Texts* (University of Illinois Press, 1996). The ubiquitous nature of film allows a larger percentage of the population to understand the themes.

than to provide a "CLS for Dummies".[134] The paper is short, only sixteen pages, and while it discusses an interesting theory it never moves beyond a surface-level analysis.

Within "Law School Enters the Matrix" Anderson presents himself as reminding the reader of US-CLS, but instead he provides an introduction to PCLS. Openly, Anderson invokes the constricted and regressive PCLS, a version of Critical Legal Studies that simply leaves the difficulties of US-CLS behind. These difficulties are in the first instance replaced by Oscar-winning special effects, which as a teaching tool has merit. However, by the end of the article Anderson has given some specific classroom examples of PCLS, and a fitting analogy to US-CLS, but not much beyond this, concluding with no real insight into achieving the critical aims he has outlined.

Still, could this have been done any better? "Law School Enters the Matrix" spends roughly two-thirds of its content introducing and demonstrating the potential of PCLS. It is not until the final five pages that Anderson turns to "*Using* The Matrix *to Teach CLS*".[135] Under this heading, Anderson leaves the "how"-to-teach PCLS examples, and focuses on comparing US-CLS with *The Matrix*. There is an earlier mention of the film in the paper, proposing its purpose as a mechanism to introduce students to US-CLS. This mention, with a minor error regarding dates (he misremembers it as being released in 1996, not 1999), is the only mention of *The Matrix* until the section on how his teaching mechanism can be applied. Unlike for Peter and Duncan in "Roll Over Beethoven", the inclusion of popular culture is not nuanced throughout the article, but introduced and then applied. This difference in technique, in and of itself, is not problematic; however, the simplicity in its application demonstrates the haunted nature of this PCLS paper. Despite Anderson's unique US-CLS comparison, at the time of his article's publication the film was not new to academic work, with a host of resources available to further develop its application.

The Matrix was released in 1999, placing it within a significant cultural shift in technology against the impending new millennium. In the lead up to the end of the twentieth century, a time before smartphones and with limited social media, the online world held a subcultural status for those who engaged with it—a status repeatedly highlighted through film. For example, in 1995 both *Hackers* and *The Net* presented similar themes of the power of technology and how it could be manipulated by those able to use it.[136]

---

[134] Anderson (n 2) 202.
[135] Ibid 211.
[136] *Hackers*, dir. Iain Softley (United Artists, 1995); *The Net*, dir. Irwin Winkler (Columbia Pictures, 1995).

These films showed a shift in the depiction of the online world with their focus on "reality". This is especially evident when compared to previous science-fiction computer-based dystopias, such as the *Terminator* franchise,[137] or life-and-death virtual realities, such as *TRON*.[138] Although *The Matrix* is science fiction, it is contextually conditioned by this subcultural grouping and view of "reality" for underground hackers and technophiles. The movie's release sits within a moral panic about "Y2K", and the associated uncertainty about technology, machines, and data.[139] All of this helped solidify *The Matrix* as a well-known and influential cultural artefact.

By 2006, a collected edition of articles addressing *The Matrix* was published: *Matrix in Theory*.[140] Despite being published two years after Anderson's article, the works contained within the collection make reference to earlier phenomena, such as "conference papers, symposia, journal articles, edited collections . . . and university courses on philosophy and *The Matrix*", which predate Anderson's article.[141] As a cultural artefact, *The Matrix* has had a continued effect,[142] which had begun before Anderson's article was published. Within the legal field, this effect was evident in a practical rather than theoretical sense. In the early 2000s there were a number of criminal cases involving pleas of insanity related to defendants believing they were in *The Matrix*. From CNN in 2003:

> Hamilton, Ohio, resident Tonda Lynn Ansley was found not guilty by reason of insanity after claiming she thought her landlord was part of a conspiracy to brainwash and kill her. Ansley shot the woman several times in the head in July 2002. [Quoting Ansley] "They commit a lot of crimes in 'The Matrix,' . . . That's where you go to sleep at night and they drug you

---

[137] See *The Terminator*, dir. James Cameron (Hemdale, 1984); *Terminator 2: Judgement Day*, dir. James Cameron (Carolco Pictures, 1991).

[138] *TRON*, dir. Steven Lisberger (Walt Disney Productions, 1982).

[139] See, e.g., John Quiggin, "The Y2K Scare: Causes, Costs and Cures" (2005) 64(3) *Australian Journal of Public Administration* 46.

[140] Myriam Diocaretz and Stefan Herbrechter (eds), *The Matrix in Theory* (Rodopi, 2006); See also Kirsty Duncan, "Tracing the Law Through the Matrix" (2001) 10(2) *Griffith Law Review* 160.

[141] Chris Falzon, "Philosophy in *The Matrix*" in Diocaretz and Stefan Herbrechter (n 140) 97, 97–112. This collection came out in 2006; however, the references Falzon and other authors use are from previous years, including many that predate Anderson's article.

[142] See, e.g., the "red pill" from *The Matrix* co-opted for an extreme men's rights group on the website Reddit: "The Red Pill", *Reddit* (Web Page, accessed 7 November 2023) <https://www.reddit.com/r/theredpill>.

and take you somewhere else and then they bring you back and put you in bed and, when you wake up, you think that it's a bad dream."[143]

Whilst legal in nature, these cases are not directly relevant to Anderson's thesis. However, they were discussed publicly, and could have been used to compare and contrast the legal impact of the film.

A more applicable area from which Anderson could have drawn was *The Matrix*'s focus on philosophy, and then philosophy's focus on *The Matrix*. From a philosophical standpoint, an immediate connection can be drawn to Jean Baudrillard's *Simulacra and Simulation*.[144] Not only does the book appear in the film,[145] but there are direct connections in *The Matrix* to Baudrillard's concept of "the real".[146] The concept, which draws on people's connection to virtual or hyperrealities (TV, film, et cetera) compared to reality itself, is dominant in *The Matrix* and compounded by a line from the character Morpheus to the protagonist Neo: "Welcome to the desert of the real."[147] The connection between Baudrillard and *The Matrix* was discussed further by Slavoj Žižek in his 2002 book, *Welcome to the Desert of the Real*.[148] In either Baudrillard's original use or Žižek's updated interpretation, Anderson would have found stronger grounding for his attempt to connect US-CLS and *The Matrix*.

There are a number of reasons why Anderson did not need to use any of these materials which engaged with *The Matrix*. Under the argument that Anderson was constricted through his writing about US-CLS/PCLS, the limited level and scope of engagement throughout makes sense. An initial reading of "Law School Enters the Matrix" presents a seemingly acceptable way to teach law students about an existing mode of critique and keep them engaged through film. However, once it is read in conjunction with other works on US-CLS or *The Matrix*, the lack of development in the article is notable. Read on its own, this leads to the conclusion that Anderson's premise was novel and worth developing—but due to its PCLS status, "Law School Enters the Matrix" is in fact constricted and regressive.

---

[143] Matt Bean, "'Matrix' Makes Its Way into Courtrooms as Defense Strategy", *CNN* (online, 21 May 2003) <http://edition.cnn.com/2003/LAW/05/21/ctv.matrix.insanity>; Mark Schone, "The Matrix Defense", *The Boston Globe* (online, 9 November 2003) <http://archive.boston.com/news/globe/ideas/articles/2003/11/09/the_matrix_defense>.

[144] Jean Baudrillard, *Simulacra and Simulation*, tr. Sheila Faria Glaser (University of Michigan Press, 1994) [trans of: *Simulacres et Simulation* (1981)] 1.

[145] *The Matrix* (n 3), 00:08:27.

[146] Baudrillard (n 144) 1.

[147] *The Matrix* (n 3) 00:41:13.

[148] Slavoj Žižek, *Welcome to the Desert of the Real* (Verso, 2002).

When reading "Roll Over Beethoven"—as either a verbatim transcript, a script to be performed, or as a Performance—different levels of insight were gained, demonstrating what US-CLS was, and what it could and could not do. In "Law School Enters the Matrix", only one plausible reading is possible, one that deliberately shies away from the intricacies in US-CLS, and embraces the constricted and regressive PCLS.

Despite approaching similar themes and closely aligned cultural artefacts, the papers are separated by the ways in which they interact with these subjects. In "Roll Over Beethoven", the authors face the troubles and difficulties of US-CLS, challenging and critiquing its position with the aim to move forward. Conversely, "Law School Enters the Matrix" harks back to US-CLS, but presents a weaker PCLS as the preferred method of enquiry. The similarly themed papers are understandably different in their approaches, but the constricted nature of "Law School Enters the Matrix" is evident and emblematic of all works of PCLS.

7

Navigating US-CLS

Into this wild Abyss the wary Fiend
Stood on the brink of Hell and looked a while, Pondering his voyage;
  for no narrow frith
He had to cross.

John Milton, Paradise Lost (1674)

The passive haunting of Posthumous Critical Legal Studies (PCLS) does not exonerate the foibles and failures of US-CLS. Instead, it provides a way to think through and reimagine the current state of Critical Legal Studies in the United States. Just because US-CLS was not regressive or constricted does not mean it did not face its own issues; according to its critics this ranged from the way the Crits dressed,[1] to the universities they taught at,[2] and the more substantial issue of what their work actually meant.

US-CLS faced critiques from a wide range of critics and sympathisers, from liberals to both broad and narrow Critical Legal scholars. These critiques range from meaningful interactions with US-CLS to *ad hominem* criticism of individual Crits, but can be generally divided into two camps: those outside US-CLS (primarily legal liberals) and critiques within Critical Legal Studies (both broad and narrow categories). The critiques approach US-CLS differently in both style and theme, but there are identifiable trends in both camps.

Generally, the critiques levelled at US-CLS from those outside the movement were more critical of US-CLS as a whole, not engaging with any nuance or subtleties in individual works. Collectively, the critiques from outside US-CLS position the movement as illegitimate, resulting in the critiques

---

[1] See *The New Republic* (Washington DC, 17 March 1986). The front page bears the heading, "Invasion of the Punk Professors".
[2] James D. Gordon III, "Law Review and the Modern Mind" (1991) 33(2) *Arizona Law Review* 265.

themselves being less substantial or intricate. There are exceptions to this, however they are a minority in the literature.[3]

Conversely, those critiquing US-CLS from within Critical Legal Studies are more inclined to view US-CLS as a legitimate enterprise, but take issue with certain approaches or theorists. It should be noted, however, that any connection or affiliation of the Crit critics does not lead to sympathy or sycophancy.

Liberal Critiques

In 1984, at the height of US-CLS, Paul Carrington published "Of Law and the River",[4] a short article in which he contrasts Mark Twain's *Life on the Mississippi* with nihilistic legal teaching. The article assesses the professional training in Twain's book and the author's preference for law schools to train future lawyers, something which he believes "legal nihilism" hinders. Carrington gives no definition of what he means by legal nihilism, but he does equate it with disbelief and incompetence in the individual.[5] The author does not openly name US-CLS as the nihilism in the law school; however, the only reference in the article which is not to Twain is to Roberto Unger's *The Critical Legal Studies Movement*.[6] Unger is referenced on the second-to-last page of the article, from which a thinly-veiled attack on US-CLS can be drawn:

> In an honest effort to proclaim a need for revolution, nihilist teachers are more likely to train crooks than radicals. If this risk is correctly appraised, the nihilist who must profess that legal principle does not matter has an ethical duty to depart the law school, perhaps to seek a place elsewhere in the academy.[7]

The article's pernicious approach to US-CLS drew a raft of criticism and concern from those associated with US-CLS, including Robert Gordon, Paul Brest, Guido Calabresi, and Owen Fiss.[8] This concern focused on academic freedom, a perceived return to "red baiting",[9] and Carrington's dichotomy

---

[3] See e.g., Andrew Altman, *Critical Legal Studies: A Liberal Critique* (Princeton University Press, 1990); Richard Bauman, *Ideology and Community in the First Wave of Critical Legal Studies* (University of Toronto Press, 2000).
[4] Paul D. Carrington, "Of Law and the River" (1984) 34 *Journal of Legal Education* 222.
[5] Ibid 226–7.
[6] Ibid 227 nn 21; Roberto Unger Mangabeira, *The Critical Legal Studies Movement* (Harvard University Press, 1983).
[7] Carrington (n 4) 227.
[8] Peter W. Martin, "'Of Law and the River,' and of Nihilism and Academic Freedom" (1985) 35 *Journal of Legal Education* 1.
[9] Ibid 16.

between the university and the law school.[10] Gordon's response to Carrington is the most detailed. Despite this, it can be summed up in his exasperation at Carrington's unfounded conclusions: "Just as I cannot think of anyone in American law teaching who thinks law is nothing but official whim, I can't think of anyone either who preaches the revolutionary overthrow of legality. This seems to be another imaginary bogey-man."[11] In response to Gordon, Carrington also wrote at length, but instead of doubling down, he acknowledged the underdeveloped nature of his original argument:

> If you are right about that, then my comments to which you take offense have little point. I am certainly aware that my concern is not appropriate with respect to all the persons having some sympathy or connection with [US-]CLS; it is for that reason that I tried to avoid referring to [US-]CLS as a corporate body, and chose to comment instead on Legal Nihilism, a phrase which I had thought likely to claim for their banner, but which may nevertheless apply to some.[12]

The response Carrington provides is not one of staunch opposition, as Gordon states in his next reply: "Your letter helps considerably to clarify the issues between us, as well as revealing more agreement than I would first have suspected to exist."[13]

Carrington appears to vindicate Gordon's argument of an "imaginary bogey-man".[14] His critique of US-CLS is not in and of itself concerning; instead what is concerning is the total lack of substance or engagement with US-CLS in his critique. His original article demonstrates a reactionary and dichotomous approach, which in spite of his later admission of the fact, spawned similar reactionary and dichotomous responses, praising the author's opposition to US-CLS.

For example, in response to Brest's concerns with the article, Louis Schwartz replied that he "found Carrington's piece brilliant, civilized, and insightful".[15] "Of Law and the River" is only eight pages long and, whether it does or does not unfairly target US-CLS, it is underdeveloped and objectively hard to call brilliant or insightful. However, for those in support of Carrington, the calm "correspondence in so leisurely 18th century fashion"[16]

---

[10] Ibid 26.
[11] Ibid 4.
[12] Ibid 10.
[13] Ibid 13.
[14] Ibid 4.
[15] Ibid 19.
[16] Ibid 13.

that occurred between the author and Gordon was replaced with more general criticisms that do not offer any real engagement with US-CLS. This can be seen further in another response to Brest's concerns. Phillip Johnson stated:

> The first thing that strikes me about your letter is its pure liberalism, so incongruous coming from a prominent member of a movement dedicated to exposing the mystification and reification of liberal legalism. Your letter expressly or impliedly incorporates a variety of concepts that I thought critical legal scholars had consigned to the trash can—academic freedom, rights, the marketplace of ideas that produces professional competence and moral development as if by an invisible hand, and especially the vision of the university as a neutral palace of learning which allows no orthodoxy to interfere with the pursuit of truth. Are you not at least a little embarrassed to invoke these long-since-deconstructed concepts on behalf of [US-]CLS?[17]

Johnson's response shifts the focus from the subject of Carrington's "Of Law and the River" to an argument about US-CLS issues with liberalism. In Johnson's context they are related, but the choice to begin his argument in this way deflects any real engagement with the issues the Crits raised with Carrington's article. Johnson's broad and dismissive "engagement" is emblematic of the liberal critiques of US-CLS, both at its peak and well into the PCLS era.

At the turn of the millennium, Arthur Austin published a listicle-type law review article: "The Top Ten Politically Correct Law Review Articles".[18] As the title makes clear, Austin's compilation is of specific articles that demonstrate "Law Political Correctness" or "LPC", something he sees as an approach and symptom of three connected sources: "Critical Race theorists composed of Blacks and females, feminists, plus the remnants of the Critical Legal Studies movement [US-CLS]".[19] In contrast to Carrington's "Of Law and the River", Austin provides more detailed engagement. Still, while his arguments are rooted in fact, they are hyperbolic and do not interact with the substance of his chosen subject.

> The control of scholarship is a critical avenue to the ultimate subversion of the Liberal establishment. The strategy is to scorch the earth: attack the assumed certainty of linearity with deconstruction, and replace the doctrinal model with the narrative genre—storytelling, allegory, and parable.[20]

---

[17] Ibid 18.
[18] Arthur Austin, "The Top Ten Politically Correct Law Review Articles" (1999) 27 *Florida State University Law Review*, 233.
[19] Ibid 234–5.
[20] Ibid 236.

Aside from scorching the earth (Blackstone survived US-CLS)[21] and giving definitive replacements,[22] Austin's assessment does accurately describe some elements of US-CLS and critical race theory. Within the top-ten list, Austin selects "Roll Over Beethoven" as his primary US-CLS choice, although he sadly adds little to the existing dialogue around this paper. However, Austin's analysis of Mary Joe Frug's "A Postmodern Feminist Legal Manifesto (An Unfinished Draft)" provides insight into the way liberals perceived the elite nature of those involved in US-CLS.[23] In terms of category, Frug's article sits comfortably within the broad Critical Legal Studies limb of the family tree; however, she was also an active member of US-CLS.[24] The article's publication during the decline of US-CLS, and its themes of postmodernism and feminist legal theory position it as a emblematic of a shift in critical legal scholarship at the time.

Austin's analysis takes a deliberately offensive and crude tone, notably when outlining the debate around the decision to publish Frug's paper posthumously after her murder. This debate gives context to the analysis, but the way in which it is approached demonstrates the flippancy with which he believes US-CLS and other critical scholars "should" be treated:

> She was stabbed to death near her home in an exclusive section of Cambridge, inflicted with five wounds in her chest and groin. The murderer has not been apprehended and rumors over motive continue to circulate, including the belief by some of her ardent supporters that she was targeted by a patriarchal conspiracy.[25]

Highlighting where and how she was killed—that is, that she lived in an "exclusive" neighbourhood and that she was stabbed in "her chest and groin"—adds no value to Austin's critique but confers a sexualisation on her death and her position within the legal elite. There is an implication that Frug either deserved to die due to her politics, or that women are murdered and it is nothing to do with the patriarchy; both are unpleasant positions to take and neither adds to the critique of Frug's writing.

---

[21] See, e.g., Duncan Kennedy, "The Structure of Blackstone's Commentaries" (1979) 28 *Buffalo Law Review* 205.

[22] See Richard Michael Fischl, "The Question that Killed Critical Legal Studies" (1992) 17(4) *Law & Social Inquiry* 779.

[23] Austin, "The Top Ten" (n 18) 237–8; Mary Joe Frug, "A Postmodern Feminist Legal Manifesto (An Unfinished Draft)" (1992) 105(5) *Harvard Law Review* 1,045.

[24] See Mary Joe Frug, "Re-Reading Contracts: A Feminist Analysis of a Contracts Casebook", (1985) 34 *American University Law Review* 1,065.

[25] Austin, "The Top Ten" (n 18) 238.

Austin continues by citing "[a] colleague of Frug [who] said: 'They engaged in a necrophiliac gang bang upon the living body of her work'", in response to the *Harvard Law Review*'s decision to publish "A Postmodern Feminist Legal Manifesto (An Unfinished Draft)". Of itself this quotation adds context; however, Austin begins the very next sentence by calling Frug's "Manifesto" "a terrorist exercise in self-flagellation".[26]

This theme of dismissing rather than engaging with the text continues in response to Frug's argument that the female body "cringes from the culture of oppression created by a system that uses linguistic ploys to render the female rapeable."[27] Austin replies that this result is the thinking of a concussed LPC, before admonishing Frug for citing Madonna and using both "fuck" and "cunt" in her assessment. Finding both words too confrontational to repeat, Austin refuses to engage with them and instead says the "'F' and 'C' words".[28]

Whilst childish, Austin's act of self-censorship exemplifies the liberal distaste for critical approaches to law. Throughout his critique, Austin sexualises and dehumanises Frug; the violence to which she was subjected is paired with her assessment of systemic violence, which is then ridiculed. The sexualisation implied in Austin's account of her death, the stabbing in "her chest and groin", and the "self-flagellation" of Frug's article, are all deemed fine by the author, but "cunt" and "fuck" are deemed too vulgar to repeat.

In the critiques of both Austin and Carrington, the same churlish responses can be seen to US-CLS and other limbs of Critical Legal Studies. Both authors, and those writing in agreement with Carrington, pride themselves on an ascetic approach to law. Law's issues should not be named, and critique should not be levelled at structures that reinforce them, unless you're training crooks. Unfortunately, the authors are seemingly unable to grasp, or deliberately miss, the points they want to refute. Cornel West makes an argument to the latter effect, stating that liberals such as

> Richard Posner, Robert Bork, and others view [US] critical legal studies as calling into question the very ends of Western civilization and the ends of traditional legal education. Thus, they conclude it ought to be pushed outside the academy completely.[29]

---

[26] Ibid.
[27] Ibid.
[28] Ibid.
[29] Cornel West, "Reassessing the Critical Legal Studies Movement" (1988) 34 *Loyola Law Review* 265, 271 nn 15.

It's a long bow to draw, but it is possible that these types of "critique" by liberals are deliberately weak so as to delegitimise US-CLS further. Whatever the reasons might be, these underdeveloped critiques demonstrate a lack of cogent or engaged analysis, which gives no insight into the problems with, or issues faced by, US-CLS.

Critical Critiques

The weakness of liberal critiques is perhaps seen most clearly when contrasted with Critical critiques of US-CLS. For example, Peter Goodrich gives a damning assessment of the theory and politics that underpinned US-CLS from a UK-CLS perspective:

> Aside from an early and now dated Marxist sociology of law which has been largely abandoned and which was itself imported, the defining feature of the critics was arguably that of a naive and somewhat bowdlerised translation of continental social theory into an American legal idiom. One consequence of such a characteristic of the literature was the limited audience which such a product or positivity was likely to have in the legal academy itself. Its success was its failure, its external visibility was its strongest form of internal secession, its text was its context.[30]

In this brief excerpt, Goodrich moves past simple critiques of whether nihilism will destroy legal training colleges,[31] or rebutting the idea that law draws from and influences power and structural hierarchies.[32] Instead, he gets to the heart of a real critique of US-CLS: its Americanised nature and reduced theoretical basis. These two issues can be seen in Goodrich's opening line, and his reference to a sociology of law, which harks back to the failed attempt by Roscoe Pound to move past Langdellianism. In referencing this, Goodrich is also critiquing the Crits who built upon Pound's approach to Karl Marx, before abandoning it—affirming Alan Freeman's insight that US-CLS scholars had a fear of being associated with Marxism.[33] Goodrich then moves on to identify the repetition of this failure through the limited understanding and application of contemporary social theory by the Crits.

---

[30] Peter Goodrich, *Law in the Courts of Love: Literature and Other Minor Jurisprudences* (Routledge, 1996) 192.
[31] Martin (n 8) 16.
[32] See generally, Duncan Kennedy, *Legal Education and the Reproduction of Hierarchy: A Polemic Against the System* (New York University Press, 2004).
[33] Alan D. Freeman, "Truth and Mystification in Legal Scholarship" (1981) 90(5) *Yale Law Journal* 1,229.

Goodrich's critique garnered a different response from the Crits than that given to their liberal critics. The dialogue between Gordon and Carrington, for example, stands in contrast to Goodrich's retelling of his interaction with Duncan Kennedy after presenting the above statement at a conference. Discussing their personal interactions over the years in his book review of Kennedy's *Critique of Adjudication (fin de siècle)*, Goodrich states:

> I met him [Kennedy] next at a critical networks conference in Boston in 1992. He did not attend my presentation but did discuss it with me and pronounce that my criticisms of U.S. critical legal studies ("[US]cls") were too strident and too loud.[34]

The reaction to Goodrich's critique continued with Goodrich's co-panellist at the conference, Peter Gabel, being "upset" by the criticism of Kennedy and US-CLS.[35]

Amongst the retelling of these interactions, Goodrich inadvertently touches on why his critique is more developed than liberal critiques of US-CLS:

> I also should admit, and in equally positive tones, that I have read *Critique* as part of a theoretical trajectory that began with what I believe to be a brilliant book about the politics of law school: *Legal Education as Training for Hierarchy*. Indeed, I have taught that text for many years. I have read it repeatedly with students, with colleagues, with intensity, with love.[36]

His sentiment can be contrasted with that of Carrington in "Of Law and the River":

> The nihilist teacher threatens to rob his or her students of the courage to act on such professional judgment as they may have acquired.

---

[34] Peter Goodrich, "Duncan Kennedy as I Imagine Him: The Man, the Work, His Scholarship, and the Polity" (2001) 22 *Cardozo Law Review* 971, 976. See also Tor Krever, Carl Lisberger, and Max Utzschneider, "Law on the Left: A Conversation with Duncan Kennedy" (2015) 10(1) *Unbound* 1, 32. Kennedy remembers the event within this article, discussing Richard Posner's review but not mentioning Goodrich by name:

> It [*Critique of Adjudication*] was received by complete overwhelming silence, except that within the community of Critical Legal Studies there was an amazing event organised by Michael Fischl and Pierre Schlag. This was a symposium at the University of Miami, an astonishingly elaborate, serious response by some people to whom I was close and others to whom I wasn't.

[35] Goodrich, "Duncan Kennedy as I Imagine Him" (n 34) 976 nn 12.
[36] Ibid 978.

> Teaching cynicism may, and perhaps probably does, result in the learning of the skills of corruption: bribery and intimidation.[37]

Whilst Goodrich might disagree with Kennedy's brand of US-CLS, his critique is derived from a place of genuine engagement rather than mere ideological stance. This approach provides critique that takes seriously its subject, in turn affording a more useful analysis. Goodrich's interaction with US-CLS, and Kennedy specifically, provides a clear contrast to the interactions of Carrington and Austin.

Goodrich's position as part of UK-CLS (despite his geographic location across the Atlantic) aids in the type of critique he gives. The initial excerpt above is taken from "Sleeping with the Enemy: An Essay on the Politics of Critical Legal Studies in America",[38] a paper that positions Goodrich as an outsider looking in. This motif can be seen in other works,[39] and is a possible reason why liberal critiques coming from within the same higher education space found it difficult to engage in a similar way.

Other "Critical" critiques, for example those of Catharine MacKinnon in the broad CLS category of feminist legal theory, also benefit from the distance between themselves and US-CLS. This can be seen in MacKinnon's 1989 article, "Feminism in Legal Education":

> Feminism also criticizes existing intellectual approaches to explaining law. Feminists have exposed objectivity as a figleaf for misogyny. The legal realists' famous aphorism – that you can tell more about what a judge will decide based on what he had for breakfast than on legal doctrine – leaves out who cooked the breakfast and who served it, far less what he did last night in bed. [US] Critical legal studies, while taking more cognizance of women's claims, is not unproblematic. Often the theories inhabit a legal world of looseness and motion that does not exist for women. Women's treatment, to put it another way, is all too determinate. Nor is male power a determinant in the system as it is viewed by much of critical legal studies. It is, rather, a constraint that one occasionally encounters in a system which is otherwise determined or is in random intellectual motion.[40]

---

[37] Carrington (n 4) 27.

[38] Peter Goodrich, "Sleeping with the Enemy: An Essay on the Politics of Critical Legal Studies in America" (1993) 68(2) *New York University Law Review* 389.

[39] Peter Goodrich, "Europe in America: Grammatology, Legal Studies, and the Politics of Transmission" (2001) 101(8) *Columbia Law Review* 2033. There are similar themes in Goodrich's tribute to Penny Pether: Peter Goodrich, "Mos Americanus or Common Law In Partibus Infidelium" (2015) 21 *Villanova Law Review* 521.

[40] Catharine MacKinnon, "Feminism in Legal Education" (1989) 7 *Legal Education Review* 85, 92.

MacKinnon then continues with a theory for why US-CLS might have escaped more stringent critique: "I must confess some suspicion that one of the reasons critical legal studies is not more sharply criticized is that none of its members, to my knowledge, is on the bench. Few mix in practice at all."[41] MacKinnon engages with US-CLS materials, particularly the claim of law being indeterminate, but this only forms part of a bigger argument on legal education and the identification of a determinate hierarchy for women.

Whilst illuminating, MacKinnon is not writing a piece on feminist legal theory approaches to US-CLS. Instead, her article is a feminist legal theory approach to legal education, which touches on US-CLS. MacKinnon is very aware of this distinction and addresses this limitation in her footnotes, providing two pertinent critiques of US-CLS as suggested reading.[42] The articles MacKinnon identifies are arguably some of the strongest critiques of US-CLS from future critical race scholars (the articles preceding the mantle of critical race theory). MacKinnon cites Mari Matsuda's "Looking to the Bottom: Critical Legal Studies and Reparations" and Patricia Williams's "Alchemical Notes: Reconstructing Ideals From Deconstructed Rights".[43] Whilst both pieces defiantly critique from a personal position related to the authors' identity and experiences, they both offer broad solutions to the problems they perceive. Both papers were published in the *Harvard Civil Rights–Civil Liberties Law Review* and were "originally presented as part of a panel discussion on the minority critique of [US-]CLS. These pieces reflect both the promise and the frustration which [US-]CLS holds for minority scholarship and politics."[44] The nature of the articles, their time within the US-CLS timeline, and their impact offer an engaged and focused critique of US-CLS.

There is necessary background information to understand the compounded and real nature of these theorists' frustration with US-CLS. The panel discussion of which Matsuda and Williams were part happened on 7 January 1987, at the tenth annual Critical Legal Studies Conference (CCLS). The theme of the conference was "Sounds of Silence: Racism and Legal Scholarship". In the December 1986 CCLS newsletter, Richard Abel

---

[41] Ibid 92–3.
[42] MacKinnon (n 40) 92 nn 18; Goodrich, *Law in the Courts of Love* (n 30) 203 nn 72. Goodrich mentions Williams's later work, *The Alchemy of Race and Rights*, in passing, in context of autobiography and the way critical legal work is moving forward.
[43] Mari J. Matsuda, "Looking to the Bottom: Critical Legal Studies and Reparations" (1987) 22 *Harvard Civil Rights–Civil Liberties Law Review* 323; Patricia J. Williams, "Alchemical Notes: Reconstructing Ideals from Deconstructed Rights" (1987) 22 *Harvard Civil Rights–Civil Liberties Law Review* 401.
[44] José A. Bracamonte, "Minority Critiques of the Critical Legal Studies Movement" (1987) 22 *Harvard Civil Rights–Civil Liberties Law Review* 297, 297.

addressed the impending conference and its theme on behalf of the CCLS planning committee:

> If [US-]CLS conferences in the past had devoted relatively little attention to feminism, they have devoted even less to racism. We decided to begin the meeting with lectures and discussions among non-lawyers on race in contemporary America. Then a number of minority law teachers will present a critique of [US-]CLS scholarship (and silences) on race. The second full day of the meeting will offer workshops that attempt to raise questions about race in the context of our research and teaching about law that deal with two central issues that confront all of us within the law school environment: the racism that minority law teachers confront (especially in the classroom); and the disadvantages that minority law students encounter in standardized tests—for admission to law school, at the end of courses, and for entry to the bar.[45]

Abel's explanation appears self-reflective of US-CLS as a whole. He acknowledges the issues caused by paying little attention to feminism, and that this conference was there to support minority scholars and people of colour who might feel similarly ostracised from US-CLS.[46] However, in spite of the intentions of US-CLS, the conference appears to have been a tipping point for an already strained relationship. As Alfredo Mirandé recalled in 2000, "the Conference intensified the schism between [US-]CLS and people of color who had not been invited to participate in the planning of the Conference."[47] Mirandé's reflective statement echoes José A. Bracamonte's conclusion to the 1987 edition of the *Harvard Civil Rights–Civil Liberties Law Review*:

> What the Critical Legal Studies movement currently has to offer therefore only partially fits the articulated historical needs of minorities. The reality of our existence and needs must find a more developed and nuanced treatment in critical scholarship and practice. By imposing an ideological paradigm without accommodating our personal, social and political needs, [US-]CLS adherents seek to impose leadership without a genuine understanding of the minority community.[48]

---

[45] Richard Abel, "Los Angeles National CLS Conference, January 6–8 1987", *Newsletter of the Conference on Critical Legal Studies* (Buffalo New York, December 1986) 1–2.

[46] The title "minority scholar" is used in accordance with the CCLS and the publications that came from it. The title is also used to differentiate the authors from the not-yet-formed title of critical race scholar/theorist.

[47] Alfredo Mirandé, "'Revenge of the Nerds,' or Postmodern 'Colored Folk'? Critical Race Theory and the Chronicles of Rodrigo" (2000) 4(1) *Harvard Latino Law Review* 153, 153.

[48] Bracamonte (n 44) 299.

The aftereffects of the conference led to the development of critical race theory in 1989.[49] However, at the time of the conference and the publication of the *Harvard Civil Rights–Civil Liberties Law Review*, Matsuda and Williams were writing on, and to some extent within, US-CLS. Fellow critical race theorist, Kimberlé Crenshaw, outlines this unique position for minority scholars:

> In the mid-1980s, [US-]CLS was the place to be for progressive, left wing, and other non-conformist law folks. [US-]CLS conferences were a mix of heavy theory, whimsical aspiration, dramatic performances, and other remnants of 1960s counter-culturalism. For a range of left-leaning people of colour in the legal academy looking for an ideological home, [US-]CLS was attractive.[50]

Reminiscent of Laura Kalman's identification of Harvard Law School as a "home" for Kennedy, Morton Horwitz, and Unger,[51] Crenshaw identifies US-CLS as offering similar hope to minority scholars. However, the similarities continue with the earlier critique of Kalman's "home" for US-CLS at Harvard, with minority scholars not feeling the common associations that a home should bring for them. As Abel's entry in the *Newsletter of the Conference on Critical Legal Studies* outlined, there were tensions before the conference, which Bracamonte and Mirandé identify were not quelled by the CCLS's theme and focus.

As such, the position that Matsuda and Williams write from provides a unique insight into US-CLS, from those looking for an ideological home, and critiquing with the aim of improvement rather than denigration or analytical distance. However, alongside this goal of improvement, there are issues which sit at odds with US-CLS, notably on the topic of "rights"—and, in Matsuda's article particularly, the prescriptive nature of the outcomes she would like to see. To analyse these critiques of US-CLS, Matsuda will be addressed first, before moving to Williams.

Mari Matsuda—"Looking to the Bottom: Critical Legal Studies and Reparations

From the title alone, the goal of improvement through critique can be seen in Matsuda's article. The loaded terms outline the location of Matsuda as a minority scholar, and the need for US-CLS to make reparations with those,

---

[49] See Kimberlé Williams Crenshaw, "Twenty Years of Critical Race Theory: Looking Back to Move Forward" (2011) 43(5) *Connecticut Law Review* 1,253, 1,297: "The conference was a precursor to the eventual emergence of the CRT [critical race theory] workshop both substantively and institutionally."
[50] Ibid 1,288.
[51] Laura Kalman, *Yale Law School and the Sixties: Revolt and Reverberations* (University of North Carolina Press, 2005) 7.

like her, who are at the "bottom". Matsuda's critiques of US-CLS generally should be separated from her specific critique of US-CLS's interaction with rights.[52] The latter argument does not engage enough with the existing US-CLS critiques of rights to successfully challenge their position. While Matsuda presents a compelling case for understanding and developing rights, the benefit of the article is a more general critique of US-CLS.

Drawing on the work of Antonio Gramsci, Matsuda outlines an overarching issue with US-CLS's engagement with those at "the bottom":

> The imagination of the academic philosopher cannot recreate the experience of life on the bottom. Instead we must look to what Gramsci called "organic intellectuals", grass roots philosophers who are uniquely able to relate theory to the concrete experience of oppression.[53]

Here, Matsuda addresses a broad area of critique that other US-CLS critics had already made,[54] but instead of focusing her critique only on the perceived "elitism" of US-CLS,[55] Matsuda goes further, stating that "a consciousness-raising dialogue between critical legal scholars and people of color provides an important methodological response to those critiques".[56] To further affirm Matsuda's level of engagement, the critique she offers can be contrasted against a similar liberal critique:

> Crits argue that the law is hypocritical, and they deconstruct it to expose the hidden values it refuses to acknowledge. Then, after taking us into the

---

[52] On the topic of rights in US-CLS, see generally Mark Tushnet, "An Essay on Rights" (1983–1984) 62 *Texas Law Review* 1,363, 1,382:

> The language of rights attempts to describe how people can defend the interests they have by virtue of their humanity against efforts by others to suppress those interests or to live indifferent to the suffering caused by failing to recognize the interests of others . . . I could not sensibly deny the importance of experiences of independence and solidarity. They are central parts of our humanity. But the reification critique claims that treating those experiences as instances of abstract rights mischaracterizes them.

See also Mark Tushnet, "The Critique of Rights" (1994) 47(1) *Southern Methodist Law Review* 23. While Matsuda refers to Tushnet in her article, she does not refer specifically to "An Essay on Rights". She does, however, cite Peter Gabel and Duncan Kennedy's "Roll Over Beethoven" ((1984) 36(1/2) *Stanford Law Review* 1), which makes similar claims to Tushnet on the topic.

[53] Matsuda (n 43) 325.

[54] Arthur D. Austin, *The Empire Strikes Back: Outsiders and the Struggle over Legal Education* (New York University Press, 1998); Gordon, "Law Review and the Modern Mind" (n 2).

[55] Matsuda (n 43) 345.

[56] Ibid 326.

wilderness and leaving us there, they zoom off in their BMWs and Jaguars to continue their class struggle against hierarchy and privilege.[57]

In his critique, liberal James Gordon highlights the same issues with elitism in US-CLS, but offers no engagement or potential ways to work through it. Conversely, throughout her article, Matsuda offers a pragmatic approach, with her focus on how US-CLS could fix itself. As the title implies, the reparations needed can be gained by looking to the bottom and engaging with minority scholars. Matsuda takes US-CLS to task on the "standard" critiques levelled at it, and describes how meaningful interaction with minority scholars would allow a progression past the problem:

> The standard critique of critical legal scholarship paints the movement as non-programmatic, over-idealized, inaccessible, cynical, anti-rational, and nihilistic. This critique is made artfully from and inartfully from without the movement. [US-]CLS theorists acknowledge the validity of at least parts of the critique, and strive for a transcendence that, as yet, remains illusory ... A bottom-up perspective would both inform the [US-]CLS movement and help it transcend the standard critique. Reference to this alternative intellectual tradition would help move [US-]CLS beyond trashing into the next stage of reconstruction.[58]

In Matsuda's proposed method, the expansion of US-CLS to not only acknowledge but engage with and repair its relationship with minority scholars would result in a transcendence and would be the next logical step for US-CLS. Matsuda proposes "reconstruction", making reference to trashing, and creating an antonym for deconstruction. She alludes to the need for reconstruction in her introduction when she praises US-CLS for their ability to deconstruct, likening them to termites within trees of law, before pointing out that no one is engaging with the discarded sawdust when they are done.[59] Matsuda provides a clearer explanation later in the article when she highlights the lack of positive development and instead the "emphasis of [US-]CLS literature on detailed deconstruction of existing legal concepts, rather than on reconstruction of new concepts and strategies".[60] She continues that "critical legal scholars stumble in depicting Utopia".[61]

---

[57] Gordon, "Law Review and the Modern Mind" (n 2) 269.
[58] Ibid 330–1.
[59] Matsuda, (n 43) 330.
[60] Ibid 345.
[61] Ibid; see also, e.g., Kennedy, *Legal Education and the Reproduction of Hierarchy* (n 32) 136, where Kennedy presents a US-CLS utopian proposal.

Her approach benefits from being seen in two distinct ways: first, highlighting the need for US-CLS to engage with minority scholars; and second, offering a prescriptive outcome including a "message of hope and inspiration" that might come from this.[62] Whilst the former part of Matsuda's approach is compatible with US-CLS, the latter and its "reconstruction" sit at odds with the existing US-CLS literature.[63]

The incompatibility in Matsuda's approach can be seen in relation to Gabel and Kennedy's "Roll Over Beethoven".[64] Matsuda makes reference to the article in her introductory footnotes as part of a general reference dump of US-CLS works which critique rights; a subsequent reference is later made to its exclusive language barriers.[65] In another footnote, Matsuda includes a quotation from Peter in "Roll Over Beethoven", which touches on the US-CLS critique of rights[66] but does not engage with the resolution he and Duncan reach several pages later.[67]

For example, Peter states that, "They [rights] don't exist. They have no existence. They are shared, imaginary attributes that the group attributes to its members that don't in fact exist. It's a hallucination."[68] When questioned by Duncan as to "why" people believe the hallucination, Peter responds, "Because in the pain of our isolation we become attached to the utopian content in legal imagery. This is why I think it's dream-like."[69] Before concluding this section of "Roll Over Beethoven", Peter responds to Duncan's question of whether there is any point in trying to get people their rights.[70] Peter's response is nuanced, arguing that the question is too simple:

> [E]very time you bring a case and win a right, that right is integrated within an ideological framework that has as its ultimate aim the maintenance of collective passivity. *That doesn't mean you don't bring the case – it means you keep your eye on power and not on rights.*[71]

---

[62] Matsuda (n 43) 249.
[63] Contra, Roberto Mangabeira Unger, *The Critical Legal Studies Movement: Another Time, a Greater Task* (Verso, 2015).
[64] Gabel and Kennedy (n 52).
[65] Matsuda (n 43) 330 nn 30, 342.
[66] Ibid 331 nn 31.
[67] Gabel and Kennedy (n 52) 36.
[68] Ibid 34.
[69] Ibid 36. See Tushnet, "The Critique of Rights" (n 52) 26–7 on the issue of rights and isolation.
[70] Gabel and Kennedy (n 52) 36.
[71] Ibid (emphasis added).

There is a clear impasse between how Crits and minority scholars view and interact with rights. Although Matsuda engages broadly with the benefits of rights and their historical use for good,[72] she overlooks the key point relating to passivity and individuality, which disrupts her method of reconstruction and "good" rights. This does not mean that Matsuda does not engage with the negative aspects of rights, but even when faced with these truths, she, like fellow minority scholar Derrick Bell, believes rights and associated legal structures can work towards a just end.[73] The paper's theme of interacting with minority scholars,[74] those at the bottom, however, is a clear critique that US-CLS should have heeded. Unfortunately, its conflation with Matsuda's focus on rights detracts from her insights analysing issues of race, specifically the post–World War II treatment of Asian Americans.[75] Instead, Matsuda's reconstruction utopia conforms to the hallucination described in "Roll Over Beethoven".[76]

Patricia J Williams—"Alchemical Notes: Reconstructing Ideals from Deconstructed Rights"

The crossover in themes between "Looking to the Bottom" and "Alchemical Notes" is such that, read together, the pair complement each other, strengthening the individual calls for a bottom-up reassessment of US-CLS. However, Williams comes from a different position to Matsuda, using allegorical stories as well as her own personal history to anchor her analysis. By itself, the power of Williams's reflective style leads to an effective structural analysis of US-CLS, specifically through the allegorical story, "The Brass Ring and the Deep Blue Sea",[77] which introduces the article, presenting a broad overview of US-CLS history.

Williams addresses several important ideas in "Alchemical Notes", but it is primarily about rights. As Williams outlines, "Alchemical Notes" is "an attempt to detail my discomfort with that part of [US-]CLS which rejects rights-based theory, particularly that part of the debate and critique which applies to the black struggle for civil rights."[78] It is also about grassroots membership and a need to look to the bottom.[79] Williams identifies the benefit of

---

[72] Matsuda (n 43) 338.
[73] Ibid 192, citing Derrick A. Bell, *Race, Racism, and American Law* (Little Brown, 1981).
[74] Ibid 349.
[75] Ibid 373–88.
[76] Gabel and Kennedy (n 52) 34.
[77] Williams, "Alchemical Notes" (n 43) 401–2.
[78] Ibid 404.
[79] Ibid 402.

the US-CLS position on rights, but then argues clearly why this position is not always applicable or viable for people of colour.[80]

To support the arguments she makes against the US-CLS critique of rights, Williams discusses her experiences as a young lawyer in Los Angeles,[81] her reflections on finding an apartment in New York at the same time as Gabel,[82] and her historical position as both a lawyer and the great-great-granddaughter of a woman sold into slavery to a lawyer.[83] In the latter reflection, Williams addresses some very real positive aspects of rights: "[T]his failure of rights discourse, much noted in [US-]CLS scholarship, does not necessarily mean that informal systems will lead to better outcomes. Some structures are the direct products of people and social forces who wanted them that way."[84] The result of this powerful rhetoric is a stance that can challenge the rights critique by Gabel and Kennedy, through a tangible, personal perspective, one not as evident in Matsuda's argument.[85]

"Alchemical Notes" also introduces Williams's titular concept of alchemy.[86] The term, which Williams uses again in her 1991 book *The Alchemy of Race and Rights*,[87] is initially a way for the author to convey the multiplicity of influences and factors that make up an individual—an inward rather than outward intersectionality.[88] The term is not fully developed until Williams's book, but her description of it there provides retrospective insight into the way the author approached the issue of rights in "Alchemical Notes":

> As I write, my editor at Harvard University Press is waging something of a struggle with the people at the Library of Congress about how this book is to be categorized for cataloguing purposes. The librarians think "Afro-Americans – Civil Rights" and "Law Teachers" would be nice. I told my editor to hold out for "Autobiography," "Fiction," "Gender Studies," and "Medieval Medicine." This battle seems appropriate enough, since for me the book is not exclusively about race or law but also about boundary.

---

[80] Ibid 404–5.
[81] Ibid 402–3.
[82] Ibid 406.
[83] Ibid 420.
[84] Ibid 423.
[85] Contra, issues of Japanese American internment, but these were not addressed in the same way.
[86] Williams, "Alchemical Notes" (n 43) 406.
[87] Patricia J. Williams, *The Alchemy of Race and Rights* (Harvard University Press, 1991).
[88] See Kimberlé Crenshaw, "Demarginalizing the Intersection of Race and Sex: A Black Feminist Critique of Antidiscrimination Doctrine, Feminist Theory and Antiracist Politics" (1989) 1(8) *University of Chicago Legal Forum* 139.

> While being black has been the most powerful social attribution in my life, it is only one of a number of governing narratives or presiding fictions by which I am constantly reconfiguring myself in the world. Gender is another, along with ecology, pacifism, my peculiar brand of colloquial English, and Roxbury, Massachusetts. The complexity of role identification, the politics of sexuality, the infections of professionalized discourse – all describe and impose boundary in my life, even as they confound one another in unfolding spirals of confrontation, deflection, and dream.[89]

The lengthy statement by Williams on categorisation gets to the heart of alchemy in "Alchemical Notes". The author's alchemical approach affects her interaction with topics including US-CLS and rights, while also providing an example of the sheer number of intersecting aspects or "alchemical elements" that position and develop a perspective, most of which are subsequently discarded for one dominant title.

Aside from this concept, "Alchemical Notes" and *The Alchemy of Race and Rights*, also share a connection through "The Brass Ring and the Deep Blue Sea", which prefaces the book and begins the article. Not only is "The Brass Ring and the Deep Blue Sea" a valid critique of US-CLS, but in creating this allegorical world Williams provides tools to imagine a way for US-CLS to continue.

"The Brass Ring and the Deep Blue Sea" is in two parts, part "A. The Meta-Story" and part "B. The Story", with each part offering a different perspective of the same event. There is also a subtitle, "A Bit of CLS Mythology", a play on words that foreshadows the story's themes of clarifying US-CLS myths and methodology. "The Brass Ring and the Deep Blue Sea" appears in "Alchemical Notes" exactly as it is presented below:

> A. The Meta-Story
> *Once upon a time, there was a society of priests who built a Celestial City whose gates were secured by Word-Combination locks. The priests were masters of the Word, and, within the City, ascending levels of power and treasure became accessible to those who could learn ascendingly intricate levels of Word Magic. At the very top level, the priests became gods; and because they then had nothing left to seek, they engaged in games with which to pass the long hours of eternity. In particular, they liked to ride their strong, sure-footed steeds, around and around the perimeter of heaven: now jumping word-hurdles, now playing polo with the concepts of the moon and of the stars, now reaching up to touch*

---

[89] Williams, *Alchemy of Race and Rights* (n 87) 258.

that pinnacle, that fragment, that splinter of Refined Understanding which was called Superstanding, the brass ring of their merry-go-round.

In time, some of the priests-turned-gods tired of this sport, denounced it as meaningless. They donned the garb of pilgrims, seekers once more, and passed beyond the gates of the Celestial City. In this recursive passage, they acquired the knowledge of Undoing Words.

Beyond the walls of the City lay a Deep Blue Sea. The priests built themselves small boats and set sail, determined to explore the uncharted courses, the open vistas of this new and undefined domain. They wandered for many years in this manner, until at last they reached a place that was half-a-circumference away from the Celestial City. From this point, the City appeared as a mere shimmering illusion; and the priests knew that at last they had reached a place which was Beyond the Power of Words. They let down their anchors, the plumb lines of their reality, and experienced godhood once more.

B. The Story
Under the Celestial City, dying mortals called out their rage and suffering, battered by a steady rain of sharp hooves whose thundering, sound-drowning path described the wheel of their misfortune.

At the bottom of the Deep Blue Sea, drowning mortals reached silently and desperately for drifting anchors dangling from short chains far, far overhead, which they thought were life-lines meant for them.[90]

The title of the story puts together two distinct images of aspiration and helplessness. First the brass ring refers to an American colloquialism about striving for a goal—based on a challenge added to early carousel rides, where riders won if they reached out and touched the brass ring.[91] With this image Williams presents the idea of succeeding within law, but constantly having to aspire further, or being unable to use law and drowning in the Deep Blue Sea. This image of constantly spinning and repetitively circling a prize is then paired with an allusion to the phrase, "Between the devil and the deep blue sea". Combining them, Williams creates a unique idiom about

---

[90] Williams, "Alchemical Notes" (n 43) 401–2.
[91] Most references for the origins of this phrase are located online via user-generated sites such as Wikipedia. Some sources are given at World Wide Words, see Michael Quinion, "Brass Ring", *World Wide Words* (Web Page, 14 January 2023) <http://www.worldwidewords.org/qa/qa-bra4.htm>. There is consistency in academic and peer-reviewed papers that use this phrase: generally it represents an aspirational goal or direction to take. However, no clear definition is given within papers using this term. The image of the carousel is prevalent in Williams's "The Brass Ring and the Deep Blue Sea".

law, one that can be summed up as "to sink or spin", highlighting the unappealing nature of both locations.

The Celestial City represents the heavenly and sacred nature of law, while the Deep Blue Sea represents a place for the layman. Williams uses this allegory to illustrate the different worlds occupied by those within and those outside of law. The hierarchy between these groups is visually structured, with those at the bottom being trampled by the effects of law but still reaching for it, while those within the Celestial City are seemingly unaware or not concerned with those deep below.

The Celestial City was built by priests who were masters of the "Word" and "Word Magic",[92] with Williams imagining the institution of law as a walled city. Her priests are lawyers and legal theorists, and their Word and Word Magic are the law. There is a depth to Williams's insight around this idea: not only is law fortified and exclusive, but those within it speak a different language. She continues the idea of fortification with Word-Combination locks that keep the gates sealed,[93] reiterating the necessity of a specific linguistic base to access the institution of law. This deterrent can also be read further, first that one needs the correct words to enter the City, but also that they need the correct voice, ensuring that the "wrong" type of people do not have access.

Once inside the City's walls, Williams discusses the notion that priests can ascend within the City, moving to the status of Gods, rather than mere men of the cloth. These Gods move beyond the solemn nature of law and begin to play games. The Gods use other related concepts, represented by Williams as moons and stars, playthings used to engage in polo matches within the Celestial City. The games Williams describes invoke imagery of a celestial elite, but their meaning goes further than this, appealing closely to the concepts and relationships of "Law and" jurisprudential movements. These movements are different from US-CLS, representing sensible and appropriate combinations like law and economics, or law and society. After outlining this tier of Priests-turned-Gods, Williams identifies a subgroup within them who don the garb of pilgrims and leave the Celestial City: the Crits.

Williams describes the Crits leaving the City and, in doing so, finding something new, the "Undoing Words".[94] A connection to the various US-CLS ideas of deconstruction, demystification, and trashing can be seen in the discovery of the Undoing Words. However, Williams argues that the power of the Undoing Words only lasts so long, and so the Crits sail from the

---

[92] Williams, "Alchemical Notes" (n 43) 401.
[93] Ibid 401.
[94] Ibid.

Celestial City across the Deep Blue Sea in search of new methods. Williams describes how as the Crits move farther from the City their power wanes, and they decide to settle in a place she names "Beyond the Power of Words".

For Williams, the status and journey of the Crits is clear. They did not come from the Deep Blue Sea, but were part of Celestial City, part of law. Their real power came when they challenged the hierarchy and left the City, discovering the Undoing Words, the ability to demystify law. However, similar to the concerns voiced by Gabel and Kennedy about US-CLS being co-opted,[95] the power or even the novelty of demystification was seen to lose its impact. As the Crits moved further from their critiques on law, their relevance and impact slowed, and by 1995 it had stopped.

"The Brass Ring and the Deep Blue Sea" is the foundation of "Alchemical Notes", underpinning Williams's critique and offering the Crits a new location to renew their critical edge, at the bottom of the Deep Blue Sea. Williams highlights the issue with the direction of US-CLS in Part B of 'The Brass Ring and the Deep Blue Sea'. She identifies the disconnection between where US-CLS should be going and instead where it has gone. Despite this plea for a directional change from Williams, Matsuda, and other minority scholars at the 1987 CCLS, the different opinions on rights led to an impasse and eventually the creation of critical race theory in 1989.[96] Crenshaw outlines the direct impact of minority scholarship presented at the conference on the development of critical race theory:

> The conference was an important transitional moment. It moved to center stage a variety of debates about race both within [US-]CLS and also within the academy more broadly. The conference clarified that an emergent collective existed that occupied a unique intersection, a space both within and between [US-]CLS and liberal race discourses. We were of course aligned with [US-]CLS in terms of its overall orientation toward the institutionalized reproduction of hierarchy. Yet it was in the moments of contestation over the racial contours of this commitment that efforts to further refine the race turn in [US-]CLS became a viable intellectual project.[97]

---

[95] Gabel and Kennedy (n 52) 4–5.
[96] See, e.g., Crenshaw, "Twenty Years of Critical Race Theory" (n 49) 1,263; David M. Trubek, "Foundational Events, Foundational Myths, and the Creation of Critical Race Theory, or How To Get Along with a Little Help from Your Friends" (2011) 43(5) *Connecticut Law Review* 1,503.
[97] Crenshaw, "Twenty Years of Critical Race Theory" (n 49), 1,297.

Sadly, the Crits did not heed the warnings at the 1986 CCLS. Instead, the minority scholars, "outsiders" to US-CLS, went on to form critical race theory, focusing on (re)connecting with those at the bottom of Williams's Deep Blue Sea.[98] This loss of allies weakened the position of US-CLS, and is another reason why a few years later, US-CLS was dead as a doornail.

---

[98] Derrick Bell, "Strangers in Academic Paradise: Law Teachers of Color in Still White Schools" (1985) 20 *University of San Francisco Law Review* 385, 392–3; Andrew W. Haines, "The Critical Legal Studies Movement and Racism: Useful Analytics and Guides for Social Action or an Irrelevant Modern Legal Scepticism and Solipsism?" (1987) 13(4) *William Mitchell Law Review* 685, 685–90.

8

American Gods

Cui bono?

Marcus Tullius Cicero, *Pro Roscio Amerino*

At the end of the US-CLS journey, with the facts laid out in order, questions still arise: was it a question that killed US-CLS, as Richard Michael Fischl proposed? Or was it Duncan Kennedy's declaration that US-CLS was dead as a doornail that finally finished it off? What about the Crits' acknowledgement that they had lost the feminist legal theorists, only to lose the emerging critical race theorists too? In reality, all of these issues led to significant challenges and the eventual downfall of US-CLS. Paired with the disparate nature of the work under the Critical Legal Studies banner, the movement lost its momentum. The very breadth and lack of doctrine that made US-CLS "US-CLS" have ensured that attempts to resuscitate it never work. Instead, Posthumous Critical Legal Studies (PCLS) continues in a half-life, referring to aspects of the original US-CLS for contemporary or continuing issues, but simultaneously wondering where the original US-CLS has gone.

Still, with a theoretical click of his fingers, Kennedy could aid in the return of US-CLS. But as both he and Roberto Unger have stated, this is not on the cards. For both theorists, US-CLS was something that happened, but not something built to continue. This understanding is woven into the movement's history: US-CLS was only possible due to extraneous factors; it was a political location; the current conferences are just like any other law conference. And because of those who said so, the works that have come after its death seem naïve: "Why bother? Don't you know we tried this at the most prestigious law schools and still couldn't make it work!"

So PCLS works grapple with a desire to reanimate a corpus that does not want to return, while reifying those who have acted as its coffin nails. Still, there have been several resurgent conferences, bringing back together original and new Crits along with feminist legal and critical race scholars. PCLS and adjacent works continue, as do new collectives that owe a debt to US-CLS. There are podcasts, documentaries, and reimaginations of US-CLS, keeping this dead theory in the spotlight. The result is a paradox where demand is high, but despite the participation of the suppliers, the supply cannot exist.

To overcome this paradox, divergence from the dominant history of US-CLS is necessary. To put it into terms at the heart of US-CLS, a trashing must ensue. Such an approach might reflect the ideal that Alan Freeman espoused: "I am not defending a form of scholarship that simply offers another affirmative presentation; rather I am advocating negative, critical activity as the only path that might lead to a liberated future."[1] Similarly, Mark Kelman states that, "We will lead silly lives if we ever stop raging against the usual."[2] This conclusion comes after a detailed account weaving through the benefits and purpose of not only questioning the usual, or the generally accepted—but taking it to task and presenting that it, and not the trasher, is silly.

In Kelman and Freeman's terms, to "trash" US-CLS requires an investigation of the movement, taking its claims seriously, and exposing possibilities that better express reality.[3] The acts of demystification that have preceded this chapter, whilst taking novel approaches, stay within the general remit of US-CLS's dominant history. This is necessary to understand what US-CLS was and what it continues to be. From this perspective it is now possible to question this "usual" or "generally affirmative" presentation of US-CLS—to understand its legacy.

US-CLS: Legacy

It may seem fatalistic to state that US-CLS was doomed from the start. However, it is a sentiment seen in the work of key Crits since its death.[4] In turn, this statement is more at odds with the optimism of PCLS than the original US-CLS. The fatalistic nature of the movement is evident from an expansion of the literary analogies that can be applied to the US-CLS journey—for example, the mythic pulling back of the curtain in *The Wonderful Wizard of Oz*.[5] This is an image, to borrow from corporate law, that may be expanded to piercing the "legal" veil, a way to conceive of legal realists, Crits,

---

[1] Alan D. Freeman, "Truth and Mystification in Legal Scholarship' (1981) 90(5) *Yale Law Journal* 1,229, 1,231.
[2] Mark G. Kelman, "Trashing" (1984) 36 *Stanford Law Review* 296, 348.
[3] Freeman (n 1) 1,230–1.
[4] See generally, Duncan Kennedy, *Legal Education and the Reproduction of Hierarchy: A Polemic Against the System* (New York University Press, 2004); Roberto Mangabeira Unger, *The Critical Legal Studies Movement: Another Time, a Greater Task* (Verso, 2015).
[5] L. Frank Baum, *The Wonderful Wizard of Oz* (Geo M Hill, 1899) 156.

and law and economics, revealing the function or purpose of law. Further, the story's content reiterates a theme of revelation. For Dorothy and friends, their return to the Emerald City to redeem Oz's promise of brains, heart, courage, and home leads to the discovery that Oz's magic is nothing more than papier-mâché and green spectacles. Oz the Great and Powerful is merely a lost ventriloquist from Omaha.

Other analogous texts that engage with this theme of revelation include everything from *The Emperor's New Clothes* to *The Matrix*; the analogy to US-CLS is not a long bow to draw. Each of these tales shares a common theme of discovery that an existing truth or reality is not as it seems, a theme which goes back to Plato's allegory of the cave. At this stage the texts and their theme of revelation are useful, as Jerry Anderson details;[6] the connection to US-CLS and *The Matrix* presents a way for students to understand US-CLS through a correlation between Kennedy and Morpheus. Similarly, one may declare that the "law has no clothes" and law's real truth is bared for all to see—although it is generally unacknowledged due to the power of law and those who it protects. This type of analogy is simplistic, but it is perceived as a good way to understand US-CLS.

While they are less discussed, the endings of these stories reinforce the fatalistic nature of US-CLS. For example, Oz sails off in a hot air balloon remembered as "wonderful", the Emperor marches on with pride rather than admit he is nude, and the *Matrix* franchise continues to spawn sequels with Neo getting older but still fighting against the matrix. And this is to be expected, just like Plato's freed prisoner who escapes the cave only to be disbelieved upon their return to the darkness. It is expected that US-CLS follows the same path. These analogies promote the idea that speaking truth to power changes little (Oz), is co-opted (the Emperor), is disbelieved (Plato), or at its most extreme has the speaker cast out (Lucifer).

The fatalistic nature of the literary analogies to US-CLS reinforces that US-CLS was destined to end. While these are posthumous applications, which neaten the narrative of the US-CLS journey, they echo the fatalistic undercurrent within US-CLS. PCLS works by Kennedy and Unger highlight why the movement was likely to end, but a reflection on a US-CLS symposium shows this thread was alive and well in the movement's mid-1980s heyday. "Psycho-Social CLS: A Comment on the Cardozo Symposium" is a 1985 afterword to a US-CLS symposium edition of the *Cardozo Law Journal*.[7]

---

[6] Jerry L. Anderson, "Law School Enters the Matrix: Teaching Critical Legal Studies" (2004) 54(2) *Journal of Legal Education* 201.

[7] Duncan Kennedy, "Psycho-Social CLS: A Comment on the Cardozo Symposium" (1985) 6(4) *Cardozo Law Review* 1,013.

Penned by Kennedy in response to the papers presented and their critiques of US-CLS, "Psycho-Social CLS" sees the presented and published papers from the symposium as both institutionalising and highlighting the institutional nature of US-CLS. Kennedy's initial gripe is about US-CLS works focusing on US-CLS, rather than attacks on liberal and conservative doctrinal methods.[8] He continues that, through the expansion of US-CLS as a network and community, divisions have grown between members. For Kennedy, this is discussed through a dichotomy between old-timers and youngsters. Kennedy sees this relationship as both Oedipal and hierarchical, which goes against the movement's ethos.

After presenting these issues without solution, Kennedy concludes by warning the emerging Crits, the "youngsters", about association with US-CLS and issues securing a tenured job. This comes in spite of an explicit mention that tenured faculty are joining the US-CLS ranks.[9] Still, without a hint of irony, Kennedy states that the liberal centre and right wing in academia have moved beyond intellectual discussions with the left, as is evident in its institutional processes: "The basic mechanism of control is to communicate to radical scholars, especially the young, that their association with the radical movement will be harmful to their careers."[10]

The tone of the article does not reflect this direct negativity. There is padding and humour, but in the overarching themes, Kennedy not only disparages the work of emerging critical scholars, but advises that mentoring them is problematic. This sits at odds with the optimism of the editorial board in their introduction to the symposium. The board states that their aim for the edition is to "further enhance [the] spirit of openness and community participation".[11]

Kennedy flags that his afterword will raise serious concerns with a vaguely cryptic forewarning in the introduction to "Psycho-Social CLS":

> [US-]Cls writing is like [US-]cls movement practice in that it takes as an important theme the unity of political, professional, and personal life. It is this characteristic that makes it particularly difficult to discern the fate of the movement from our position in the belly of the whale.[12]

Thematically a link can be drawn to Kennedy's concerns in "Roll Over Beethoven" about US-CLS being co-opted by "others". Still, where the earlier

---

[8] Ibid 1,014–15.
[9] Ibid 1,013–14.
[10] Ibid 1,029.
[11] Editorial Board, "Introduction" (1985) 6(4) *Cardozo Law Review* 691, 691.
[12] Kennedy, "Psycho-Social CLS" (n 7) 1,013.

piece was focused on liberals, "Psycho-Social CLS" is an exercise in gatekeeping for younger fellow travellers. Taken at face value, Kennedy's allusion to Jonah may lead the reader to sympathise with him. However, given the article's admonishment of new US-CLS work, the fate of US-CLS seems fairly clear.

This symposium edition came out in the United States in the summer of 1985, about eighteen months before Richard Abel's note in the Conference on Critical Legal Studies Newsletter calling for a concerted effort to address issues of race.[13] It also arrived roughly a year after the US-CLS *Stanford Law Review* edition in 1984. Following this timeline, Kennedy appears to be actively discouraging new adherents to US-CLS—along the lines that no one but the original "oldtimers" (note that Kennedy was in his early forties here) really understand how to critique—at the peak of US-CLS's popularity.

The disparate nature of US-CLS ensures that one article, one Crit, or one concept is not representative of the whole. And in certain contexts, this makes sense.[14] However, as a catch-all excuse it is not something that holds up to trashing. In 1985, it is clear that Kennedy was actively trying to dissuade new Crits from aligning with US-CLS. To understand this self-sabotage it helps to know more about the sociopolitical context of when US-CLS came about and those who helped create it.

Unpacking the Narrative

> It will also help us to relativize our understanding of the past's relation to the present if we see that our conventional views of that relation are mediated by familiar narrative story-lines, that are so deeply entrenched in our consciousness that we are often unaware of their rule over our conception of reality. These story-lines, like other mentalities, have a history filled with ideological purposes, and there always exist—and so we always may draw upon—competing stories that impress the same historical experience with radically divergent meanings.[15]

In February 2020, just prior to the COVID-19 pandemic, Princeton University held a conference on US-CLS.[16] The in-person event brought

---

[13] Richard Abel, "Los Angeles National CLS Conference, January 6–8 1987" *Newsletter of the Conference on Critical Legal Studies* (Buffalo New York, December 1986) 1–2.
[14] See generally Akbar Rasulov, "CLS and Marxism: A History of an Affair" (2014) *Transnational Legal Theory* 5(4) 623.
[15] Robert W. Gordon, "Critical Legal Histories" (1984) 36 *Stanford Law Review* 57, 101–2.
[16] *Critical Legal Studies: Intellectual History and History of the Present*, (27–28 February 2020) CLS Conference <https://clsconference.princeton.edu>.

together Crits, feminist legal scholars, critical race theorists, and a gaggle of other critically or theoretically adjacent onlookers. The event was the first of its kind in a number of years, premiering a short film on the Crits by Jeannie Suk Gersen and opening a US-CLS archive at the Princeton Mudd Library. Given the age of the participants and at least one death of a Crit since then, the conference is likely to be the last time a majority of the founding members of US-CLS were all together.[17]

The structured panels and talks reinforced the divisions between the Crits and other broad Critical Legal Studies. The spaces in between these panels offered more human glimpses of the Crits themselves. For example, Peter Gabel briefly mentioned the Doors and early US-CLS following their lead to "break on through to the other side", while Mari Matsuda asked whether, in the face of fascism, liberalism was worth revisiting. However, the most interesting comment overheard throughout the day was one by David Trubek. Trubek was discussing something with a fellow panellist on stage before the panel started. During this chat, he gestured to Robert Gordon in the crowd and said something along the lines of, "In the 60s we all followed Bob's dad down to South America." A few nods and smiles were given, but no further mention was made of this.

Robert Gordon's father, Abraham Lincoln Gordon (referred to as Lincoln Gordon), embodied a certain type of US public servant in World War II and the post-war period.[18] Educated at Harvard before completing his DPhil at Oxford as a Rhodes scholar, Lincoln Gordon held positions in government and academia. In the 1960s, the era Trubek briefly reminisced about in 2020, Lincoln Gordon was the US ambassador to Brazil implementing the Marshall Plan. In the abstract, this family history is interesting, but not part of US-CLS history. And why would it be? Robert Gordon is not his father, much like Lincoln Gordon was not a Crit. However, as an act of demystification, these connections matter; they breathe colour and context into otherwise black-and-white areas. Or, another way, when an individual moves from the personal to the mythic, we lose the context that makes them *them*.

This can be seen when an individual's name represents their domination in a field as a whole. Of course this is not unique to law, or even the academe, but within those confines, monoyms like Dworkin, Posner, or Raz require little expansion. Similarly, in US-CLS, Kennedy, Unger, and Gordon

---

[17] Peter Gabel passed away in October 2022. Roberto Unger and Morton Horwitz were notably absent from the conference.

[18] Bruce L. R. Smith, *Lincoln Gordon: Architect of Cold War Foreign Policy* (University of Kentucky Press, 2015).

represent different aspects of the movement, their ideas and dominance in their respective fields understood by surname alone.

Whether it is Kennedy's polemics, Unger's thoughts on liberalism, or Gordon's critical histories, within US-CLS these names symbolise distinct threads of the movement. However, with this mythic status there is an erasure of the individual and a further distinction between US-CLS and critical race theory. While Patricia Williams outlines her personal history as a mechanism to understand where she sits in relation to law, the Crits are less forthcoming. This lack of personal genealogy is not some conspiracy to hide their pre-US-CLS existence, but something less related to existing histories or understandings of US-CLS. Having an ambassador for a father, or television-star parents,[19] while not common, was not outside the realms of normalcy for privately educated, Ivy-League men in the 1960s. Excluding these historical aspects—or, more rightly, not including them—leads to a homogenisation of US-CLS history. A disinterested or objective account is harder to create when the materials come from those with an interest: Crits, anti-Crit liberals, minority scholars, new Crits, and so on. The inclusion of family histories does not alleviate this, but it adds to the history, providing context and background.

An example already mentioned is Williams's use of personal history to give context to her own struggles on admission to law school. Here in more detail is the power of personal history:

> [W]hen I decided to go to law school, my mother told me that "the Millers were lawyers so you have it in your blood." Now the Millers were the slaveholders of my maternal grandmother's clan. The Millers were also my great-great-grand-parents and great-aunts and who knows what else. My great-great-grandfather Austin Miller, a thirty-five-year-old lawyer, bought my eleven-year-old great-great-grandmother, Sophie, and her parents.[20]

While the Crits aimed to demystify law, critical race theorists like Williams took it further by presenting their own histories and relationships with law in their work. This method is often paired with other nontraditional approaches, such as the narrative structure Williams uses: "Critical Race Theorists have built on everyday experiences with perspective, viewpoint, and the power

---

[19] Peter Gabel's parents, Arlene Francis and Martin Gabel, starred on screen and stage. Francis was a panellist on the CBS series *What's My Line?* for almost twenty years.

[20] Patricia J. Williams, "Alchemical Notes: Reconstructing Ideals from Deconstructed Rights" (1987) 22 *Harvard Civil Rights–Civil Liberties Law Review* 401, 418.

of stories."[21] Although this method has been criticised,[22] its use in critical approaches to law adds necessary dimensions to critiques of the effect of the human element in legal systems.

On one level, the inclusion of an outline of an existing relationship with law, such as the one Williams describes, echoes foundational elements of law. For example, when Williams presents her family history with lawyers, she is coming to the critique and assessment of law and law school with clean hands; those who seek equity must do equity. Certain Crits have been sceptical of this approach, notably Mark Tushnet.[23] Amongst others who use narrative and personal history, Tushnet critiques Williams, heralding some of her stories as useful, while overall finding their subjectivity to invalidate the objective standards Williams appeals for.[24] This critique has validity, but it does seem to miss the purpose of such writing—wanting, instead, a more palatable universality in an individual's personal history.

These critiques demonstrate that an author's predilections, preferences, or purposes are rarely critiqued unless they come in an unfamiliar form. A black-letter law piece is unlikely to be chastised for the personal politics behind it, if it is written in the third person—critiques by the Crits are an exception. What Williams shows in her writing is that, through personal history and interactions with law, a more composite understanding of critique is possible. The illuminating nature of this approach builds on the analogies to US-CLS, that through these personal histories and interaction with the law, the curtain can be pulled back further to reveal a more "real" US-CLS.

Quoting Alain Badiou in a discussion on the unique features of the twentieth century, Slavoj Žižek argues that, unlike utopian or scientific plans for the future evident in earlier centuries, the twentieth century focused on the "real".[25] There are obvious correlations between this theory and the emergence of both legal realism and US-CLS. However, a more composite

---

[21] Richard Delgado and Jean Stefancic, *Critical Race Theory: An Introduction* (New York University Press, 3rd ed, 2017) 45.

[22] The "critical" nature of this narrative approach has been challenged. See especially Anne M. Coughlin, "Regulating the Self: Autobiographical Performances in Outsider Scholarship" (1995) 81(5) *Virginia Law Review* 1,229, 1,259. Coughlin argues that the narrative approach conforms rather than rebels: "The storytellers' opposition to law concludes by reaffirming the core values of our legal system."

[23] Mark Tushnet, "The Degradation of Constitutional Discourse" (1992–1993) 81 *Georgetown Law Journal* 251.

[24] Ibid 270–1.

[25] Slavoj Žižek, *Welcome to the Desert of the Real* (Verso Books, 2002) 1. Žižek employs a capital "R" for real, which is useful in context, but not here.

reality is evident in the work of Williams.²⁶ To further pull the curtain back on US-CLS, personal histories and context are needed. There are not many US-CLS works that provide a similar degree of personal history to that of Williams. However, a personal history can be constructed through other sources and interviews, which provide more context, especially around the formation of US-CLS.

Clandestine Legal Studies

One historical link that has never really been explored in US-CLS discussions is the effect of the Central Intelligence Agency (CIA) on US-CLS. Kennedy's work for the organisation has been mentioned to varying degrees, but is seemingly disconnected from US-CLS. Kennedy's employment preceded his JD at Yale Law School and functioned as a catalyst for his change in politics. Kennedy discusses this period at length in a 2015 interview, detailing his leftist optimism during his undergraduate studies, before a return to his Cold-War liberal roots in the CIA.²⁷ Kennedy worked for the National Student Association (NSA),²⁸ a CIA front that was exposed by the magazine *Ramparts* in 1967. By this stage Kennedy had left his position and was undertaking his JD. As Kennedy states, "I was radicalized between 1966 and 1969."²⁹

The story Kennedy tells is logical and linear: he grew up with educated, Cold-War liberal parents, and attends elite institutions, but always as a bit of an outsider. An anti-Communist who joined the CIA to avoid the war in Vietnam, all the while he was flirting with radicalism. Kennedy highlights generational tales between his cohort at Yale and his left-leaning professors, with a schism between the slightly older generation and those coming through university in the late 1960s. Kennedy's specific example is Alexander Bickel, a liberal professor who introduced him to legal realism.³⁰ The way both parties thought and engaged with the politics of the time provided Kennedy with a clear line between the old guard and what would eventually be US-CLS.

However, at the time Kennedy was rediscovering his radical roots and seeing generational lines forming, Charles Reich was also teaching at Yale

---

26 While the focus here is on Williams and her writing on alchemy, this narrative approach is taken in other critical race works. See C. K. Doreski, *Writing America Black: Race Rhetoric in the Public Sphere* (Cambridge University Press, 1998) 187–210.
27 Tor Krever, Carl Lisberger, and Max Utzschneider, "Law on the Left: A Conversation with Duncan Kennedy" (2015) 10(1) *Unbound* 1.
28 Ibid 5–6.
29 James R. Hackney Jr., *Legal Intellectuals in Conversation: Reflections on the Construction of Contemporary American Legal Theory* (New York University Press, 2012) 20.
30 Krever, Lisberger, and Utzschneider (n 27) 9; Duncan Kennedy, "Boola!" (1996) 49 *Social Text* 31.

Law School. Reich, famous for his bestselling work *The Greening of America*,[31] seems to fall outside of the divide Kennedy discusses with Bickel. *The Greening of America* is a countercultural text focusing on the failure of systems and structures in the US, reframing them in terms of social positions and consciousness. Reflecting on his book the year it was released, Reich states:

> [T]he revolution of the new generation ... is now spreading rapidly, & already our laws, institutions, & social structure are changing in consequence. Its ultimate creation could be a higher reason, a more human community, & a new & liberated individual.[32]

There are immediate similarities with US-CLS, and yet there is no mention of Reich in Kennedy's work, with only minor comparisons between Reich and US-CLS in a later generation of US-CLS work.[33] Laura Kalman highlights that Reich was not a radical but a legal liberal, concerned with the stifling nature of traditional law school education for idealistic students.[34] This places Reich as a logical conversation partner of Kennedy or other Crits in their own reimagination of law schools.

Still, there are a multitude of reasons why Kennedy did not interact with Reich. US-CLS did not have to reflect on a *New York Times* bestselling book that dealt with some similar themes. But this lack of acknowledgement and interaction colours the "us vs them" divide of a newly re-radicalised Kennedy—especially when Reich dedicates his book, "For the students at Yale, who made this book possible, and for their generation."[35] At the same time, outside of the law faculty, the dean of Yale's drama school, Robert Brunstein, published *Revolution as Theatre*, a sympathetic but critical analysis of young radicals.[36] All of this challenges the isolation in Kennedy's radicalisation.

Kennedy also made some questionable choices during and after law school, first working a summer for a Republican mayor of New York, and then clerking for Justice Potter Stewart, an Eisenhower-nominated judge. For each bit of history that sits at odds with the image of a founder of US-CLS, Kennedy has a narrative building on these diversions which led him back to

---

[31] Charles A. Reich, *The Greening of America* (Penguin, 1972).
[32] Charles A. Reich, "Reflections: The Greening of America", *The New Yorker* (New York, 26 September 1970) 42.
[33] Brigitte Fleischmann, "A Cultural Historian's Reading of Charles Reich's Impact on the Contemporary Discourse on 'Welfare'" (1989–1990) 31(2) *William & Mary Law Review* 307.
[34] Laura Kalman, *Yale Law School and the Sixties: Revolt and Reverberations* (University of North Carolina Press, 2005) 62–3.
[35] Reich, *The Greening of America* (n 31) 7.
[36] Robert Brunstein, *Revolution as Theatre* (Liveright, 1971).

critical righteousness. However, the details are fragmented. Kennedy's foray into the CIA is mentioned in earlier interviews, like in James Hackney's 2005 *Legal Intellectuals in Conversation*, where it warrants only a paragraph. In a 1994 interview with a student at Suffolk University in Boston, Kennedy makes no mention of his pre-law history.[37] This personal history would not be out of place in the 1994 interview, especially given the casual way it is mentioned in the 2005 piece.

A possible reason why the CIA is suddenly included by Kennedy in 2005 is two other interviews from that year. First, there is Kalman's *Yale Law School and the Sixties*, which makes a passing mention of Kennedy's CIA involvement prior to law school.[38] Second is an interview for Karen Paget's book *Patriotic Betrayal*.[39] *Patriotic Betrayal* details Paget's experience of the NSA through recently declassified documents and her personal history as the wife of a staff member. While both she and her husband knew about the CIA-NSA connection,[40] the majority of those involved in the NSA did not. Paget describes how, when *Ramparts* received the tip that the CIA was involved, the magazine's editors were flummoxed:[41]

> The NSA was a liberal organization. It supported the civil rights movement, raised bail money for jailed activists, condemned the anticommunist witch hunts of the House of Un-American Activities, and at its last Congress had debated supporting civil disobedience against the draft and the Vietnam war.[42]

A select number of those working for the NSA did know about the connection, including Kennedy. Paget interviewed Kennedy for the book in 2005, the same time Kennedy started discussing his CIA connection elsewhere.[43] The NSA itself was vital to post-war anti-Communist security. Louis Menand summarises its power:

> [T]he N.S.A. functioned as a glove that concealed the American government's hand and allowed it to do business with people who would never knowingly have done business with the American government. These

---

[37] Gerard J. Clark, "A Conversation with Duncan Kennedy" (1994) 24(2) *Suffolk University Law School Journal* 56.
[38] Kalman (n 34) 70.
[39] Karen M. Paget, *Patriotic Betrayal* (Yale University Press, 2015).
[40] Ibid ix.
[41] Ibid 4.
[42] Ibid 4–5.
[43] Hackney (n 29).

people thought that they were dealing with a student group that was independent of the government. They had no idea that the N.S.A. was a front.[44]

Information on influential students who took roles in foreign governments was invaluable to the CIA and those it shared information with, including information on student dissidents shared with authoritative regimes. For his part, Kennedy "is one of those who worries about the information pipeline inside the agency",[45] aligned with other former CIA-NSA workers concerned that the information collated on student activists would go to Iranian or South African officials.

Kennedy's other statements throughout *Patriotic Betrayal* synthesise with his law school interviews in 2005 and 2015: *Yale Law School and the Sixties* was published in 2005, with *Patriotic Betrayal* coming out in 2015 (Kennedy's interview for the book was undertaken a decade earlier). His general narrative is that, during his time at the NSA, he realised the magnitude of what the work was really about. In spite of this, after his year in France as part of the NSA delegation, Kennedy returned to Langley, commencing law school after his second year at the CIA ended. And Kennedy was not alone, with other disaffected CIA analysts participating in anti–Vietnam War marches.[46] Kennedy's story is a sympathetic one of a politically interested law student finding his feet to "transition" from anti-Communist Cold-War liberal to Crit.

Similarly, when Trubek talked about following "Bob's dad down to South America", he was referencing his time as a legal development advisor, first in Washington DC and then in Rio de Janeiro, between 1962 and 1966. Trubek goes into some detail about his time in Brazil, working at the embassy:

> We were lending huge amounts of money to Latin America, to Latin American countries to support development. And, to the extent possible, to promote the political factions that we thought were likely to oppose communism. This meant pouring a huge amount of money into Chile in order to forestall the election of [Salvador] Allende the first time around, in '65 I guess, or '64. It meant allocating our money in Brazil, initially, to governors who opposed the very left-leaning president. And of course there were all sorts of covert things going on that I had no idea about.[47]

---

[44] Louis Menand, "A Friend of the Devil', *The New Yorker* (online, 16 March 2015) <https://www.newyorker.com/magazine/2015/03/23/a-friend-of-the-devil>.
[45] Paget (n 39) 400.
[46] Tim Weiner, *Legacy of Ashes: A History of the CIA* (Anchor, 2008) 329.
[47] Betsy Draine, "Oral History with David M. Trubek", *University of Wisconsin Law School Oral Histories* (Wisconsin Law School, 23 & 24 July, 1 August 2008) 36–7.

While Trubek claims that he was unaware of the specifics of the covert operations going on, Robert Gordon's father did know. In September 1961 Lincoln Gordon was confirmed as ambassador to Brazil by the US Senate. During his time as ambassador, João Goulart was president of Brazil. Their initially cordial relationship continued until the Brazilian coup d'état in 1964, which removed the elected Brazilian Labour Party president and installed a military dictatorship. The dictatorship, which was more sympathetic to US interests than the left-of-centre president had been, remained in place until 1985.[48]

Lincoln Gordon was instrumental in the coup. In a 1962 discussion with John F. Kennedy, Lincoln Gordon "discussed spending $8 million to swing the next elections and to prepare the ground for a military coup against Goulart—'to push him out if necessary'".[49] It was after Lincoln Gordon's discussions with President Kennedy that "CIA money began pouring into Brazil".[50] This approach continued after Kennedy was assassinated, with declassified cables between Lincoln Gordon and President Lyndon Johnson highlighting the movement of naval ships and weaponry for "anti-Goulart forces".[51]

Between completing his Bachelor of Arts at Harvard College and commencing at Harvard Law School, Robert Gordon, enrolled in the military. Gordon served with the 3rd Infantry Division of the US army from 1963 to 1964, after a stint as a reporter at the Louisville Courier-Journal. In 1966 and 1967, Gordon took a job at *Newsweek* in their Boston and Rio de Janeiro bureaus, arriving in Brazil after the coup and during the early years of the military dictatorship.

In 1968 Gordon undertook his JD at Harvard Law School, a year before Unger began in 1969. The latter's grandfather had been exiled from Brazil by Goulart's mentor, and former president of Brazil, Getúlio Vargas. Unger's liberal grandfather remains the greatest influence on the founding Crit, offering insight into Unger's own foray into Brazilian politics,[52] but also aligning him

---

[48] Smith (n 18) chapters 13, 14, and 15. See also "Lincoln Gordon Personal Papers", *John F. Kennedy Presidential Library and Museum* <https://www.jfklibrary.org/asset-viewer/archives/LGPP>.

[49] Weiner (n 46) 218.

[50] Vincent Bevins, *The Jakarta Method* (Public Affairs, 2020) 194.

[51] Peter Kornbluh (ed) "CIA, Secret Memorandum of Conversation on 'Meeting at the White House 1 April 1964 Subject-Brazil', 1 April 1964", *National Security Archive* (Audio Recording, 1964) <https://nsarchive2.gwu.edu/NSAEBB/NSAEBB118/index.htm#audio>.

[52] Romano Carlin, "Boss Nova" *Chronicle of Higher Education* (online, 6 June 2008) <https://www.chronicle.com/article/boss-nova>.

with the other Crits and their disdain of Karl Marx and anything connecting them with Communists.

Kennedy states this clearly: "I was not a Marxist and knew nothing about Marxism except for the wildly distorted parodies dished out at the beginning of Harvard economics classes."[53] Kennedy's attitude towards Marx can be seen through the praise of one of his heroes, Paul Sweezy. Sweezy, who like Kennedy was an Exeter and Harvard graduate, worked for the Office of Strategic Service (the OSS, a precursor to the CIA), and influenced the young Kennedy through pamphlets that Kennedy's elementary school teacher had given him. For Kennedy, Sweezy "represented a non-Communist, radical leftism advocating socialism premised on state ownership of the means of production to achieve class justice as well as rational growth."[54]

Unger was more sympathetic to those disagreeing with Brazil's dictatorship. However, their praise of revolutionaries like Che Guevara added to his disdain and general repulsion at their frame of mind.[55] While Unger engaged more with Marx than most other Crits, he disagreed with the neo-Marxist direction of US-CLS and was "never really attracted to the content of Marxism".[56] Tushnet is also lumped into this group, with Kennedy referring to him as a "post-Marxist".[57] Politically, then, the roots of US-CLS are not only less radical than most of the histories present, but much more liberal than the founders probably believed.

***

Recent historic examinations of the US during the post-war period have shown how influential the CIA was in shaping the culture of the twentieth century. Largely, this was due to concerns about the attraction of Communism to the working class, and fears about its spread to the intelligentsia in Europe:

> [I]n these countries the best people of science, art, and literature belong to the Communist Party, are heading the movement of progressive struggle among the intelligentsia and by their creative and tireless struggle, are winning more and more intellectuals to the cause of Communism.[58]

---

[53] Krever, Lisberger, and Utzschneider (n 27) 9.
[54] Ibid 2.
[55] Carlin (n 52) 3.
[56] Ibid 4–5.
[57] Krever, Lisberger, and Utzschneider (n 27) 8.
[58] Frances Stonor Saunders, *Who Paid the Piper? The CIA and the Cultural Cold War* (Granta, 1999) 27, citing Andrei Zhdanov, "Report on the International Situation" in *Politics and Ideology* (Moscow, 1949).

The CIA were not the only group concerned about the spread of Communism to the US. Education, educators, and educational institutions were also concerned about the rise of communism. Menand argues that roughly 600 teachers and professors lost their jobs due to this fear. Universities changed their policies and introduced loyalty oaths for faculty. Philosophers like Sidney Hook reinvigorated liberal anti-Communist organisations.[59] In broader circles, the CIA realised that strategies like the Marshall Plan were not enough, and a turn to cultural warfare was needed.[60]

"The use of philanthropic foundations was the most convenient way to pass large sums of money to Agency projects without alerting recipients to their source."[61] Well-known foundations, Ford, Rockefeller, and Carnegie, were used. Industrialists like J. M. Kaplan volunteered to assist in the fight against communism and the Kaplan Foundation was soon an asset too. The Museum of Modern Art and its board were also connected to the CIA,[62] with famous artists Jackson Pollock, Mark Rothko, and Adolph Gottlieb in support of anti-Communist measures.[63] Funding ran to a range of covert operations, including "youth groups, labor unions, universities, publishing houses, and other private institutions".[64] And behind the scenes, those running the CIA were generally of a specific type, with "more liberal intellectuals per square inch at the CIA than anywhere else in government".[65]

Although staffing wasn't exclusively from the Ivy League, these universities were well represented. Historically, Ivy League universities were the places from which the OSS drew their adherents: J. P. Morgan's children were in the OSS, as were those from the DuPont and Vanderbilt families.[66] This continued with the CIA: "It was this historic elite, the Ivy-Leaguers who cast their influence over America's boardrooms, academic institutions, major newspapers and media, law firms and government, who now stepped forward to fill the ranks of the fledgling Agency."[67] These measures continue to this day, and have grown; since 1985, the CIA has had an "Officer in Residence" programme where CIA officers take a two-year break to teach at universities.[68]

---

[59] Louis Menand, *The Free World: Art and Thought in the Cold War* (Picador, 2021) 188–91.
[60] Stonor Saunders (n 58) 30–1.
[61] Ibid 134.
[62] Ibid 260.
[63] Ibid 276–7.
[64] Ibid 135.
[65] Ibid 236.
[66] Ibid 34–5.
[67] Ibid 36.
[68] Valerie Strauss and Vernon Loeb, "CIA Sends Agents to Schools—to Teach", *The Washington Post* (online, 18 April 2000) <https://www.washingtonpost.com/archive/

As well as being more candid about their position at universities, the CIA has declassified information that offers some context to the way US-CLS operated.

One example from the OSS, a few years prior to the formation of the CIA, offers insight into the ways in which workers could cause "simple sabotage". These techniques were not created for law professors, but they align with the way US-CLS disrupted law schools. The manual highlights that a saboteur should use the "materials he might normally be expected to possess as a . . . worker in his particular occupation",[69] and that the "targets of his sabotage are usually objects to which he has normal and inconspicuous access in everyday life."[70] The links to US-CLS are more apparent when the manual states that a "non cooperative attitude may involve nothing more than creating an unpleasant situation among one's fellow workers, engaging in bickerings, or displaying surliness."[71] This continues until the saboteur finds colleagues who aid them in greater acts of sabotage.

The CIA has connections to the universities, occupations, and families of key Crits. But these connections also exist with a number of other students from prominent families who graduated from elite institutions, as well as students from non-prominent families and non-elite institutions. Such was the threat of Communism in the US that there are tangential connections in a number of places. However, to once again employ a test from private law, one may ask if the relationship between US-CLS and the CIA is farfetched or fanciful? To which the answer must be no. There have been far stranger CIA connections drawn in recent years,[72] and less powerful groups infiltrated—for example, animal rights groups by the UK's Special Demonstration Squad. In fact, the connection is likely to be less conspiratorial,[73] but this relationship provides context to the formation of US-CLS. It attaches personal histories to the dominant voices in its ranks, who shaped what US-CLS would become. Rather than being due to a larger conspiracy, Kennedy actively dissuading fellow travellers in the 1980s can be understood as being due to his

---

politics/2000/04/18/cia-sends-agents-to-schools-to-teach/c63cc800-ba18-4dd2-83e7-3d07b0d1f793>; John Hollister Hedley, "Twenty Years of Officers in Residence CIA in the Classroom" (2005) 49(4) *Studies in Intelligence* 31.

[69] Director of Strategic Services, *Simple Sabotage Field Manual – Strategic Services (Provisional)* (Office of Strategic Services, 1944) 1.

[70] Ibid.

[71] Ibid.

[72] Tom O'Neill with Dan Piepenbring, *CHAOS: Charles Manson, the CIA, and the Secret History of the Sixties* (Back Bay, 2019).

[73] See generally Michael Butter, *The Nature of Conspiracy Theories* (Polity, 2020).

lack of control. US-CLS was moving away from the disaffected, Cold-War, anti-Communist, liberal view that it started with.

These histories also help explain the lack of interaction with others working in similar areas—not only those already highlighted at Yale during Kennedy's studies, but those working on law-specific critiques. In 1971, Robert Lefcourt published *Law Against the People: Essays to Demystify Law, Order and the Courts*, which received a review in the *California Law Review*.[74] Despite covering topics that would later be addressed by US-CLS, there was apparently no interaction between the parties. In a similar vein, but perhaps more telling, is Derrick Bell's publication of *Race, Racism and American Law* in 1970.[75] The vacuum that US-CLS created and its place in US law schools as the "left alternative" made it very difficult for other approaches to claim space. It was not until 1986 that US-CLS acknowledged its issues with race, by which time the civil rights movement was closer to twenty years old, rather than the two or three years old that it had been when Bell published his work.

***

The legacy of US-CLS is best aligned with a folklore quotation about the Velvet Underground: they didn't sell many records, but everyone who bought one went out and started a band. In the Critical Legal Studies family tree, the impact of US-CLS can be seen directly. However, an indirect mapping of the movement's influence would be near impossible to create. Even in related but rival schools of thought, brief glimmers of influence are often overlooked.[76] At the same time, US-CLS was not always a positive influence. Those more radical adherents looking for belonging had to battle against the hegemonic law and fellow Critical travellers. Liberals who could not align with a theory that offered fewer solutions than problems were similarly ostracised.

Conspiratorial legal studies has its appeals: the rejection of rights, just as civil rights activists are causing ripples in law schools; a deliberate lack of structure that first and foremost promoted the "white male heavies"; putting off new Crits; and the now-known CIA connections. This version of the history of US-CLS has all the trappings of a John le Carré novel, with Kennedy cast not as the famous protagonist George Smiley, but as Roy Bland, undercover as "a minor left-wing intellectual in search of light", writing for leftish papers and tiny magazines subsidised by the CIA.[77] "Tinker, Tailor, Soldier,

---

[74] Malcolm S. Burnstein, "Review" (1972) 60(5) *California Law Review* 1,485.
[75] Derrick Bell, *Race, Racism, and American Law* (Little Brown, 1981).
[76] Susan S. Silbey and Austin Sarat, "Critical Traditions in Law and Society Research" (1987) 21(1) *Law & Society Review* 165.
[77] John le Carré, *Tinker Tailor Soldier Spy* (Penguin, 1974) 165–6.

Crit" sits somewhere between *The Paper Chase* and a Cold-War spy film.[78] But this, too, is a posthumous declaration, a neatening of the history of US-CLS. It serves to categorise and reduce rather than clarify.

The personal histories of the Crits, much like their reframing as a legal subculture, are there to demystify not to proselytise. US-CLS was complicated, and deliberately so. It had the makings of a cult, with enigmatic leaders and secret language,[79] it shocked polite society, it inspired and disappointed, and, much to its founders' relief, it died.

CLS mortuus est, vivat CLS—CLS is dead, long live CLS

---

[78] *The Paper Chase*, dir. James Bridges (20th Century Fox, 1973).
[79] Amanda Montell, *Cultish: The Language of Fanaticism* (Harper Wave, 2021).

Bibliography

Secondary Sources

Abbott, Martin and Jennifer McKinney, *Understanding and Applying Research Design* (John Wiley & Sons, 2013)

Agamben, Giorgio, "Friendship" (2004) 5 *Contretemps* 1

Alexander, Peter, *Hamlet: Father and Son* (Oxford University Press, 1955)

Altman, Andrew, *Critical Legal Studies: A Liberal Critique* (Princeton University Press, 1990)

Altman, Andrew, "Legal Realism, Critical Legal Studies and Dworkin" (1986) 15(3) *Philosophy & Public Affairs* 205

Anderson, Jerry L., "Law School Enters the Matrix: Teaching Critical Legal Studies" (2004) 54(2) *Journal of Legal Education* 201

Austin, Arthur D., *The Empire Strikes Back: Outsiders and the Struggle over Legal Education* (New York University Press, 1998)

Austin, Arthur D., "Life At Harvard Law School: 'Sometimes It's Tough To Get Out Of Bed When You're Wearing Silk Pajamas'" (1993) 78 *Iowa Law Review* 427

Austin, Arthur, "The Top Ten Politically Correct Law Review Articles" (1999) 27 *Florida State University Law Review*, 233

Bankowski, Zenon and Geoff Mungham, *Images of Law* (Routledge, 1976)

Barish, Evelyn, *The Double Life of Paul de Man* (Liveright, 2014)

Barr, Olivia, *A Jurisprudence of Movement: Common Law, Walking, Unsettling Place* (Routledge, 2016)

Baudrillard, Jean, *Simulacra and Simulation*, tr. Sheila Faria Glaser (University of Michigan Press, 1994) [trans of: *Simulacres et Simulation* (1981)]

Bauman, Richard, *Ideology and Community in the First Wave of Critical Legal Studies* (University of Toronto Press, 2000)

Becker, Ernest, *The Denial of Death* (Free Press Paperback, 1997)

Bell, Derrick, *Race, Racism, and American Law* (Little Brown, 1981)

Bell, Derrick, "Strangers in Academic Paradise: Law Teachers of Color in Still White Schools" (1985) 20 *University of San Francisco Law Review* 385

Bevins, Vincent, *The Jakarta Method* (Public Affairs, 2020)

Bix, Brian H. (ed), *Philosophy of Law: Critical Concepts in Philosophy* (Routledge, 2016) vol 6

Blalock, Corinne, "Neoliberalism and the Crisis of Legal Theory" (2014) 77 *Law and Contemporary Problems* 71

Boal, Augusto, *Games for Actors and Non-Actors*, tr. Adrian Jackson (Routledge, 1999)

Boal, Augusto, *Theatre of the Oppressed*, tr. Charles A. McBride (Theatre Communications Group, 1993)
Boyle, James (ed), *Critical Legal Studies* (Dartmouth, 1992)
Bracamonte, José A., "Minority Critiques of the Critical Legal Studies Movement" (1987) 22 *Harvard Civil Rights–Civil Liberties Law Review* 297
Brinkley, Alan, *Liberalism and its Discontents* (Harvard University Press, 1998)
Brown, Wendy, *Politics Out of History* (Princeton University Press, 2001)
Brown, Wendy, *Undoing the Demos: Neoliberalism's Stealth Revolution* (ZoneBooks, 2015)
Brunstein, Robert, *Revolution as Theatre* (Liveright, 1971)
Burnstein, Malcolm S., "Review" (1972) 60(5) *California Law Review* 1,485
Buse, Peter and Andrew Stott (eds), *Ghosts: Deconstruction, Psychoanalysis, History* (Macmillan, 1999)
Butter, Michael, *The Nature of Conspiracy Theories* (Polity, 2020)
Carrington, Paul D., "Of Law and the River" (1984) 34 *Journal of Legal Education* 222
Carroll, Noël, *The Philosophy of Horror or Paradoxes of the Heart* (Routledge, 1990)
Chase, Anthony, "The Birth of the Modern Law School" (1979) 23(4) *American Journal of Legal History* 329
Clark, Gerard J., "A Conversation with Duncan Kennedy" (1994) 24(2) *Suffolk University Law School Journal* 56
Clarke, J. J., "'The End of History': A Reappraisal of Marx's Views on Alienation and Human Emancipation" (1971) 4(3) *Canadian Journal of Political Science* 367
Clark, Robert, *Corporate Law* (Little Brown, 1986)
CLC Middlesex University, "One-Day Conference: What Is Critical Legal Studies" (Call for Papers, 1985) <https://www.kent.ac.uk/law/research/clc-2016/archive.html>
CLC Organizing Group, "Critical Legal Conference" (Meeting Minutes, 1985) <https://www.kent.ac.uk/law/research/clc-2016/archive.html>
Coase, Ronald H., "Law and Economics at Chicago" (1993) 36(1) *Journal of Law & Economics* 239
Coase, Ronald H., "The Problem of Social Cost" (1960) 3 *Journal of Law and Economics* 1
Cogan, Brian and Thom Gencarelli (eds), *Baby Boomers and Popular Culture: An Inquiry into America's Most Powerful Generation* (Praeger, 2015)
Cohen, Stanley, *Folk Devils and Moral Panics: The Creation of the Mods and Rockers* (Paladin, 1973)
Coughlin, Anne M., "Regulating the Self: Autobiographical Performances in Outsider Scholarship" (1995) 81(5) *Virginia Law Review* 1,229
Crenshaw, Kimberlé, "Demarginalizing the Intersection of Race and Sex: A Black Feminist Critique of Antidiscrimination Doctrine, Feminist Theory and Antiracist Politics" (1989) 1(8) *University of Chicago Legal Forum* 139
Crenshaw, Kimberlé Williams, "Twenty Years of Critical Race Theory: Looking Back To Move Forward" (2011) 43(5) *Connecticut Law Review* 1,253
Critical Legal Studies: Intellectual History and History of the Present (27–28 February 2020), CLS Conference <https://clsconference.princeton.edu>
Cummings, Scott L., "Critical Legal Consciousness in Action" (2007) 120 *Harvard Law Review* 62

Dalton, Clare, "An Essay in the Deconstruction of Contract Doctrine" (1985) 94(5) *Yale Law Journal* 997

Davies, Margaret, *Asking the Law Question* (Thomson Reuters, 3rd ed, 2008)

Davis, Colin, "Hauntology, Spectres and Phantoms" (2005) 59(3) *French Studies* 373

Deleuze, Gilles and Félix Guattari, *Kafka: Towards a Minor Literature*, tr. Dana Polan (University of Minnesota Press, 1986) [trans of: *Kafka: pour une literature mineure* (1975)]

Deleuze, Gilles and Félix Guattari, "What is a Minor Literature?", tr. Robert Brinkley (1983) 11(3) *Mississippi Review* 13

Delgado, Richard and Jean Stefancic, *Critical Race Theory: An Introduction* (New York University Press, 3rd ed, 2017)

Denvir, John (ed), *Legal Reelism: Movies as Legal Texts* (University of Illinois Press, 1996)

Derrida, Jacques, *Of Grammatology*, tr. Gayatri Chakravorty Spivak (Johns Hopkins University Press, 1976) [trans of: *De la Grammatologie* (1967)]

Derrida, Jacques, *Specters of Marx: The State of the Debt, the Work of Mourning and the New International*, tr. Peggy Kamuf (Routledge, 1994) [trans of: *Spectres de Marx* (1993)]

Desautels-Stein, Justin and Christopher Tomlins (eds), *Searching for Contemporary Legal Thought* (Cambridge University Press, 2017)

Diocaretz, Myriam and Stefan Herbrechter (eds), *The Matrix in Theory* (Rodopi, 2006)

Director of Strategic Services, *Simple Sabotage Field Manual – Strategic Services (Provisional)* (Office of Strategic Services, 1944) 1

Doreski, C. K., *Writing America Black: Race Rhetoric in the Public Sphere* (Cambridge University Press, 1998)

Douzinas, Costas, "A Short History of the British Critical Legal Conference or, the Responsibility of the Critic" (2014) 25 *Law and Critique* 187

Douzinas, Costas, "Oubliez Critique" (2005) 16(1) *Law and Critique* 47

Douzinas, Costas and Adam Gearey, *Critical Jurisprudence: The Political Philosophy of Justice* (Hart, 2005)

Douzinas, Costas, Peter Goodrich and Yifat Hachamovitch (eds), *Politics, Postmodernity, and Critical Legal Studies: The Legality of the Contingent (and Sport)* (Routledge, 1994)

Douzinas, Costas and Lynda Nead (eds), *Law and the Image: The Authority of Art and the Aesthetics of Law* (University of Chicago Press, 1999)

Douzinas, Costas and Colin Perrin (eds), *Critical Legal Theory* (Routledge, 2012)

Draine, Betsy, "Oral History with David M. Trubek" *University of Wisconsin Law School Oral Histories* (Wisconsin Law School, 23 & 24 July, 1 August 2008)

Duncan, Kirsty, "Tracing the Law Through the Matrix" (2001) 10(2) *Griffith Law Review* 160

Duxbury, Neil, *Patterns of American Jurisprudence* (Clarendon Press, 1995)

Duxbury, Neil, "The Reinvention of American Legal Realism" (1992) 12(2) *Legal Studies* 137

Dworkin, Ronald, "Is Wealth a Value?" (1980) 9(2) *Journal of Legal Studies* 191

Editorial Board, "Introduction" (1985) 6(4) *Cardozo Law Review* 691

Erlich, Avi, *Hamlet's Absent Father* (Princeton University Press, 1977)

Esposito, Roberto, "The *Dispositif* of the Person" (2012) 8(1) *Law, Culture and the Humanities* 17

Farber, Daniel A. and Suzanna Sherry, "Beyond All Criticism" (1999) 83 *Minnesota Law Review* 1,735

Farber, Daniel A. and Suzanna Sherry, *Beyond All Reason: The Radical Assault on Truth in American Law* (Oxford University Press, 1997)

Fellmeth, Robert C., "State-Lovers, State-Haters, and Orly Lobel" (2007) 120 *Harvard Law Review* 36

Fischl, Richard Michael, "The Question That Killed Critical Legal Studies" (1992) 17(4) *Law and Social Inquiry* 779

Fisher, Mark, "What Is Hauntology?" (2012) 66(1) *Film Quarterly* 16

Fisher, William W., III, Morton J. Horwitz, and Thomas A. Reed (eds), *American Legal Realism* (Oxford University Press, 1993)

Fiss, Owen M., "Death of the Law" (1986) 72(1) *Cornell Law Review* 1

Fitzpatrick, Peter and Alan Hunt (eds), *Critical Legal Studies* (Basil Blackwell, 1987)

Fleischmann, Brigitte, "A Cultural Historian's Reading of Charles Reich's Impact on the Contemporary Discourse on 'Welfare'" (1989–1990) 31(2) *William & Mary Law Review* 307

Foucault, Michel, *The History of Sexuality: Volume One and Introduction*, tr. Robert Hurley (Pantheon Books, 1978)

Foucault, Michel, *Power/Knowledge*, ed. Colin Gordon, tr. Colin Gordon et al. (Harvester Press, 1980)

Fraser, David, "What a Long, Strange Trip It's Been: Deconstructing Law from Legal Realism to Critical Legal Studies" (1988–89) 5 *Australian Journal of Law and Society* 35

Freeman, Alan D., "Truth and Mystification in Legal Scholarship" (1981) 90(5) *Yale Law Journal* 122

Frug, Mary Joe, "A Postmodern Feminist Legal Manifesto (An Unfinished Draft)" (1992) 105(5) *Harvard Law Review* 1,045

Frug, Mary Joe, "Re-Reading Contracts: A Feminist Analysis of a Contracts Casebook" (1985) 34 *American University Law Review* 1,065

Fukuyama, Francis, "The End of History?" (1989) 16 *National Interest* 3

Fukuyama, Francis, "The 'End of History' 20 Years Later" (2013) 30(4) *New Perspectives Quarterly* 31

Fukuyama, Francis, *The End of History and the Last Man* (Free Press, 1992)

Gabel, Peter and Duncan Kennedy, "Roll Over Beethoven" (1984) 36(1/2) *Stanford Law Review* 1

Gearey, Adam, "'Change Is Gonna Come': Critical Legal Studies and the Legacies of the New Left" (2013) 24 *Law and Critique* 211

Giddens, Thomas (ed), *Graphic Justice: Intersections of Comics and Law* (Routledge, 2015)

Giddens, Thomas, *On Comics and Legal Aesthetics: Multimodality and the Haunted Mask of Knowing* (Routledge, 2018)

Glahn, Philip, *Bertolt Brecht* (Reaktion Books, 2014)

Golder, Ben and Peter Fitzpatrick, *Foucault's Law* (Routledge-Cavendish, 2009)

Goode, Erich and Nachman Ben-Yehuda, *Moral Panics: The Social Construction of Deviance* (Wiley-Blackwell, 2nd ed, 2009)

Goodrich, Peter, "Duncan Kennedy as I Imagine Him: The Man, the Work, His Scholarship, and the Polity" (2001) 22 *Cardozo Law Review* 971

Goodrich, Peter, "Europe in America: Grammatology, Legal Studies, and the Politics of Transmission" (2001) 101(8) *Columbia Law Review* 2,033

Goodrich, Peter, *Law in the Courts of Love: Literature and Other Minor Jurisprudences* (Routledge, 1996)

Goodrich, Peter, "Mos Americanus or Common Law in Partibus Infidelium" (2015) 21 *Villanova Law Review* 521

Goodrich, Peter, "Satirical Legal Studies: From the Legists to the Lizard" (2004) 103(3) *Michigan Law Review* 397

Goodrich, Peter, "Screening Law" (2009) 21(1) *Law and Literature* 1

Goodrich, Peter, "Sleeping with the Enemy: An Essay on the Politics of Critical Legal Studies in America" (1993) 68(2) *New York University Law Review* 389

Gordon, James D., III, "Law Review and the Modern Mind" (1991) 33(2) *Arizona Law Review* 265

Gordon, Robert W., "Bargaining with the Devil" (1992) 105(8) *Harvard Law Review* 2,041

Gordon, Robert W., "Critical Legal Histories" (1984) 36 *Stanford Law Review* 57

Gordon, Robert W., "Critical Legal Studies as a Teaching Method, against the Background of the Intellectual Politics of Modern Legal Education in the United States" (1989) 59 *Legal Education Review* 59

Gordon, Robert W., "'Critical Legal Histories Revisited': A Response" (2012) 37(1) *Law & Social Inquiry* 200

Gregory, David L., "A Guide to Critical Legal Studies" (1987) 1987(6) *Duke Law Journal* 1,138

Hackney, James R., Jr, *Legal Intellectuals in Conversation: Reflections on the Construction of Contemporary American Legal Theory* (New York University Press, 2012)

Hägglund, Martin, *Radical Atheism: Derrida and the Time of Life* (Stanford University Press, 2008)

Haines, Andrew W., "The Critical Legal Studies Movement and Racism: Useful Analytics and Guides for Social Action or an Irrelevant Modern Legal Scepticism and Solipsism?" (1987) 13(4) *William Mitchell Law Review* 685

Hall, Mark A. and Ronald F. Wright, "Systematic Content Analysis of Judicial Opinions" (2008) 96 *California Law Review* 63

Hartnoll, Phyllis, *A Concise History of the Theatre* (Thames and Hudson, 1978)

Hartog, Hendrik, "Introduction to Symposium on 'Critical Legal Histories': Robert W. Gordon. 1984. Critical Legal Histories. Stanford Law Review 36:57–125" (2012) 37(1) *Law & Social Inquiry* 147

Harvey, David, *A Brief History of Neoliberalism* (Oxford University Press, 2005)

Hasnas, John, "Back to the Future: From Critical Legal Studies Forward to Legal Realism, or How Not to Miss the Point of the Indeterminacy Argument" (1995) 45(1) *Duke Law Journal* 84

Haverkamp, Anselm, "The Ghost of History: Hamlet and the Politics of Paternity" (2006) 18(2) *Law and Literature* 171

Hebdige, Dick, *Subculture: The Meaning of Style* (Routledge, 1989)

Hollister Hedley, John, "Twenty Years of Officers in Residence" (2005) 49(4) *Studies in Intelligence* 31

Holmes, Oliver Wendell, Jr, *The Common Law* (Dover Publications, 1991)

Holmes, Oliver Wendell, Jr, "The Path of the Law" (1897) 8 *Harvard Law Review* 61
Honig, Bonnie, *Antigone, Interrupted* (Cambridge University Press, 2013)
Horowitz, Helen Lefkowitz, "The 1960s and the Transformation of Campus Cultures" (1986) 26(1) *History of Education Quarterly* 1
Horsman, Yasco, *Theaters of Justice: Judging, Staging, and Working Through in Arendt, Brecht, and Delbo* (Stanford University Press, 2011)
Horwitz, Morton J., *The Transformation of American Law 1780–1860* (Harvard University Press, 1977)
Hughes, Chris, "Dialogue between Fukuyama's Account of the End of History and Derrida's Hauntology" (2012) 7(18) *Journal of Philosophy: A Cross-Disciplinary Inquiry* 13
Hutchinson, Allan C. and Patrick J. Monahan, "The 'Rights' Stuff: Roberto Unger and Beyond" (1984) 62(8) *Texas Law Review* 1,477
Kahlenberg, Richard D., *Broken Contract: A Memoir of Harvard Law School* (University of Massachusetts Press, 1992)
Kahn, Victoria, "Hamlet or Hecuba: Carl Schmitt's Decision" (2003) 83(1) *Representations* 67
Kalman, Laura, *Yale Law School and the Sixties: Revolt and Reverberations* (University of North Carolina Press, 2005)
Kelman, Mark, *A Guide to Critical Legal Studies* (Harvard University Press, 1987)
Kelman, Mark G., "Trashing" (1984) 36(1/2) *Stanford Law Review* 293
Kennedy, Duncan, *A Critique of Adjudication (fin de siècle)* (Harvard University Press, 1998)
Kennedy, Duncan, "Boola!" (1996) 49 *Social Text* 31
Kennedy, Duncan, "Critical Labor Law Theory: A Comment" (1981) 4 *Industrial Relations Law Journal* 503
Kennedy, Duncan, "Form and Substance in Private Law Adjudication" (1989) 89 *Harvard Law Review* 1685
Kennedy, Duncan, "How the Law School Fails: A Polemic" (1971) 1 *Yale Review of Law and Social Action* 77
Kennedy, Duncan, *Legal Education and the Reproduction of Hierarchy: A Polemic Against the System* (New York University Press, 2004)
Kennedy, Duncan, "Psycho-Social CLS: A Comment on the Cardozo Symposium" (1984–1985) 6 *Cardozo Law Review* 1013
Kennedy, Duncan, "Remembering Keith Aoki's 'Casual Legal Studies: Art During Law School'" (2012) 45(5) *University of California Davis Law Review* 1,817
Kennedy, Duncan, *The Rise and Fall of Classical Legal Thought* (BeardBooks 2006)
Kennedy, Duncan, *Sexy Dressing Etc.* (Harvard University Press, 1993)
Kennedy, Duncan, "The Stakes of Law, or Hale and Foucault!" (1991) 15(4) *Legal Studies Forum* 327
Kennedy, Duncan, "The Structure of Blackstone's Commentaries" (1979) 28 *Buffalo Law Review* 209
Kennedy, Duncan, "Two Globalizations of Law & Legal Thought: 1850–1968" (2003) 36(3) *Suffolk University Law Review* 631
Kennedy, Duncan and Corinne Blalock, "Provocation as Strategy" (2022) 121(2) *South Atlantic Quarterly* 377
Kennedy, Duncan and Karl E. Klare, "A Bibliography of Critical Legal Studies" (1984) 94(461) *Yale Law Journal* 461

Kenyon, Andrew T. and Peter D. Rush (ed), *An Aesthetics of Law and Culture: Text, Images, Screens* (*Studies in Law, Politics, and Society*) (JAI Press, 2004)

König, René, "WIKIPEDIA: Between Lay Participation and Elite Knowledge Representation" (2013) 16(2) *Information, Communication and Society* 160

Kornbluh, Peter (ed) "CIA, Secret Memorandum of Conversation on 'Meeting at the White House 1 April 1964 Subject-Brazil,' April 1, 1964", *National Security Archive* (Audio Recording, 1964) <https://nsarchive2.gwu.edu/NSAEBB/NSAEBB118/index.htm#audio>

Krever, Tor, Carl Lisberger and Max Utzschneider, "Law on the Left: A Conversation with Duncan Kennedy" (2015) 10(1) *Unbound* 1

Lacan, Jacques, *Écrits: The First Complete Edition in English*, tr. Bruce Fink (W. W. Norton, 2006)

Lee, Newton (ed), *Google It* (Springer, 2016)

Lefcourt, Robert, *Law Against the People* (Random House, 1971)

Leitch, Thomas, *Wikipedia U: Knowledge, Authority, and Liberal Education in the Digital Age* (Johns Hopkins University Press, 2014)

Levine, Norman, *Marx's Discourse with Hegel* (Palgrave Macmillan, 2012)

Lévi-Strauss, Claude, *Myth and Meaning* (Routledge, 1989)

"Lincoln Gordon Personal Papers", *John F. Kennedy Presidential Library and Museum* <https://www.jfklibrary.org/asset-viewer/archives/LGPP>

Livingston, Debra A., "'Round and 'Round the Bramble Bush: From Legal Realism to Critical Legal Scholarship" (1982) 95(7) *Harvard Law Review* 1,669

Lobel, Orly, "The Paradox of Extralegal Activism: Critical Legal Consciousness and Transformative Politics" (2007) 120 *Harvard Law Review* 937

Loizidou, Elena, "Sex @ the End of the Twentieth Century: Some Re-Marks on a Minor Jurisprudence" (1999) 10 *Law and Critique* 71

Luban, David, "Legal Modernism" (1986) 84(8) *Michigan Law Review* 1,656

MacKinnon, Catharine, "Feminism in Legal Education" (1989) 7 *Legal Education Review* 85

MacNeil, William P., *Lex Populi*: *The Jurisprudence of Popular Culture* (Stanford University Press, 2007)

MacNeil, William P., "'You Slay Me!': Buffy as Jurisprude of Desire" (2003) 24(6) *Cardozo Law Review* 2,421

Madison, D. Soyini, *Critical Ethnography: Method, Ethics, and Performance* (Sage, 2nd ed, 2012)

Manza, Jeff, "Critical Legal Studies" (1990) 35 *Berkeley Journal of Sociology* 137

Marcus, Daniel, *Happy Days and Wonder Years: The Fifties and the Sixties in Contemporary Cultural Politics* (Rutgers University Press, 2004)

Martin, Peter W., "'Of Law and the River,' and of Nihilism and Academic Freedom" (1985) 35 *Journal of Legal Education* 1

Marx, Karl and Friedrich Engels, *The Communist Manifesto* (Penguin Classics, 2002)

Matsuda, Mari J., "Looking to the Bottom: Critical Legal Studies and Reparations" (1987) 22 *Harvard Civil Rights–Civil Liberties Law Review* 323

McLaughlin, Eugene, "See Also Young, 1971: Marshall McLuhan, Moral Panics and Moral Indignation" (2014) 18(4) *Theoretical Criminology* 422

McLeod, Ian, *Legal Theory* (Palgrave Macmillan, 5th ed, 2010)

Menand, Louis, *The Metaphysical Club* (Farrar Straus and Giroux, 2001)

Mettler, Meghan Warner, "'If I Could Drive You Out of Your Mind': Anti-Rationalism and the Celebration of Madness in 1960s Counterculture" (2015) 9(2) *Journal of Literary & Cultural Disability Studies* 171
Meyerson, Denise, *Essential Jurisprudence* (Routledge Cavendish, 2008)
Miéville, China, *Between Equal Rights: A Marxist Theory of International Law* (Brill, 2005)
Miller, John J., Karl Zinsmeister, and Ashley May, *Agenda Setting: A Wise Giver's Guide to Influencing Public Policy* (Philanthropy Roundtable, 2015)
Minda, Gary, *Postmodern Legal Movements: Law and Jurisprudence at Century's End* (New York University Press, 1995)
Minkkinen, Panu, "The Radiance of Justice: On the Minor Jurisprudence of Franz Kafka" (1994) 3 *Social & Legal Studies* 349
Mirandé, Alfredo, "'Revenge of the Nerds,' or Postmodern 'Colored Folk'? Critical Race Theory and the Chronicles of Rodrigo" (2000) 4(1) *Harvard Latino Law Review* 153
Mirowski, Philip and Dieter Plehwe (eds), *The Road from Mont Pèlerin: The Making of the Neoliberal Thought Collective* (Harvard University Press, 2009)
Montell, Amanda, *Cultish: The Language of Fanaticism* (Harper Wave, 2021)
Mootz, Francis J., III (ed), *On Philosophy in American Law* (Cambridge University Press, 2009)
Moyn, Samuel, *The Last Utopia* (Belknap Press, 2010)
Neacsu, E. Dana, "CLS Stands for Critical Legal Studies, If Anyone Remembers" (2000) 8(2) *Journal of Law and Policy* 415
Nietzsche, Friedrich, *On the Genealogy of Morals*, tr. Michael A. Scarpitti (Penguin Classics, 2013)
O'Neill, Tom, with Dan Piepenbring, *CHAOS: Charles Manson, the CIA, and the Secret History of the Sixties* (Back Bay, 2019)
Paget, Karen M., *Patriotic Betrayal* (Yale University Press, 2015)
Paul, Jeremy, "CLS 2001" (2001) 22 *Cardozo Law Review* 701
Pigou, Arthur C., *The Economics of Welfare* (Macmillan, 4th ed, 1932)
Posner, Richard A., *Economic Analysis of Law* (Little Brown, 1973)
Posner, Richard A., *The Economics of Justice* (Harvard University Press, 1981)
Posner, Richard A., *The Problematics of Moral and Legal Theory* (Belknap Press, 1999)
Quiggin, John, "The Y2K Scare: Causes, Costs and Cures" (2005) 64(3) *Australian Journal of Public Administration* 46
Raban, Ofer, *Modern Legal Theory and Judicial Impartiality* (Glasshouse Press, 2003)
Rancière, Jacques, *The Emancipated Spectator*, tr. Gregory Elliott (Verso, 2011)
Rasulov, Akbar, "CLS and Marxism: A History of an Affair" (2014) 5(4) *Transnational Legal Theory* 622
Reich, Charles A., *The Greening of America* (Penguin, 1972)
Richardson, John and Brian Leiter (eds), *Nietzsche* (Oxford, 1978)
Rorty, Richard, "The Banality of Pragmatism and the Poetry of Justice" *Southern California Law Review* 63 (1990) 1,811
Russell, J. Stuart, "The Critical Legal Studies Challenge to Contemporary Mainstream Legal Philosophy" (1986) 18(1) *Ottawa Law Review* 1
Salojärvi, Juhana Mikael, "A Counter-Culture of Law: Jurisprudential Change and the Intellectual Origins of the Critical Legal Studies Movement" (2019) 59(4) *American Journal of Legal History* 409

Sarat, Austin, Lawrence Douglas, and Martha Merrill Umphrey (eds), *Law on the Screen* (Stanford University Press, 2005)

Schlag, Pierre, "US CLS" (1999) 10 *Law and Critique* 199

Schlegel, John Henry, "CLS Wasn't Killed By a Question" (2007) 58(5) *Alabama Law Review* 967

Schmitt, Carl, "Hegel and Marx" (2014) 22(3–4) *Historical Materialism* 388

Shapiro, Fred R. and Michelle Pearse, "The Most-Cited Law Review Articles of All Time" (2012) 110(8) *Michigan Law Review* 1,483

Sharp, Cassandra and Marett Leiboff (eds), *Cultural Legal Studies: Law's Popular Cultures and the Metamorphosis of Law* (Routledge, 2015)

Shepherd, Simon and Mick Wallis, *Drama/Theatre/Performance* (Routledge, 2004)

Silbey, Susan S. and Austin Sarat, "Critical Traditions in Law and Society Research" (1987) 21(1) *Law and Society Review* 165

Smith, Bruce L. R., *Lincoln Gordon: Architect of Cold War Foreign Policy* (University of Kentucky Press, 2015)

Solum, Lawrence B., "On the Indeterminacy Crisis: Critiquing Critical Dogma" (1987) 54 *Chicago Law Review* 462

Stewart, James Gilchrist, "CLS Is Haunted! A Perspective on Contemporary Critical Legal Studies" (2020) 36(1) *Law and Literature* 135

Stewart, James Gilchrist, "Demystifying CLS: A Critical Legal Studies Family Tree" (2020) 41(1) *Adelaide Law Review* 121

Stewart, James Gilchrist, "Panic at the Law School! A Critical Case for Legal Subcultures" (2002) 33(2) *Law and Critique* 195

Stewart, Michael, *Keynes and After* (Pelican, 2nd ed, 1968)

Stone, Matthew, Illan rua Wall, and Costas Douzinas (eds), *New Critical Thinking: Law and the Political* (Routledge, 2012)

Stonor Saunders, Frances, *Who Paid the Piper? The CIA and the Cultural Cold War* (Granta, 1999)

Teles, Steven M., *The Rise of the Conservative Legal Movement: The Battle for Control of the Law* (Princeton University Press, 2008)

Thacker, Eugene, *In the Dust of This Planet: Horror of Philosophy Volume One* (Zero, 2011)

Thornton, Margaret, "Gothic Horror in the Legal Academy" (2005) 14(2) *Social & Legal Studies* 267

Tomlins, Christopher, "Law As . . . IV: Minor Jurisprudence in Historical Key. An Introduction" (2017) 17 *Law Text Culture* 1

Trubek, David M., "Foundational Events, Foundational Myths, and the Creation of Critical Race Theory, or How to Get Along with a Little Help from Your Friends" (2011) 43(5) *Connecticut Law Review* 1,503

Tushnet, Mark, "An Essay on Rights" (1983–1984) 62 *Texas Law Review* 1,363

Tushnet, Mark, "Critical Legal Studies: A Political History" (1991) 100(5) *Yale Law Journal* 1,515

Tushnet, Mark, "Critical Legal Studies: An Introduction to its Origins and Underpinnings" (1986) 36 *Journal of Legal Education* 505

Tushnet, Mark, "The Critique of Rights" (1994) 47(1) *Southern Methodist Law Review* 23

Tushnet, Mark, "The Degradation of Constitutional Discourse" (1992–1993) 81 *Georgetown Law Journal* 251

Unger, Roberto Mangabeira, *The Critical Legal Studies Movement* (Harvard University Press, 1983)
Unger, Roberto Mangabeira, *The Critical Legal Studies Movement: Another Time, a Greater Task* (Verso, 2015)
Unger, Roberto Mangabeira, *Knowledge and Politics* (Free Press, 1975)
Unger, Roberto Mangabeira, *Law in Modern Society: Toward a Criticism of Social Theory* (Free Press, 1976)
University of Kent, "Critical Legal Conference, First Annual Conference: Law, Critique and Social Transformation" (Call for Papers, 1986) <https://www.kent.ac.uk/law/research/clc-2016/archive.html>
Vaidhyanathan, Siva, *The Googlization of Everything (And Why We Should Worry)* (University of California Press, 2012)
Ward, Ian, *Introduction to Critical Legal Theory* (Routledge Cavendish, 2nd ed, 2004)
Weiner, Tim, *Legacy of Ashes: A History of the CIA* (Anchor, 2008)
West, Cornel, "Reassessing the Critical Legal Studies Movement" (1988) 34 *Loyola Law Review* 265
Williams, Patricia J., "Alchemical Notes: Reconstructing Ideals From Deconstructed Rights" (1987) 22 *Harvard Civil Rights–Civil Liberties Law Review* 401
Williams, Patricia J., *The Alchemy of Race and Rights* (Harvard University Press, 1991)
Worthen, W. B., *The Wadsworth Anthology of Drama* (Thomson Wadsworth, 4th ed, 2004)
Young, Jock, "Moral Panic: Its Origins in Resistance, Ressentiment and the Translation of Fantasy into Reality" (2009) 49(1) *British Journal of Criminology* 4
Young, Jock, *The Drugtakers: The Social Meaning of Drug Use* (MacGibbon and Kee, 1971)
Žižek, Slavoj, *Welcome to the Desert of the Real* (Verso, 2002)

Media

Fiction

Baum, L. Frank, *The Wonderful Wizard of Oz* (Geo M Hill, 1899)
Dickens, Charles, *A Christmas Carol and Other Christmas Writings* (Penguin Classics, 2003)
Eliot, T. S., *Collected Poems 1909–1962* (Harcourt Brace Jovanovich, 1991)
Le Carré, John, *Tinker Tailor Soldier Spy* (Penguin, 1974)
Stoker, Bram, *Dracula* (Penguin Classics, 2003)

Film and Television

A Christmas Carol, dir. Clive Donner (Entertainment Partners, 1984)
Coffee and Cigarettes, dir. Jim Jarmusch (Asmik Ace Entertainment, 2003)
Coffee and Cigarettes III, dir. Jim Jarmusch (Cinesthesia Productions, 1993)
Hackers, dir. Iain Softley (United Artists, 1995)
Invasion of the Body Snatchers, dir. Don Siegel (Walter Wanger Productions, 1956)
Invasion of the Body Snatchers, dir. Philip Kaufman (Solofilm, 1978)
It's a Wonderful Life, dir. Frank Capra (Liberty Films, 1946)
Jaws, dir. Steven Spielberg (Universal Studios, 1975)
The Matrix, dir. the Wachowskis (Warner Brothers, 1999)
The Net, dir. Irwin Winkler (Columbia Pictures, 1995)

The Paper Chase, dir. James Bridges (20th Century Fox)
South Park, dir. Trey Parker (Comedy Central, 1997)
South Park: Bigger, Longer & Uncut, dir. Trey Parker (Scott Rudin Productions, 1999)
The Terminator, dir. James Cameron (Hemdale, 1984)
Terminator 2: Judgement Day, dir. James Cameron (Carolco Pictures, 1991)
TRON, dir. Steven Lisberger (Walt Disney Productions, 1982)

Theatre

Ibsen, Henrik, *A Doll's House* (CreateSpace, 2013)
Miller Arthur, *Death of a Salesman: Certain Private Conversations in Two Acts and a Requiem* (Penguin, 2000)
Shakespeare, William, *Hamlet*, ed. Bernard Lott (Longman, 1997)
Strindberg, August, *Three Plays*, tr. Peter Watts (Penguin, 1975)
Williams, Tennessee, *The Glass Menagerie* (Penguin, 2009)

Dictionaries and Encyclopedias

Berkman Klein Center for Internet and Society at Harvard University, "Critical Legal Studies Movement", *The Bridge* (Web Page, 23 October 2023) <https://cyber.harvard.edu/bridge/CriticalTheory/critical2.htm>
Berkman Klein Center for Internet and Society at Harvard University, *The Bridge* (Web Page, 1 March 2023) <https://cyber.harvard.edu/research/bridge>
Butt, Peter (ed), *Concise Australian Dictionary* (LexisNexis Butterworths, 4th ed, 2011)
Encyclopedia.Com, *Critical Legal Studies* (Web Page, November 2023) <https://www.encyclopedia.com/law/encyclopedias-almanacs-transcripts-and-maps/critical-legal-studies>
Garner, Bryan A. (ed), *Black's Law Dictionary* (Thomas West, 9th ed, 2014)
Larkin, Ralph W., "Counterculture: 1960s and Beyond" (2015) 5 *International Encyclopedia of the Social & Behavioral Sciences 2nd Edition* 73
Legal Information Institute, *Critical Legal Theory* (Web Page, August 2022) <https://www.law.cornell.edu/wex/critical_legal_theory>
Mann, Trischa (ed), *Australian Law Dictionary* (Oxford, 2010)
Quinion, Michael, "Brass Ring", *World Wide Words* (Web Page, 14 January 2023) <http://www.worldwidewords.org/qa/qa-bra4.htm>
Wikipedia, *Critical Legal Studies* (Web Page) <https://en.wikipedia.org/wiki/Critical_legal_studies>

Newspapers and Websites

Abel, Richard, "Los Angeles National CLS Conference, January 6–8 1987", *Newsletter of the Conference on Critical Legal Studies* (Buffalo New York, December 1986)
Atlas, James, "The Case of Paul de Man", *New York Times* (online, 28 August 1988) <https://www.nytimes.com/1988/08/28/magazine/the-case-of-paul-de-man.html>
Bean, Matt, "'Matrix' Makes Its Way into Courtrooms as Defense Strategy", *CNN* (online, 21 May 2003) <http://edition.cnn.com/2003/LAW/05/21/ctv.matrix.insanity>
Beinart, Peter, "Why Trump Is Accusing Obama of Wiretapping" *Politics, The Atlantic* (online, 7 March 2017) <https://www.theatlantic.com/politics/archive/2017/03/why-trump-is-accusing-obama-of-wiretapping/518793>

Bernstein, Fred A., "Derrick Bell, Law Professor and Rights Advocate, Dies at 80", *The New York Times* (online, 6 October 2011) <https://www.nytimes.com/2011/10/06/us/derrick-bell-pioneering-harvard-law-professor-dies-at-80.html>

Carlin, Romano, "Boss Nova" *The Chronicle of Higher Education* (online, 6 June 2008) <https://www.chronicle.com/article/boss-nova/>

Deerfield Academy, "Peter Gabel '64", Alumni (Web Page, 5 June 2015) <https://deerfield.edu/alumni/class-notes/2015/06/peter-gabel-64/10223689>

Drake Law School, "Jerry Anderson Profile", *Faculty and Staff* (Web Page, 2023) <http://www.drake.edu/law/facstaff/directory/jerry-anderson>

Fox, Margalit, "Walter Bowart, Alternative Journalist, Dies at 68", *New York Times* (online, 14 January 2008) <https://www.nytimes.com/2008/01/14/arts/14bowart.html>

Fox, Steven M., "The Collected Trashman" (2013) *Underground Comix Joint* <https://comixjoint.com/collectedtrashman.html>

Fukuyama, Francis, "The History at the End of History', *The Guardian* (online, 3 April 2007) <https://www.theguardian.com/commentisfree/2007/apr/03/thehistoryattheendofhist>

Glaser, Eliane, "Bring Back Ideology: Fukuyama's 'End of History' 25 Years On", *The Guardian* (online, 21 March 2014) <https://www.theguardian.com/books/2014/mar/21/bring-back-ideology-fukuyama-end-history-25-years-on>

Gold, Allan, "Traditionalist Is Named As Harvard Law Dean", *The New York Times* (online, 18 February 1989) <https://www.nytimes.com/1989/02/18/us/traditionalist-is-named-as-harvard-law-dean.html>

Granetz, Marc, "Duncan the Doughnut", *The New Republic* (Washington DC, 17 March 1986) 22

"Invasion of the Punk Professors", *The New Republic* (Washington DC, 17 March 1986), 1

Ivanov, Avel, "The Student's Dilemma: Conformity or Education", *Quillette* (online, 15 May 2018) <https://quillette.com/2018/05/15/students-dilemma-conformity-education>

Kelaidis, Katie, "The Enlightenment's Cynical Critics", *Quillette* (online, 15 June 2018) <https://quillette.com/2018/06/15/the-enlightenments-cynical-critics>

Kelman, Andrew, "Beyond All Warnings: The Radical Assault on Truth in the Law", *Quillette* (online, 2 April 2018) <http://quillette.com/2018/04/02/beyond-warnings-radical-assault-truth-law>

Kelman, Andrew, "Walking the Tightrope Between Chaos and Order—An Interview with Jordan B. Peterson", *Quillette* (online, 27 January 2018) <https://quillette.com/2018/01/27/walking-tightrope-chaos-order-interview-jordan-b-peterson>

Kingson, Jennifer A., "Harvard Tenure Battle Puts 'Critical Legal Studies' on Trial", *The New York Times* (online, 30 August 1987) <https://www.nytimes.com/1987/08/30/weekinreview/harvard-tenure-battle-puts-critical-legal-studies-on-trial.html>

Legal Information Institute, *Who We Are* (Web Page) <https://www.law.cornell.edu/lii/about/who_we_are>

McManus, Matt, "In Defence of Critical Legal Theory: A Reply to Andrew Kelman', *Quillette* (online, 14 April 2018) <https://quillette.com/2018/04/14/defence-critical-legal-theory-reply-andrew-kelman/>

Menand, Louis, "A Friend of the Devil', *The New Yorker* (online, 16 March 2015) <https://www.newyorker.com/magazine/2015/03/23/a-friend-of-the-devil>

Menand, Louis, "Francis Fukuyama Postpones the End of History", *The New Yorker* (online, 3 September 2018) <https://www.newyorker.com/magazine/2018/09/03/francis-fukuyama-postpones-the-end-of-history>

Menand, Louis, "The de Man Case", *A Critic at Large*, *The New Yorker* (online, 24 March 2014) <https://www.newyorker.com/magazine/2014/03/24/the-de-man-case>

Menand, Louis, "What is 'Critical Legal Studies': Radicalism for Yuppies" *The New Republic* (Washington DC) 17 March 1986, 20

Mishra, Pankaj, "Jordan Peterson & Fascist Mysticism", *The New York Review of Books* (online, 19 March 2018) <https://www.nybooks.com/daily/2018/03/19/jordan-peterson-and-fascist-mysticism/>

Posner, Richard A., "Bookshelf: A Manifesto for Legal Renegades", *The Wall Street Journal* (New York, 27 January 1987)

Presser, Stephen B., "What American Law Professors Forgot and What Trump Knew", *Opinion*, *Chicago Tribune* (online, 17 November 2016) <https://www.chicagotribune.com/news/opinion/commentary/ct-law-professors-trump-scalia-supreme-court-conservative-perspec-1118-md-20161117-story.html>

Quillette, *What is Quillette?* (Web Page, 6 November 2022) <https://quillette.com/about>

"The Red Pill", Reddit (Web Page, accessed 7 November 2023) <https://www.reddit.com/r/theredpill>

Reich, Charles A., "Reflections: The Greening of America" *The New Yorker* (New York, 26 September 1970) 42

Rodriguez, Miguel, "'Politicized' Faculty Affects Tenure, Teaching, Research" *Harvard Law Record* (Cambridge, 9 March 1984)

Schone, Mark, "The Matrix Defense", *The Boston Globe* (online, 9 November 2003) <http://archive.boston.com/news/globe/ideas/articles/2003/11/09/the_matrix_defense>

Strauss, Valerie and Vernon Loeb, "CIA Sends Agents to Schools—to Teach", *The Washington Post* (online, 18 April 2000) <https://www.washingtonpost.com/archive/politics/2000/04/18/cia-sends-agents-to-schools-to-teach/c63cc800-ba18-4dd2-83e7-3d07b0d1f793>

"Vorenberg, Former Law School Dean, Dies at 72", *The Harvard Crimson* (online, 14 April 2000) <https://www.thecrimson.com/article/2000/4/14/vorenberg-former-law-school-dean-dies>

Wikipedia, *Wikipedia Contributors* (Web Page) <https://en.wikipedia.org/wiki/Wikipedia:About#Wikipedia_contributors>

Yen, Hope, "As HLS Mulls Its Mission, CLS Scholars Remain Quiet", *Harvard Law Record* (Cambridge, 1 December 1995), 2

Yen, Hope, "Crits at HLS a Dying Breed?", *Harvard Law Record* (Cambridge, 1 December 1995), 4

Index

A Christmas Carol, 82, 87
Anderson, J., 93–5, 117–25
Austin, A., 51–2, 55, 67, 129–31

Bell, D., 20
Birkbeck College, 29, 63
Boal, A., 113–14
broad Critical Legal Studies, 23–5, 34–5, 49; *see also* narrow Critical Legal Studies
Brown, W., 81

Carrington, P., 18, 67, 127–9
Central Intelligence Agency, 156
    CIA, 156, 161–3
Clark, R., 32, 44, 45–6, 47
Coase, R., 40–1, 44
Cohen, S., 14, 16
comics, 10
Conference on Critical Legal Studies, 14, 33, 57
    CCLS, 33, 57, 66
Cornell University Law School, 60, 61, 63
    Legal Information Institute, 63
counterculture, 1–3, 6–7, 8, 11, 13–14; *see also* subculture
Crenshaw, K., 137, 146
critical race theory, 23, 25, 52, 67

Dalton, C., 18, 43, 46
Davies, M., 23, 24–7, 30, 49
Deleuze, G., 12
demystification, 1–2, 59, 62
Derrida, J., 52, 74, 76, 79–81
Dickens, C., 74
Douzinas, C., 23, 25, 27, 28, 30, 49, 63
Duxbury, N., 41, 50

Farber, D., 67, 68, 71; *see also* Sherry, S.
feminist legal theory, 25, 52, 67–8

Fischl, R.M., 51, 52, 107
Fiss, O., 67
Fitzpatrick, P., 27, 29, 30
Foucault, M., 8, 23, 105
Freeman, A., 8–9, 149
Fukuyama, F., 75, 76–9

Gabel, P., 93, 98–117, 121, 140; *see also* Kennedy, D.
Gearey, A., 23, 25, 27, 47, 49
genealogy, 23, 47
Goodrich, P., 10, 12–13, 28, 30, 132–4
Gordon, A.L., 153, 160
Gordon, R., 3–4, 43, 64, 127–9, 160
Guattari, F., 12–13

Harvard Law School, 16–17, 18, 32, 33, 36–37, 38, 42–3, 44–5, 65
haunting, 74–5, 83–5
    hauntology, 75, 80, 81, 90
Holmes Jr., O.W., 38–9
Horwitz, M., 32, 33, 34, 36–7, 39, 46, 47, 66
Hunt, A., 28, 30

Kafka, F., 12–13
Kalman, L., 37, 39, 157
Kant, E., 63
Kelman, M., 4, 8–9, 41–2, 54–5, 66, 69–70, 149
Kennedy, D., 3–4, 5, 10–11, 18, 19–20, 32, 33–5, 36–7, 46, 48, 73, 89, 93–7, 117, 121, 140, 151–2, 156–9, 161

Langdell, C.C., 38–9
    Langdellism, 38–9
law and economics, 32, 39–40, 41, 42, 45
law schools, 3, 4, 7, 16
legal realism, 37–8, 39
liberalism, 22, 36, 39–40, 41, 42, 77

MacKinnon, C., 134–5
Matsuda, M., 137–40, 141
Minkkinen, P., 12–13
minor literature, 12
minor jurisprudence, 11–13
moral panic, 1, 14, 16–18, 19–21
mystification, 6, 7, 56–7, 66, 68, 69

narrow Critical Legal Studies 24–5; *see also* broad Critical Legal Studies
Neacsu, E.D., 93–5
neoliberalism, 42, 80

Posner, R., 41–2
Posthumous Critical Legal Studies, 31, 73
  PCLS, 31, 47, 48, 52, 64, 73–4, 85, 88, 89, 122

Reich, C., 156–7
rights, 9, 141–2

Shakespeare, W., 74
Sherry, S., 67, 68, 71; *see also* Farber, D.
subculture, 2, 6–7, 8, 11, 13–14, 20; *see also* counterculture

The Bridge, 62, 65–70
The Matrix, 122–4

trashing, 1, 8–9–11, 149; *see also* Trashman
Trashman, 9–10, *see also* trashing
Trubek, D., 18, 43, 46, 159–60
Tushnet, M., 89, 155, 161

UK-CLS, 28, 29, 30
  British Critical Legal Studies, 25, 27
Unger, R., 6, 7, 32, 33, 35–7, 39, 63, 64, 66, 90, 160–1
US-CLS, 27, 28, 30, 31, 33–7, 39, 41, 42, 45–6, 48, 52–3, 57–9, 62, 64, 66, 126
  Brit Crits, 25, 27
  death of US-CLS, 30–1, 32, 42, 48–53, 60, 73
  US-based Critical Legal Studies, 25, 27

Ward, I., 99–100
Wex, 63–5
Wikipedia, 61–3, 68, 69
Williams, P., 14, 141–6, 154–5

Yale Law School 19, 37, 43
Yale, 39
Yen, H., 32, 45–7
Young, J., 14–15

EU representative:
Easy Access System Europe
Mustamäe tee 50, 10621 Tallinn, Estonia
Gpsr.requests@easproject.com

www.ingramcontent.com/pod-product-compliance
Lightning Source LLC
Chambersburg PA
CBHW071846230426
43671CB00012B/2085